THE SECRET OF MENTAL MAGIC

THE SECRET OF MENTAL MAGIC

A Course of Seven Lessons

By

WILLIAM WALKER ATKINSON

KALPAZ

ISBN: 978-93-5128-435-2(HB)

First Published in 1907
Indian Reprint in 2017

Published by

Kalpaz Publications
C-30, Satyawati Nagar,
Delhi – 110052
E-mail: kalpaz@hotmail.com
Website: kalpazpublications.com
Ph.: +91-9212142040

To My Friend

Helen Wilmans

whose writings gave me inspiration, courage, determination, and will, when I sorely needed them, this little volume is respectfully inscribed.

EPIGRAPH

"... but, one day, the sturdy lion, the monarch of the wilds, was grievously wounded by the arrows of the hunters, and crept away to seek rest and shelter. But, alas! in its hour of need, it attracted to itself the kicks from the hoofs of the wild-asses of the desert, and the malicious snaps of the jackals which formerly partook of the scraps of the feast of the monarch. Such is life, my son;—when the mighty are fallen low, then cometh the day of the lesser ones."

—*Ancient Persian Fable.*

Contents

I. Mental Magic. 3
II. The Underlying Force. 21
III. Mental Suggestion. 55
IV. Personal Influence. 97
V. The Science of Telementation. 133
VI. Mental Therapeutics. 185
VI. Mental Architecture 213

The Author's Foreword

In this book I deliver to you a Message that has been seeking expression for some time. It is a strong Message, of elemental power and primitive force. It is given to you in its original simplicity, and is not draped with airy metaphysical veils, nor by heavy theological prejudices or predilections. I have tried to get down to the bare body of the Truth concerning Mental Magic, although, in order to do so, I have had to strip away covering after covering of personal views of writers, teachers, schools, and cults. I have cast aside these discarded draperies, and now present to you the simple, natural Truth as I have found it. Some who are partial to these added draperies may resent their disuse—I can't help it if they do—I am not writing this book for such. Others may be shocked at the nakedness of the Unadorned Truth—I cannot help this either—this book was not written for mental prudes, so let them stalk off hiding their faces with the hands if they wish. (They will sneak a hasty glance over their shoulders, though, when they think that no one is looking—such people always do.)

These lessons are "solid," and contain much strong food for strong people. There is nothing of the *Charlotte Busse*, or *Meringue*, about these lessons. They are solid food, and must be partaken of as such. Partaken of properly, they will nourish and strengthen you, building up muscle, tissue and bone. But, bolted or swallowed at a gulp, they may give you a bad case of "mental dyspepsia." Hygienic laws operate on the mental as well as the physical plane. The lessons are full of concentrated, condensed information, and must be partaken of in small bites, well masticated, in order to insure perfect digestion. You must study each lesson, before you proceed to the next one. You cannot "skim-over" these lessons in a single reading, if you expect to master their contents. They need reading, and re-reading, and each time you go over them, you will find something new. I have compressed in this book, enough matter to fill six books, if properly diluted and spread out.

The original size of this book was about 200 pages, but after the original manuscript was placed in the hands of the printer, I kept on thinking of this thing, and that thing, that should "go in the book." And so, from day to day, I sent the printer enough "additional matter" to bring the book up to its present proportions (about double the original size)—the price being kept the same, of course. This "additional matter" has been inserted and dove-tailed in, among the original matter, until to the proof-readers the lessons seemed like a mosaic, or "grandmother's quilt." The advance notices were out, so I could not devote as much time as I would have liked to the work of "polishing up" the connecting joints, or "rounding up" the corners, occasioned by this insertion of new matter in the different parts of the several lessons. Consequently, there may be apparent a lack of "smoothness" and "finish" about the work, arising from this cause. I trust that you will understand, and pardon such, in view of what I have said to you.

But, after all, I must confess that I do feel that I have given you "good measure—heaped full and running over," and have managed to deliver my Message according to my best Desire. And, that's the principal thing, after all—isn't it?

To all the students of these lessons, I send a message of Good-Cheer, Courage, and Self-Confidence. You are Centres of Power in the Great Ocean of Universal Power. Realize this truth, and you will have attained that which you seek. You have attracted this book to you—now take what the Law has sent you, and use it. And, as it brought you *this*—so will it bring you THAT, which you Desire so ardently.

William Walker Atkinson.

Masonic Temple; Chicago, Ill., February 26, 1907.

My Basic Statement

There exists an Universal Dynamic Principle of Life; pervading all space; immanent in all things; manifesting in an infinite variety of forms, and life, and energy or force;—and the essential inner nature of that Universal Principle is MIND! The energy, or force, of that Principle is no respecter of persons. Its services are open to all, and it operates in response to the proper effort no matter by whom it may be exerted. But the proper effort must be exerted, consciously or unconsciously, else there will be no operation of the forces.

William Walker Atkinson.

The Secret of Mental Magic

Lesson I.

Mental Magic.

Introductory—Mysterious Mental Influencing Power—The Present Interest in Mental Magic—The Basis of Modern "Isms"—What Is "Mental Magic"?—The Persian Magi—The Occult Forces of Nature—The Esoteric Knowledge—The Ancient Use of Will Power—The Priestly Adepts—The Force Above Good and Evil—The Secret of the Force—Ignorant Use of the Force—Modern Uses of the Force—The Attempt to Monopolize the Occult Knowledge—Too Late to Deny Facts—A Mighty Power for Good or Evil—Ignorance No Protection—The Bane and the Antidote—The Coming of the Super-Man—A Scientific Presentation—Adverse Criticism Braved.

LESSON I.

MENTAL MAGIC.

BY "MENTAL Magic" I mean all of the wonderful instances of the influence of one mind over another, as evidenced in thousands of different forms, degrees and phases. Whether in the form of Personal Magnetism, or the subtle fascinating charm of one mind over another— that form of mental force that influences as if by an irresistible charm; that bewitches, allures, charms, enchants, attracts; or in what has been called Fascination, in which one person is able to influence another in an uncontrollable manner, by exercising a powerful or irresistible influence upon his or her affections, emotions, passions or thoughts; or in some of the other similar forms of the exercise of an unseen, inexplicable influence upon others; or in the phenomena known as Hypnotism, Mesmerism, Psychologism, etc., etc., with which all are more or less familiar; or in the phenomena attendant upon the revival of the Ancient Occultism in the last twenty years, under various names and forms, the fundamental principle of which consists in forms of mental "treatments" of one kind or another, present or "absent"; or in the phenomena of what has been called "Suggestion," of which we hear so much in scientific circles; or in the various forms of Mind or Faith Cures, of which so much has been heard of late years, and upon which a number of religions and cults have been built; or in the repulsive forms of Mental Influence, known as Witchcraft, Voodooism, Black Magic, etc., etc.— we have the same fundamental principle, and manifestation of some phase of the general phenomena of Mental Magic. The same cause is under all its manifestations—"good" or "bad," "black" or "white." It is all the operation of the one great Law, or Principle of Nature.

Mysterious Mental Influencing Power.

We see on all sides men who seem to exert a wonderful and mysterious mental influence upon others—upon those associated with them, or upon the public mind. Leaders spring into prominence, apparently owing their power to some mysterious influence over the minds and wills of others. Some attain power and position—others attain wealth and social state, by reason of some inner force. When we meet certain people, we become at once impressed by a Something about them that makes its power and influence felt by us. They seem to radiate a peculiar force that bends our wills captive, and causes us to fall in with their desires, to a greater or lesser extent.

We know that when some people enter a room, they bring with them an indefinable influence that becomes apparent to all. Certain houses and stores have atmospheres of their own, which are perceptible to those entering them. Some places are depressing to all who live or do business in them. Some salesmen impart a sense of confidence and trust at once, while others cause the reverse. Some persons attract—others repel.

Some people seem to have a way of influencing the minds of others with whom they come in contact, so that these others will rally around the self-constituted leader, and thus cults, religions, and "isms" are formed. We all know how far a strong "magnetic" leader may carry his followers. We have seen many instances of it during the past twenty years. People have followed some of these leaders like a flock of sheep. And they will always do so, until the underlying principle is understood and people protect themselves.

And all of these things go to form part of the phenomena of mental magic. Surely the subject is worth investigating.

THE PRESENT INTEREST IN MENTAL MAGIC.

Now, as never before, the subject of the mystic forces of the Mind is attracting the attention of the majority of thinking people. In the ages of the past the knowledge of the subject was possessed by but the few, who jealously guarded it from the minds of the masses, the latter obtaining but scraps of the hidden knowledge, and that adulterated with the grossest superstition and attributed to the particular form of primitive religion prevailing in the particular place, at that particular time. And even now, notwithstanding the popular interest in the subject, but very few have arrived at a scientific understanding of the matter, and the majority take their knowledge of the New Psychology in the capsule of Dogma and Theory advanced by some particular cult or sect.

Mental Magic has been known to the race, in one form or another, from time before history was written. In the earliest records we find many traces of it among all peoples. And, even today, it is known and practiced, in a more or less ignorant manner, by all races, from the people of the highest civilization known to us, down to the ignorant African savages or Bushmen.

Many have been turned away from a serious consideration of the subject by the fact that many of its forms have been accompanied by the grossest superstition, and the most absurd repulsive ceremonies. They have failed to see that underlying all the extravagant ideas and methods of application, there was to be found a fundamental law of Nature, as real and as constant as any other natural law or force. And, inasmuch as this law is in constant operation, and all are subject to its influence and effect, does it not become the duty of intelligent people to acquaint themselves with this mighty force or law, in order that they may understand its workings; take advantage of its benefits; and protect themselves against its misuse? Believing that there is but one answer to this question, this series of lessons has been written in order to throw light on a subject commonly left in the dark, or at least in the twilight, of the human understanding.

The Basis Of Modern "Isms."

I am fully aware of the fact that many ingenious theories have been advanced by modern writers attempting to account for the phenomena of Mental Magic. But all students of the subject are aware that these theories, cleverly as they have been designed, are more or less self-contradictory, and many a reader has thrown aside the subject in disgust after a vain attempt at reconciling the opposing views. And to make the matter worse, various cults and sects and "isms" have sprung into existence, the promulgators and leaders of which have used the accepted phenomena of Mental Magic as a foundation upon which to build airy structures of religion, philosophy, and metaphysics.

Many of these cults have practically claimed a monopoly of the great natural force, and have assumed the right to be the sole custodians of the secrets thereof, alleging that they have the "only real article —all others are base imitators," notwithstanding that all of them show that they have arrived at at least a working knowledge of the force, and are obtaining results—each obtaining about the same percentage of successes, notwithstanding the fact that each denies the other the fact of possessing the information and right to use it. Is it not apparent to any intelligent observer that they are all using the same great natural force, in spite of their conflicting theories—and that their results are obtained in spite of their theories, rather than because of them?

Mental Magic.

What Is "Mental Magic"?

Perhaps the best way to begin our consideration of the subject would be for us to take a look at the original definitions of the two words composing the title of these lessons—Mental Magic. It is always well to turn to the dictionary when you begin the consideration of any subject, for by so doing you get at the original idea in the minds of the people who first used the terms, and give to your subject-thought a firm and solid foundation. You place yourself in the position of the original thinker, and have the advantage that always comes from the possession of a new thought fresh from the mint of the mind. You are able to see the Idea free from the excrescences which afterwards attach to it.

The word "Mental" is derived from the Latin word *mentis*, the mind, and Webster defines the English word as: "Of, or pertaining to the Mind." The definitions of the word "Mind" are more or less imperfect, and unsatisfactory,—necessarily so, because men do not know the real nature of Mind, and can define it only in the terms of its own states. Perhaps this definition is as clear as any: "By Mind we mean simply that by, which we perceive, think, feel, desire and Will." So we may consider "Mental" as meaning, "Of, or pertaining to, that by which we perceive, think, feel, desire and Will. So much for the first word.

The Persian Magi.

The second word—Magic—was derived from the Persian word "mag," meaning "a priest." The Persian priests were "wonder-workers," or "magicians," the latter word being derived from the word "Magi," the name of the hereditary caste of priests of ancient Persia and Medea. This Magian order, or esoteric cult of the Zoroastrian priesthood, represented the center of Ancient Occultism at that period of the world's history, and their influence was felt in all parts of the world, and continues down to this time. So highly were its members respected and considered, that the term "Wise Men," and "Magi" were synonomous. The "Three Wise Men" mentioned as appearing at the birth of Christ (Matt. II) were known as the Magi, or "wise men from the East."

From the word "Magi" came the term "Magic," which Webster has defined as follows: "The hidden wisdom supposed to be possessed by the Magi; relating to the occult powers of nature; mastery of secret forces in nature; having extraordinary properties; seemingly requiring more than human power, etc." So we may consider the word Magic to mean: "Mastery of the occult forces of nature," the. term indicating the existence of such forces, and the possibility of the mastery or control of them.

The Occult Forces Of Nature.

But by the use of the term "Mental Magic," I mean more than the mere mental control of the "occult forces of nature." I mean that these "occult forces of nature" are themselves mental in character and nature, and that their control or mastery means simply the CONSCIOUS use, control, mastery, and application of certain mental forces, called "occult," that are possessed by the race, and are used by all, either consciously or unconsciously. The mastery or control of these forces, means that one may learn to "knowingly" apply that which all have been using blindly and unknowingly. And as knowledge and intelligent use always means Power, the knowledge of the principles of these forces, and the consequent intelligent application of them brings Power to those acquiring it.

The Esoteric Knowledge.

While it is true that that which is known as "Magic" has always heen mixed up with a mass of credulity, superstition, and meaningless forms and ceremonies. the close student will see that these excrescences and appendages necessarily arose from the superstitions of the mass of the people, and to the various forms of primitive religions that the race has fostered during the procession of the centuries and ages. The magicians were nearly always priests in the old days, that being the only career open to them, and one that enabled them to erect the barrier of primitive religious rites between their wisdom and the ignorance of the race.

The careful student will be able to trace the possession of something real and true always manifesting among the various forms and ceremonies of the various ancient cults. There was always to be found an esoteric or inner cult, within the mass of the exoteric or ignorant priesthood and followers of the temples. There was always the light of Truth burning in the holy of holies of the temples, for those who were sufficiently advanced to worship at its shrine.

THE ANCIENT USE OF WILL-POWER.

And, among the dim records of the ancient mysteries that have come down to us from ancient India, Egypt, Persia, Chaldea, Babylon, Greece, and Rome, and the other old centers of civilization and culture, we may always find the underlying principle of the existence of some mighty force connected with the human Mind—or more particularly, the Will— that was at the bottom of the mysteries, and magic, and miracles. Back of all the ceremonies, rites, and incantations was the esoteric idea that the Will was the real force employed under the mask of incantation and rites assumed to impress the imaginations and minds of the populace. Back of the amulet and charm was the working of the Will of the person wearing them, which was called into effect by the Faith or Imagination (a real power and not a fancy as many believe) of the man ignorant of the real force.

As the writer on this subject in the Encyclopædia Brittanica has truly said (although he was ignorant of the truth underlying the silly forms): "There being an evident relation between an object and the thought of it, it becomes one of the chief practices of the sorcerer to try to make things happen by thinking about them." And the same writer in another place speaks, of: "The element in Magic, not depending upon 'spirits,' depends upon imagined powers and correspondences in nature, of which the adepts avail themselves in order to discover hidden knowledge, and to act upon the world around them by means beyond the ordinary capabilities of men. Thus by mere effort of Will," etc., etc.

And the student who will look under the surface, and read between the lines, will be able to see the evidence of "Mental Magic" underlying all the forms of Magic, Mystery, and Wonder-working Miracle of all times and ages, and people—of all kinds, character or name. Behind all the masks he will see the features of this use of the Will-Force of man—always the same, in spite of the fantastic and grotesque masks and trappings.

THE PRIESTLY ADEPTS.

I could fill pages with recitals of the many disguises under which Mental Magic masquerades, but I must hurry on the telling "How," and I can do no more than to hastily call your attention to the many evidences of the use of this power in all parts of the world, and in all times. The ancient mysteries of Egypt, Greece, etc., were systems of forms and ceremonies, wherein were hidden the use of Mental Magic. The sick were brought to the temples and healed. The minds of the populace were filled with the thoughts of victory impressed upon them by the Will and subtle suggestions of the priests. What we know in these days as "Will-Force," and "Mental Suggestion," including that which we now call "Affirmations" or "Auto-suggestions," were understood and skillfully used by the priests, or magicians, in order to control the people.

And it must not be for a moment supposed that these forces were used for evil purposes. On the contrary the priests were the real governing classes—the powers behind the throne—and they felt the responsibility of power, and endeavored by their knowledge of the occult forces of the mind to lead the people in the right path. Of course, selfish men there have always been, and we hear of cases away back in the early days of history where this power was prostituted for evil and selfish purposes, just as power is always capable of wrong application.

In all ages we learn of the healing of the sick by mental power, for Mental Healing presents an unbroken line from the earliest days down to the present, concealed often under fancy trappings, but the same in principle always. And what we call "Mental Suggestion" has always been in force in the hands of the leaders of the race to influence, for good or evil, those under them. The great leaders of men have always been adepts in Mental Magic, although many of them have never suspected the sources of their power.

THE FORCE ABOVE GOOD AND EVIL.

To many it may seem almost sacrilegious to state that the highest uses of Mental Magic, such as leading the race up to higher ideals, aims and accomplishments,—to success, happiness and health—are merely higher forms of the same force that is used by the ignorant and repulsive savage in his rites of Voodooism, Sorcery, and similar dark practices. But it is true. Mental Magic is like any other great natural force—it is above good and evil. It is neither good and evil, but may be used for either. This is true of Electricity, Steam, Explosives and every other natural force. And we might as well look this fact squarely in the face, and govern ourselves accordingly.

The same force that is used by the modern "healer," when he or she "treats" a patient for health, success, or some other desirable quality, is the same used by the black Voodoo; the Congo sorcerer; the Salem witch; the Hawaiian conjure-man who prays people into sickness and death; the medicine-man of the American Indian, with his charms and incantations; the Wizards and Enchanters of the Middle Ages; the practitioner of "adverse treatments," or "malicious mental magnetism," of the modern cults. The same force pervades all, just as the same lifeblood runs through the saint and sinner; the angel and demon; the dove and the serpent; the lamb and the tiger—Nature's one force through all.

The Secret Of The Force.

And just as the Mental Magic brought into operation through the prayers of the faithful of all religions, before their shrines, images and holy objects, so may the same force be brought into operation through the fetiches, conjurations, enchantments, charms, spells and devil-worships of the ignorant and depraved minds. The secret is this: The power does not come from the supposed source, but from within the mind of the man employing it. And, still more startling, to the uninitiated, is this statement, which is equally true: The power of the mind of the person affected is the real cause of the effect, rather than the power of the mind of the supposed causer, the latter merely calling into operation the power of the mind of the person affected.

Ignorant Use Of The Force.

Passing from the past to the present age, we see in greater use than ever this wonderful Mental Magic. No longer the property of the few, the information has filtered out among the masses, through various sources, and we see the force in use on all sides. Often, the persons using it have not the true knowledge of its real nature, and such persons often involve themselves in a terrible whirlpool of effects by reason of a selfish and base employment of this power. Many are playing with this force like children playing with dynamite.

It is one of the purposes of the lessons to call the attention of such people to the nature of the force they are employing, and the possible, nay, probable results, of a misuse of it. Not that they are punished for such misuse, but rather by reason of it. Black magicians are invariably caught in the meshes of their own nets—are entangled in the psychic machinery of their own manufacture—and are blown up by their own psychic high explosives. These things will be dealt with in their proper places in these lessons.

Modern Uses Of The Force.

In concluding this little consideration of the subject, I would call the attention of the student to the fact that now, for the first time in the history of the world, Mental Magic is being employed for furthering commercial aims and ends. Treatments for Wealth are commonly known and advertised; instructions in the use of suggestions for commercial purposes are furnished both personally, and in correspondence courses; the laws and principles are explained, partially, at least, in books written for the instruction of those selling or advertising goods, and otherwise soliciting the patronage of the public.

It is true that the few strong men in business life have always made use of this ,force, consciously or unconsciously, but never before has it been taught generally as a part of a business education. It has been reserved for America to recognize the force, and to boldly apply it in this way, i. e., to the making of dollars. And other countries are fast falling in line. And in view of this fact, is it not time that those who know of the real nature, principles, and laws of this force should give to the world their knowledge, that the race may know with what they are dealing— and may be enabled to extract the good from it by proper use, and, seeing the evil possibilities of improper use, may avoid such prostitution of one of nature's greatest forces.

The Attempt To Monopolize The Occult Knowledge.

Many students of the Occult have sought to keep from the general public a knowledge of the fundamental principles of the great law of nature underlying the phenomena of Mental Magic. They have claimed that it was "dangerous" for people generally to know that such a force existed and could be used. They have held "that such knowledge should be carefully guarded by the few, and that its very existence should be denied to the many.

This may have been good reasoning in the earlier days of the world, when the masses were grossly ignorant, and when the only knowledge was locked up in the minds of the caste of priests and other leaders of the race. But the argument no longer applies, for the general intelligence of the race has refused to allow any locked doors in the Temple of Knowledge, and has insisted that all doors be thrown open to them. The result has been that a considerable body of Occult knowledge has been opened to the gaze of the public, and they are clamoring for more. Much of the knowledge possessed by the public regarding Mental Magic is but quasi-knowledge—half-truths—and the time has come when the whole truth should be taught.

TOO LATE TO DENY FACTS.

The time has arrived when the public should be made acquainted with the great force underlying the phenomena of Mental Magic. People should be instructed regarding this force; its laws and operation; its intelligent and proper use, with directions designed to protect people against its improper use against them, on the part of others—this latter a most important matter in these days of occult and psychic investigation on the part of the public, and the attempted base and selfish uses to which some are putting the occult mental forces of Nature.

It is too late to deny or ignore the existence of the mighty mental force in Nature, that underlies the various forms of phenomena that go to form the outward phase of Mental Magic, good and bad. Too much has been witnessed by the public concerning these matters for them to be hushed by the old cry, "There's nothing in it but imagination." On the one hand they have witnessed the various "treatments" of the healers, tending toward the cure of disease, the attainment of success, etc. And on the other, they have heard whispers of "adverse treatments," etc., and have heard of, or read, the various courses of instruction in Hypnotism, Mesmerism, etc., etc., and have seen evidences of the good and bad effects of what has been called " Suggestion," in all of its forms. And they are beginning to realize that all of these things, differing as they may seem, have a common root in some one natural force. And they are demanding, like the man from Missouri, to "be shown." And they have a right to demand this.

A Mighty Power For Good Or Evil.

The race has always recognized the existence of a mighty force of Nature which man has employed, consciously or unconsciously, in the direction of influencing his fellow men; other forms of life; and even the so-called lifeless things around him. In the earlier days this use of the force was called "Magic" (Black and White); Mystical Art; Divine Power; Miracle; Fascination; Charming; Enchantment; Wonder-working; Necromancy, etc., and in its more base and evil uses, Black Art; Witchcraft; Sorcery; Voodooism; Hexism, etc. For it must be remembered that this great force of nature is capable of base as well as of noble use.

Like any other great natural force—like electricity; the power of explosives; steam; the X rays; radium, etc.,—this great force is capable of the highest and most beneficial uses by man when properly applied, and is also capable of being applied to the most harmful purposes. Different as are the results arising from the varying applications, the force is the same in each case. The forces of Nature are not possessed of a sense of good and evil—their function and purpose is to act, in obedience to the laws of their nature without regard to the question of good and evil to those by whom, or against whom, they are employed. This may seem like a terrible thing, but a moment's thought will satisfy you that it is true of all natural forces, and the question of good and evil, and its reward or punishment, belongs to another plane of life.

IGNORANCE NO PROTECTION.

But it may be asked, why do I wish to inform the public about a force, unknown to many, which is capable of evil as well as of good use and results. The answer is simple: Ignorance is no protection against anything, for the knowledge is always possessed of the few who may use it on the ignorant many without suspicion; the greater publicity is given to a thing, and the better it is understood, the better may its good effects be obtained and the less the danger of its improper use—forewarned is forearmed. If a thing is good, the greater publicity given it the greater the good—if it is evil, the brighter the searchlight turned upon it, the less danger is there attendant upon it.

The danger of all evils lies in the Darkness of Concealment, not in the Daylight of Publicity. "Turn on the Light" has always been the watchword of Progress and Civilization. And more particularly is this so at this the first decade of the Twentieth Century when the interest in Occultism and kindred subjects has made a number of people acquainted with the force known as Mental Magnetism, and has acquainted them with its uses, under various names and theories. And in many cases it is being practiced upon people who are unfamiliar with the subject, and therefore it is time that some one should "turn on the light," that it may be seen by all men and known for what it is—capable of the highest and the lowest uses, but a great force of Nature.

THE BANE AND THE ANTIDOTE.

And with this exposition of it, goes the remedy and protection against improper use, as well as the knowledge of its wonderful proper uses. If it be a bane—here is the antidote. But it is not necessarily a bane, any more than steam, electricity, and explosives are a bane to mankind. What would be thought of people who would suppress knowledge of all natural laws, because of the possibility of improper use? Ignorance is no protection. Truth and Fact must be followed to the end, and it will be discovered that, in Nature, every force that may be possible of hurtful use, may be guarded against by natural means.

THE COMING OF THE SUPER-MAN.

So much for the unpleasant side. But there is a very pleasant side to this subject of Mental Magic. This force has come to man just when he most needs it. He has used the so-called mechanical forces to clear away the obstacles that Nature put into his way in order to develop him into a Man, and now he turns to higher forms of energy and work—he is crying for new worlds to conquer. And these new worlds will be conquered by the Mind, rather than by the muscle. Great things are before the race, and one of the greatest forces in Nature in the work of the building up of the Super-Man, will be this force called Mental Magic. By it man will be enabled to fight off the forces of Ignorance and Ma terialism, and to draw to himself Knowledge from the Universal Mind that will enable him to accomplish the heretofore Impossible.

A SCIENTIFIC PRESENTATION.

In these lessons I shall treat Mental Magic as I would any other great force or energy of Nature, *i. e.*, in a scientific manner, stating the principles plainly and without concealment, and also giving in full what I and other experimenters along the lines of this subject have learned of the methods beneficial, and the reverse, concerning the applications of these principles. In the case of the beneficial application, full directions will be given that the student may avail himself of the force to the fullest extent. In the cases where the subject of the harmful use of the force is alluded to, the student will be instructed how the same may be prevented, obviated, and neutralized, so that full protection is assured. This is what I should do in lessons upon Electricity, Steam, or Explosives—and that is the course I purpose following in these lessons on Mental Magic.

Adverse Criticism Braved.

It is possible that this course may bring upon me the adverse criticism of those who believe "that the public is not ready for such knowledge," and that "such things should be reserved for the few." To such people, and all others, I would say that I have no sympathy with such an attitude, and I believe that the race is ready for ALL Truth, and that that which is proper for the Few is proper for the Many. I believe that the greater the degree of Knowledge the greater the degree of power and advancement. I believe that Ignorance is not happiness; and that to keep a man ignorant of a natural fact, in order that he may escape its effect, is like allowing him to smoke when seated on a keg of powder, rather than to acquaint him with a knowledge of explosives—or, to use another figure, to advise him to bury his head in the sand like an ostrich, rather than to look upon the approach of a possible danger. I do not believe in such sophistry! I do not believe in Ignorance! I do not believe in Darkness!

Therefore, I purpose to

"TURN ON THE LIGHT."

Lesson II.

The Underlying Force.

Introductory—The "Just Why" of Things—What We "Don't Know"—The Evidence of Thought Transference—Flammarion's Theory—"Mental States" Not "Thoughts"—"Mentative Energy" the Real Force—My Terms of Expression—Mentative Induction—Telementation—The Underlying Energy—The Universal Mentative Energy—The Energy Operates Like Electricity—The Brain Is a "Transformer" of Energy—The Two Mentative Poles—Desire and Will in Evidence Always—Desire and Will in Telementation—"Thought" Not the Motive Power—The Moving Force of the Mind—Desire the Mental Inciter—The Attracting Power of Desire—The Eifect of Desire Force—The Insistent Desire—Waves of Desire-Force—What "Desire" Really Means—The Relation of Will to Desire—The Mentative Twins—The Mastery of Will—the Testimony of Wise Men—Will, the Projector of Mentative Force—The Wonders of Will—The Masculine and the Feminine Energy—The Directing Will—The Protecting Will—Mentative Induction—Mentative Currents—Mental Atmospheres of Places—The Effect of the Mentative Vibrations—Waves of "Feeling"—Mentative Cyclones—The Centers of the Mental Whirlpools—Mentative Influence—More About Mentative Influence—Personal Influence—Mental Suggestion—Nature's Protective Armor—Self-Protection—Learn How to Feel and Will.

Lesson II.

The Underlying Force.

In the preceding lesson I have mentioned that underlying all of the various phases of the phenomena of Mental Magic there was to be found one principle or force.

This underlying principle or force is of course a mental force, and operates along the lines of the now fully established scientific principle, mistakenly called "Telepathy," but which I have called "Mental Induction." After centuries of doubt, denial and ridicule on the part of Science it has at last been forced upon the scientific mind that Mind Transference, or the Circulation of Mind, is an established fact. The experiments of the London Society of Psychical Research have given to the world a volume of unimpeachable evidence regarding this fact of the transference of mental states from one mind to another, and thousands of people have demonstrated to their own satisfaction, by means of private experiments, the truth of this phenomenon.

There have been many theories advanced to account for this transference of mental conditions, from one mind to another, and we have heard much talk of man having "two minds," etc., the theories, in some cases, having grown top-heavy from the weight of their elaborations. In these lessons I shall have nothing to do with any theory of "two minds," or any similar theory attempting to account for the series of phenomena before us. Personally, I take but very little stock in many of the popular theories on the subject.

The "Just Why" of Things.

I have never met anyone who really did know the "just why," and I do not believe that anyone really does know. I make this statement, advisedly, after reading and studying about all of importance that has been written on the subject, and after a personal acquaintance with many of the leading authorities. They all have a clear understanding of the fact of the phenomena, but when it comes to the underlying cause—the "just what is Mind?" part of the question—they either frankly confess that they do not know, or else take refuge in some metaphysical or fanciful psychological theory, and hypnotize themselves and their followers by a flood of words, and play upon words.

Personally, I believe that this "just what" is locked in the subject of the "just what" of Life and Being. Until we know the latter we can•not expect to know the former. And, so I, for one, have cut loose from all the theories regarding the nature of Mind-those "soap-bubbles with which the grown-up children of science amuse themselves"-and shall make no attempt to formulate one here. You will have to take the facts as I present them, and prove them by personal experiment-if you want a theory of the nature of Mind, make one for yourself, for I have retired from the business. I have learned to say "I do not know!"

What We "Don't Know."

And for that matter, we do not know the "just what" of anything, no matter how much we may know about the phenomenal side of the thing. Nobody knows "just what is" anything—if one knew the "just what is" of a single thing, he would have the key to the Riddle of the Universe—but he doesn't know, and may never know. We know of the existence of Electricity, for example, and we know how to use it, manage it; control it—but we do not know "just what it is." Do you remember the story of the youth in college, who when asked by the Professor "What is Electricity?" replied, "Well, sir, I did know, but I have forgotten." The Professor replied, drily, "Now, isn't that too bad. Here is the only person in the world who ever knew what Electricity is, and he has forgotten it. How very sad! What a loss for mankind!"

And in view of the facts just mentioned, I am able to confess without embarrassment that "I do not know" the "just why"—or "just what is" side of the subject of Mind. But I do know the laws and principles of its operation—how it acts, and how it may be used—and I shall confine myself to the "How" side of the subject, rather than to the "Why."

The Evidences of Thought Transference.

I shall not attempt to offer evidence to prove the existence of the fact of the transference of Mentative Energy at this time and place. The evidence may be had elsewhere, if needed, but I believe that everyone who reads these lessons will have had some personal experience in his or her own life, that will render further proof unnecessary. In case, however, such proof is needed, I refer the doubter to the pages of any recent work on the subject, or the pages of the Reports of the London Society for Psychical Research, the said society being composed of men of worldwide reputation in science and learning, their honesty and capability being beyond question.

Flammarion's Theory.

I shall, however, quote the following passage from Camille Flammarion, the eminent French astronomer, who is also an investigator of this subject. He says: "We sum up, therefore, our preceding observations by the conclusion that one mind can act at a distance upon another, without the habitual medium of words, or any other visible means of communication. It appears to us altogether unreasonable to reject this conclusion if we accept the facts. This conclusion will be abundantly demonstrated. There is nothing unscientific, nothing romantic in admitting that an idea can influence a brain from a distance. The action of one human being upon another, from a distance, is a scientific fact; it is as certain as the existence of Paris, of Napoleon, of Oxygen, or of Sirius." He further states: "There can be no doubt that our psychical force creates a movement in the ether, which transmits itself afar like all movements of ether, and becomes perceptible to brains in harmony with our own. The transformation of a psychic action into an ethereal movement, and the reverse, may be analogous to what takes place on a telephone, where the receptive plate, which is identical with the plate at the other end, reconstructs the sonorous movement transmitted, not by means of sound, but by electricity. But these are only comparisons."

"MENTAL STATES" NOT "THOUGHTS."

The entire subject of Mental Magic rests upon the fact that Mental States may be transferred from one mind to another. You will notice that I say "Mental States," instead of "Thoughts"—I do this purposely, because I hold that the most powerful phases of mental action do not rise to the plane of Thought, but are far from elementary in nature, and belong to the "Feeling," or "Emotional" plane of mind. And I believe that the real FORCE has more to do with DESIRE and WILL than with Thought. I will bring out these points as I proceed.

"MENTATIVE ENERGY" THE REAL FORCE.

At this point, I wish only to call attention to the fact that there is a SOMETHING—some kind of FORCE—that is generated and then passed from one mind to another, conveying Mental States, Feelings, Emotions, Thoughts, etc., with it. Now what is this Something? We do not know "just what," as I have said, but we recognize its existence and effects, and see that it is a real

SOMETHING. We may not understand its ultimate nature—its "just what is"—but we know it IS, and we have a right to name it. What shall we call it? What name best fits its characteristics. You may call it what you like, but I purpose calling it "Mentative Energy." And the stream or current of this Energy I shall call "Mentative Currents." And the process of its affecting other minds, either by Personal Influence or by Mentative Currents, I shall call "Mentative Induction." And the act of producing this Energy I shall call "Mentation." Let us examine these terms for a moment.

MY TERMS OF EXPRESSION.

You will notice that all of these terms arise from the word "Mentation." Now, what is Mentation? Let us see! The first part of the word comes from the Latin word, *mentis,* meaning "the mind.' The second part, *"ation,"* is a suffix meaning "acting." So the word "Mentation" means "Mind-in-action."

Then, consequently, we have the following definitions:

MENTATION: Mental Activity. MENTATIVE: Relating to Mental Activity.

MENTATE: To manifest Mental Activity. MENTATOR: One who Mentates.

MENTATIVE ENERGY: The Energy arising from Mental Activity.

MENTATIVE CURRENT: A stream or current of Mentative Energy.

MENTATIVE INDUCTION: Induction by Mentation.

Please acquaint yourselves thoroughly with these terms, for they will be used very frequently in these lessons.

The term "Mentative Current" will be readily understood. The word Mentative I have defined. The word "Current" means "a flowing or passing stream."

MENTATIVE INDUCTION.

The term "Mentative Induction" will be readily understood by those familiar with the phenomena of Electricity. The word

"Induction" comes from the word "Induce," which means "to influence." In Electrical Science the word Induction is used in the sense of "the process whereby one body possessing magnetic or electrical properties reproduces that property in another body without direct contact."

In text-books on Physics a simple experiment is often given students to illustrate Magnetic Induction, as follows: A Magnet is so placed that its poles project over the edge of a table upon which it rests. An iron nail, or steel needle, is held a little distance below the magnet so that it will not actually touch the latter but will be near enough to be magnetized by "induction," that is, without direct contact. The nail, or needle, will have an induced property of magnetism produced by the current from the magnet, and will support another nail, or needle, by direct contact. This induced magnetism renders the nail, or needle, a magnet, possessing all the properties of the original magnet, so long as the current flows.

And, just as a magnet may communicate its properties by Induction so may an electrified body communicate electrical states in another body without actual contact. The text-books are full of examples to illustrate this law. The theory accepted by Science is that the Induction is the action of the electrical current through the Ether, by waves of vibration. And I hold that just as the vibratory-waves of Magnetism and Electricity pass through the Ether and produce similar properties in other bodies by means of Induction, so do the vibratory waves of Mentative Energy, from one mind, pass through the Ether, and by Induction set up similar mental states in the minds of other persons within the "field of induction." We shall see many evidences of this as we proceed in these lessons.

TELEMENTATION.

I shall use another new term in these lessons, which it may be as well to explain here at this point. I have adopted the term "Telementation" to indicate the action of the Mind over a distance by means of Mentative Currents—"long-range mental influence." The word "*Tele*" is from the Greek, and means "far," or "far off." Its uses in "telephone," "telegraph," etc., are well understood.

Some may ask why I discard the word "Telepathy," which is generally used in the sense of "Thought-Transference." My answer is that the term is improper and misleading. Telepathy, according to its root-words, really means "to suffer at a distance," the word "pathy," arising from the Greek word meaning "to suffer." It may properly be used in connection with the mental-transference of pain, or disease, or similar mental states, but its use otherwise is improper, notwithstanding its having acquired a secondary meaning. Sooner or later it will be dropped—the signs of it are apparent even now.

THE UNDERLYING ENERGY.

And, to a consideration of the nature of this Mental Energy or Activity. Let us begin at The Mind itself. As I have said, "just what" the Mind is no one *knows*, although nearly every writer on the subject has indulged in a scientific guess at it. The secret remains wrapped up in the Secret of The All, which no man knoweth. I shall not attempt to indulge in metaphysical speculation in these lessons—if you like that sort of thing, there are countless books written on the subject to be found on the shelves of every library in the land.

But we must have a beginning for our study of Mentative Energy—and here it is. Brushing aside, for the moment, all the theories as to the inner nature of Mind, I find myself unable to escape from the conclusion of Spencer and other great scientific thinkers that there is "An Infinite and Eternal Energy from which all things proceed." And I believe that all that exists in the phenomenal world is a manifestation of the Universal Energy. And, further, I am compelled to believe that as personal manifestations of Mind emanate from this Universal Energy, then this Universal Energy must contain Mind. For there is an indisputable law of logic that "whatever is evolved as a consequent,—must be involved as an antecedent"—that is, that you cannot get something out of a thing unless that something is already in it.

THE UNIVERSAL MENTATIVE ENERGY.

And moreover, I am compelled to think that the presence of Mind is perceptible in everything in Nature. I hold that there is Mind in the plant, else it could not grow and shape itself. And, further, I welcome heartily the teachings of the most advanced physical science, which holds that in the atoms, and the particles that go to make up atoms, there are to be found evidences of Life and Mind in operation. And, more than this I welcome as brothers, those who assert that as all forms and shapes of material life are seen to dissolve into the Ether, from which they arose, then, consequently, there "must be Mind in the Ether itself," else there would be no mind in any physical forms.

And, so, without asking you to attach yourself to any metaphysical, philosophical, or religious theory or teaching (suit yourself about these things) I must point you to the fact now admitted by the world's greatest thinkers that, at the last, there is to be found AN INFINITE AND ETERNAL ENERGY, MENTATIVE IN ITS NATURE, OF AND IN WHICH ALL THINGS ARE EVOLVED MANIFESTATIONS.

And, using this as a foundation, I hold that all the individual or personal manifestations of Mind, seen in ourselves or others, are but Centers of Mentative Energy in the great Substance of Universal Mentative Energy.

THE ENERGY OPERATES LIKE ELECTRICITY.

Whatever Mind may be, in its ultimate nature, the leading thinkers on the subject now hold that in its "working nature" or phase of operation it seems to work along similar lines to those followed by Electricity. Like Electricity, the Mind undoubtedly has two Poles, or phases. Like Electricity it travels in currents. Like Electricity, it operates by Induction. Like Electricity it is Vibratory in its nature. And, like the higher forms of Energy—super-electrical in nature—it possesses Radio Activity, or Radiant Energy—that is like many other forms of Radiant Energy, it is constantly throwing off streams of active energy, in the shape of "Rays"; "Vibrations," or "Waves." Recent scientific discoveries have proven this, and in the next few years the world will be startled by additional discoveries along these lines. Already we are receiving hints of "Mental Photographs," or "Radiographs," and before long we shall have "Mentometers," that will register the Telemental waves. Please mark this prophecy (made in January, 1907) and see how soon will be its fulfilment.

THE BRAIN IS A "TRANSFORMER" OF ENERGY.

The Brain I regard as in the nature of a "transformer" of the Universal Mind Energy, or possibly as a "converter" of the Energy into Thought, Desire, Will, etc. The Brain cannot *create*—its office is merely to "transform" or "convert" an existent Energy into usable forms and phases. Science agrees in the belief that in all brain-processes there is an employment of some kind of Energy, and a "burning-up" of brain substance. Just as there is a constant "burning-up" of the elements of an electrical battery in the production of Electricity, so is there a "burning-up" of brain matter, in the production of Mental Activity. And, yet Science teaches us that no Electricity is ever "created"—simply a portion of the Universal Electricity is "converted" or "transformed." And I believe that the same holds good in Mental Action in the Brain.

THE TWO MENTATIVE POLES.

And now it is time for us to begin our consideration of the Two Mentative Poles.

In these lessons I shall hold to the fact there is evident in the manifestation of Mentative Energy, in any and all forms, two distinct Poles or Phases. I find myself compelled to coin two more terms for these poles or phases, for there are none now in common use. I shall call these two Mentative Poles respectively "The Emotive Pole" and "The Motive Pole." The word "Motive" means: "that which acts; wills; moves; chooses; controls." The word "E-motive" means: "that which manifests feeling; emotion; agitation; passion; sensation, etc.". These definitions apply to my use of the terms in these lessons. You will be able to fix these two ideas connected with the Mentative Poles, by thinking of the Motive Pole as "Will"; and of the Emotive Pole as "Feeling."

The two active manifestations of the two Mentative Poles are as follows:

The Emotive Pole manifests actively as DESIRE.

The Motive Pole manifests actively as WILL.

DESIRE AND WILL IN EVIDENCE ALWAYS.

You will find these two phases, Desire and Will, manifest in every mental action. There must always be a preceding Desire, and a responding Will, even in the production of a Thought: One must "desire" to know a thing, and then "will" to know it, before the Thought is evolved. The Thought is the child of the two parents, Desire and Will. Think over this a moment. You may not always recognize the two elements, because they often follow each other so closely as to seem one impulse. And then again, the Desire may manifest outside of the conscious field, but it is always present. And your mind may be so filled with the Desire, that you do not recognize the action of the Will, but it is always there.

These two forces, Desire and Will, are manifest all through Nature. Haekel the German scientist, in his works along the lines of the most advanced scientific thought, tells us that even in the actions of the atoms, there is evident (1) the feeling or Desire of attraction, or repulsion; and (2) the impulse of Will responding thereto, causing the action in accordance with the Desire. It is a Universal Law, and its evidences may be seen everywhere.

DESIRE AND WILL IN TELEMENTATION.

And, in the Mind, these two poles play a most important part, along the lines of Telementation. Not only does Desire cause a response of Will, but both Desire and Will are active forces in themselves, and act and react upon the Desire and Will poles of mentality of others. We shall see many evidences of this as these lessons progress. In fact, the entire theory and practice of Mental Magic depends upon this underlying principle.

Your strong Desire-force is able to rouse the Will of another mind in response thereto. It may likewise set up vibrations in that other mind, awakening there similar Desires. Your Will power may arouse Desire in the mind of another, and cause action in accordance therewith. It may also overpower the Will of another, and lead it captive. Your combined Will and Desire pouring out in a Mentative Current may produce a combined effect upon the minds of others by Telemental Induction. These two poles of the mind are both active and powerful in their effect. Both may be roused into intense activity, according to well-known laws, as we shall see. Let us take a few moments' time and consider the subject of Desire-Force and Will-Power, before we proceed further.

"THOUGHT" NOT THE MOTIVE-POWER.

Those who have studied the phenomena of Mental Influence have generally accepted the theory that the effect upon other people was produced by the "Thought" of the sender, and all the teachings upon the subject have been along this line. I, too, fell into this error, and for many years taught of the power of "Thought," etc. But I have come to modify my views on the question.

Of course, everyone who has paid any attention to the subject knows that Thought-transference is a fact, Telementation being an established reality. But there is a very great difference between the fact that "thoughts" may be sent and received like telegraphic messages, on the one hand, and that persons may be influenced and affected, and bent to the Desire or Will of another, on the other hand. It is like the difference between Thinking and Doing in ordinary life. One may send his thoughts so that another may receive them—but what of this? Where does the Doing and Compelling come in? It is evident that the real Force must be looked for in some far more elementary and vital operation of the mind, than logical and reasoning thought. What is Thought, anyway? Webster defines it as "An exercise of the mind in any of its higher forms; reflection, cogitation." Nothing very forceful about this, is there? We must look for something in the mind having more elementary force and power.

THE MOVING-FORCE OF THE MIND.

Let us think a moment. What part of the mind seems to produce the greatest moving power and strength? Is it not chiefly that region of the mind" that produces what we call Emotions—Feelings—Desires—Cravings—Passions? Does not this part of the mind really cause the greatest incentive action on our part? Is not the whole moving-force largely summed up in the two words DESIRE and WILL? Think of this a moment.

Why did you do this thing, and that thing? Is it because you thought about it by cold, logical reasoning, and acted upon the impulse given thereby? Or, was it not because you WANTED to do it—DESIRED to do it—FELT like doing it? Is not always the FEELING or DESIRE precedent to and the originator of the action? And, as for Thought, is it not used merely as a judge deciding on the wisdom of the action, and as an instrument to think up the best ways of manifesting the Feeling or Desire? Think of this-is it not so? Did you ever do a thing (except under compulsion) that you did not Desire to do it? And was not the Desire the preceding cause of your every action?

Desire the Mental Inciter.

Desire is the great inciting power of the Mind. Desire is "that which incites to action." And you always act upon the strongest Desire—subject always to the restraining influence of the Reason, and the Restricting or Impelling influence of the Will. I will tell you more about this wonderful thing, the Will, in a moment or two, but let us now think of Desire, for that is the real Emotive-power.

Desire originates in the sub-conscious regions of the mind, and often we can feel her there, before she emerges into consciousness, stirring us up with feelings of vague discontent and unrest. After a bit, gathering enough force, she emerges into the conscious field, and then begins to demand expression. Now remember, that when I say Desire, I mean all kinds of Desire, high and low. Many people think of Desire as only the craving of a low nature, but Desire really means a feeling that Wants something—and that something may be the very highest aspiration of the human mind.

The Attracting Power of Desire.

Now, this Desire in all of its manifestations has a mighty power of Attraction and Influence. It manifests as the Law of Mentative Attraction which is constantly drawing toward us the things we Desire, and also drawing us toward them. Not only is this true on the conscious plane, but even on the sub-conscious. Our desires constitute our Nature, and our Nature is always operating a mighty power of Mentative Attraction.

The trouble with the most of us is that we allow our Desire-Force to be scattered, and diffused, thereby lessening its Attractive power. It is only when we learn the secret of Concentration and Focussing the Desire-Force by the Will, that we are able to get results above the average. The Will is the director and controller of the Desire-Force, and upon its training and management depends the powerful use of the latter.

The Effect of Desire-Force.

Desire-Force not only has its effect upon the person, and others near him, but it may be, and often is, sent for thousands of miles where it affects and influences others, in ways. Desire-Force is the mighty Force which makes many of the forms of Mental Magic possible. It spreads out from the mind of the person, affecting and influencing others even at other parts of the world, if concentrated and directed by the Will. It is a force beside which the X Ray and Electricity fade into insignificance. It moves not merely blind, lifeless things, but the living minds, thought, emotions, passions and actions of Men. It is the force that rules the world, and its destinies. Like any other great Natural Force it is capable of being used for good or evil. It is neither good nor evil—it is either or both, according to the mind in which it originates.

The Insistent Desire.

What phase of mental effort is more apt to be a motive-force—the cold, lifeless thought about an abstract metaphysical proposition, or a mathematical problem, on the one hand; and a warm vital wave of "feeling," emotion or passion, such as Love, Hate, Ambition, Aspiration, Courage and Desire on the other? And, remember that these last mentioned all belong to the "feeling" side of the mind, and all are manifestation of elementary Desire.

Desire is at the bottom of all feeling. Before we can love or hate, there must be Desire. Before we can have Ambition or Aspiration there must be Desire. Before we can manifest Courage and Energy there must be Desire. Desire for something must underlie all life action—Desire conscious or sub-conscious. Abstract Thought is a cold, bare thing, lacking vitality and warmth—Desire is filled with life, throbbing, longing, wanting, craving, insisting, and ever pressing outward toward action. Desire indeed is the phase of our mental action that is a motive-force.

Waves of Desire-Force.

And not only does Desire incite us to action—move us to accomplish its ends, but it also, when sufficiently strong, surges out from our minds in great waves and clouds of invisible and subtle energy or force, and travels here and there toward the object of its inner urge—affecting, attracting, drawing, forcing the desired thing into submission to its cravings and demand. In the presence of some strong man or woman—that is, in the presence of one whose Desire burns fiercely and strongly, and whose Will has learned to concentrate the Desire-Force—one may actually feel the impact of the elementary principle of mind as it vibrates in great waves from the brain and nervous system of such a one. Who has not met people who actually seemed to be Living Desire and Will?

What "Desire" Really Means.

The source of Desire-Force exists in every person, and it may be developed to a wonderful degree. The Desires of many of you—of the majority of the race, in fact—never get further than the faint "want to" stage. These people "wish" for things in a faint pink-tea way. They never want a thing hard enough to stir their Desire-force into action and make the thing come to them, or else make it take them to the thing. The majority of people do not know how to Desire. They do not know what it is to be filled with that intense, eager, longing, craving, ravenous Desire that fills them with a new and mighty force, and makes them DEMAND things instead of merely asking for them. They are like sheep, pigeons, or rabbits, and sit meekly around while the strong ones of the race—the ones filled with masterful Desire—walk around and pick up every good thing in sight. And it serves them right, too, for they are not exercising the force which Nature has given them for the purpose of self-protection and use. They have had the elementary vigor and virility bleached out of them by the "refinements" of one phase of civilization, and have nearly lost all that goes to make up Manly Men, and Natural Women. They have become beggars instead of masters—mendicants of Nature, instead of Masters of her.

The forces of Nature are at the disposal of the man of vigor and determination and Desire. Such a one has but to knock at the door of Attainment and have it opened to him. Instead of doing this, the majority of us sit around the doorsteps whining that the door shall be opened to us. In the name of Human Power, friends, get up, and fill yourself with powerful Desire, then march up to the door and smite it fiercely with your mailed fist, demanding masterfully, "Open for me, the Master!" And, lo! it will fly open at your call.

The Relation of Will to Desire.

I have shown you that Desire-Force is the great mental force underlying the phenomena of Mental Magic. But Desire-Force without the aid of the Will is like steam unconfined and directed, and gunpowder fired in the open air—both wasted energy. The Will is the lever and director of the great power of Desire, and without its aid the latter is almost inoperative and ineffectual. Let us examine into the operation of the Will.

The Will has two offices in connection with Desire. These two offices may be spoken of as (1) the Directing office; and (2) the Protecting office.

The Will acts as the arouser, director, restrainer, concentrator, and manager of the great occult force of Desire. What is generally known as Will-Power is often in reality merely Desire power strongly concentrated and directed to a focus by the power of the Will. Remember this, please, for it will enable you to form a better idea of the subject of Will-Power. Often when you hear Will-Power spoken of, whatever is attributed to it is really said of and attributed to Desire controlled, directed, and focussed by Will. The effort of the Will is operated in the direction of this directing, focussing, concentrating, etc., and in the degree that the Will is trained to do this so is the degree of "Will-Power" of the individual. Not only is the Will able to do this, but it is able also to direct the Desire-Force into the mind of other persons, awakening similar vibrations there, and then by its own power the Will is able to direct the Desire-Force of the other persons into action, taking away that office from the Will of the other persons, if their Will be not strong enough in its Protective office to resist the attack.

THE MENTATIVE TWINS.

The idea of Will-Power is more familiar to the minds of people than is that of Desire-Force. All recognize the wonderful power of the Will, and know of many instances of great accomplishment by reason of its power. And, yet, how few have stopped to consider that unless there was a preceding Desire, there could be no manifestation of Will. Unless a person desires, that is, *wants* to do a thing, he will manifest no Will-Power. But, on the other hand, one may desire to do a thing, and unless the Will is aroused and applied no action will occur. Desire arouses Will-Power; and Will may stimulate Desire. The two act and re-act upon each other. The two should work in unison, and the trained Master Mind has both under control and pulling well together, like a well-trained team.

Will-Power is more than a mere Determination to act, although that mental attitude and action is manifested in Will-Power. It is a living force. Desire is the sister, and Will the brother twin. And both, together, manifest that which we know as Mentative Influence.

Will-Power is more than a mere mental faculty-it is a mighty attribute, the influence of which may extend far beyond the mind of the person manifesting it. The greatest feats of the occult magicians depend upon Telementation operated by trained Will-Power. And the so-called "great" men of history, ancient and modern, had their source of strength in this Will-Power, which they trained and developed to an extraordinary degree.

THE MASTERY OF WILL.

The exercise of Will shows itself in two ways, (1) the Mastery of one's own Mind; and (2) the Mastery of the minds of others. The second is well nigh impossible unless the first be accomplished. One must first train his mind so that he will hold it firmly in the grasp of the Will, and prevent it from jumping this way and that way, instead of moving ahead to its purpose. When one has so trained his mind to be obedient to his Will, that it can be held steady and "one pointed," as the Hindus say, then is he in a position to direct his Mentative Currents upon others to the best advantage. But so long as his mind is in a state of disorganization, one faculty pulling this way, and another that way, and so on, he cannot hope to concentrate upon others the force that is being wasted in keeping order at home. When the mind is mastered by the Will, then may new territory be conquered.

The term, Will-Power, is commonly used in connection with the manifestation of Firmness, or Determination. The Determined Will is known as a mighty factor toward attainment and accomplishment. And I think it well to consider this fact at this point, for back of all outward manifestations of Mentative Influence along active lines, lies this Determined Will of the individual. The more determined and firm be the Will of the individual, the stronger the Mentative Influence emitted and emanated by him. This statement should not require proof, for its truth is apparent to all who have made a study of man and his powers. It has been recognized by writers in all times. Here are a few quotations that will tend to fix the matter firmly in your mind, and create in you a desire to manifest the

The Underlying Force.

Determined Will—the lever that directs and concentrates Mentative Influence.

The Testimony of Wise Men.

Buxton said: "The longer I live, the more certain I am that the great difference between men, between the feeble and the powerful, the great and the insignificant, is Energy—Invincible Determination—a purpose once fixed, and then Victory or Death. That quality will do anything that can be done in this world—and no talents, no circumstances, no opportunities will make a two-legged creature a Man without it."

Donald G. Mitchell said: "Resolve is what makes a man manifest; not puny resolve, not crude determinations, not errant purpose—but that strong and indefatigable Will which treads down difficulties and danger, as a boy treads down the heaving frost-lands of winter; which kindles his eye and brain with a proud pulse-beat toward the unattainable. Will makes men giants."

Disraeli said: "I have brought myself by long meditation to the conviction that a human being with a settled purpose must accomplish it, and that nothing can resist a Will which will stake even existence upon its fulfillment."

Sir John Simpson said: "A passionate Desire and an unwearied Will can perform impossibilities, or what may seem to be such to the cold and feeble."

John Foster said: "It is wonderful how even the casualties of life seem to bow to a spirit that will not bow to them, and yield to subserve a design which they may, in their first apparent tendency, threaten to frustrate. When a firm, decisive spirit is recognized, it is curious to see how the space clears around a man and leaves him room and freedom."

But these matters will be touched upon in other parts of this book, and I must hasten on to consider the manifestations of Will-Power as the director of Mentative Currents affecting persons and things outside of the individual manifesting it.

WILL, THE PROJECTOR OF MENTATIVE FORCE.

As we have seen, the use of the Will as the projector of Mentative Currents is the real base of all Mental Magic, under whatever name it may manifest. And the phase of Will known as Telementation is the form the results of which strike the observer with the greatest force. The Will Currents of a strong man reaches out far beyond the limits of his brain, and influences people and things, causing them to be inclined toward his wishes. Many men have worked their Will upon others far removed, and much that is known as Thought-transference, Telepathy, Mental Influence, etc., is really this working of the Will Currents over space. What occultists have called "thought-forms," etc., are really manifestations of the energy of the Will. Will is a living force, that can be projected and operated at a distance. It has a property of reacting upon others, and permeating them with a mental essence not their own, unless they repel the invasion or fortify themselves against the aggression.

THE WONDERS OF WILL.

Desire and Will are more elementary forms of mentation than Thought. They underlie Thought. Without Desire and Will there can be no Thought. "Feeling" ever precedes Thought, and Desire and Will form the Essence of what we call "Feeling." Many people live almost altogether on the Feeling plane, and exercise but little Thought. The infant Desires and Wills before it can Think. Desire and Will is really the medium from which Thought is evolved.

A modern writer on Mysticism has said: "There is no force in the universe except Will-force," meaning, of course, the great Natural Force or Energy called Will, of which Desire and Will in Man are expressions. Desire is a natural force, and can be used, managed, controlled and directed just as can be any other natural force. And what we know as Will-Power is the positive phase of directed Desire. The Orientals have trained and cultivated this Will-Power to degrees that seem miraculous to the Western mind, and by this trained Will-Power they perform the so-called "miracles" that confound the Western scientist. But even the West has its men of "Iron Will," whose influence is felt on all sides, and whose power is openly acknowledged by the public. In the East these men are generally hermits and sages, while in the West they are generally "men of action," leaders, "captains of industry," etc.

THE MASCULINE AND THE FEMININE ENERGY.

Mentative Energy is the essence of all Mental Influence and other forms of the mental control of one person by another. It includes the positive, forcing, impelling, compelling, driving phase called Will as its Motive Pole, and as its Emotive Pole it has that attracting, drawing, pulling, luring, charming, fascinating something that we call Desire. Mentative Energy manifests in the phases of both Desire and Will, as we generally use these terms, for it is composed of the elements of both. Will may be said to represent the Masculine side of Mentative Energy, and Desire the Feminine side. It may help you to fix in your mind the attributes, characteristics and nature of these two phases of Mentative Energy by associating them with the idea of Masculine and Feminine.

I wish that you would learn to think of Desire-Force as the warm, ardent, fiery, forceful energy underlying the manifestations of Mentative Energy; and of the Will-Power as the cold, keen, strong, directing, controlling projector of the Energy. By fixing these mental images in your mind, you will be better able to manifest the two phases as occasion arises.

THE DIRECTING WILL.

Besides its office as the Director of the Energy, the Will serves a very important office as the Restrainer of Desire-Force. It, when under the control of the "I" of the person, and taking the suggestion of Reason and Judgment, is able to prevent one from expressing undesirable or hurtful Desires. It refuses to project the Desire-Force, or to allow the Desire to take effect in action. It also turns back the Desire upon itself, and refuses to allow it to manifest. It is the utmost importance that the Individual acquire a mastery of his Will, for by doing so he will be able not only to express his Desires with the greatest force and effect, but will also be enabled to restrain hurtful Desires, and to prevent their manifestation upon the plane of action.

THE PROTECTING WILL.

And the Will has still another important office. It acts as a Protector. It is the Will-Power that repels the influence or vibrations of another mind, and which renders its possessor immune from undesirable thought-waves of Mentative Induction. It creates a Protective Aura around the individual, which will turn aside the thought-waves or vibrations which may reach him, whether such be sent directly to him or whether they are the vibrations emanating from the minds of others and unconsciously sent forth. The Will, when properly used, acts as an insulator for attacks upon the Desire Pole of one's mind, and prevents the vibrations from reaching their mark. And if it be well trained and strengthened it will be able also to resist the most powerful attacks upon it by the Wills of others, and will beat back the vibrations which would force their way into its stronghold to take it captive.

MENTATIVE INDUCTION.

And now let us examine into the subject of the operation of the Mentative Energy, in the phase of its employment, consciously or unconsciously, to affect the minds of others. It is true that this subject will be considered in detail in our lessons on Personal Influence and Telementation, but it will be well for us to take a glance at the general workings at this point. I shall cover the points briefly, the elaboration being made at the proper points in the lessons.

The Underlying Force.

In the first place, let us consider the matter of Mentative Induction. As you have seen in this lesson, the currents of Mentative Energy flow in vibratory waves from the mind of the individual, and act upon the minds of others according to the laws of Mentative Induction. They thus set up corresponding vibrations, and therefore corresponding Mental States or Feelings, in the minds of such people. In other words, these vibrations "induce" or set up by Induction in the minds of others, the Mental States existing in the mind of the Mentator.

These induced Mental States are similar in quality and nature to that in the original mind. But, of course, they are less in degree, for a part of the original energy has been dissipated in many directions, and then again, a certain amount of force is lost according to the degree of resistance in the receiving mind. If the receiving mind sets up, consciously or unconsciously, a considerable resistance to the vibrations, it will either entirely neutralize or repel them, or else rob them of much of their power. If, on the contrary, the receiving mind be in its nature more or less in accord with the vibrations, it will set up little or no resistance, and the induced condition will be very nearly as strong as the original impulse. A little thought will make this plain to you.

Mentative Currents.

The ether, or fine substance filling space, is constantly filled with these Mentative Currents, of all kinds and degrees, streaming out from the minds of all kinds of people. These currents, of course, come in contact with each other, and often either combine or else act to neutralize each other. For instance, currents of a certain degree or kind of vibration (that is, of a certain Mental State) when they come in contact with other currents of similar vibrations, will tend to coalesce and combine, there being a harmony and attraction existing betweeen them. But if they are opposing vibrations they will antagonize each other and act in the direction of neutralizing each other's force.

If they be of equal strength, both will lose power, but if one be much stronger than the other it will lose only in the inverse ratio of its strength, and the weaker will suffer likewise. That is, the weaker will lose twice as much power as the stronger, and the stronger will lose only half as much as the weaker—supposing that the stronger is of twice the strength of the weaker.

"Mental Atmospheres" Of Places.

In this way is accounted for the well-known fact that places, towns, cities, etc., have their own "personal atmospheres," which affect persons living in them or visiting them. These "personal atmospheres" of towns arise from a combining, neutralizing, etc., of the various vibrations arising from Mentative Currents from the minds of the people living in the town. An average vibration is struck, which is strongly felt by all within the "field of induction" of that town. A little thought will make it clear to you that this is a correct statement of the mental conditions manifest in various towns, cities, etc., all over the world.

Each place has its own individuality, which soon makes its impression on those taking up their abode in it. It is more than geographical and atmospheric condition, although, of course, these play their part, as we all know. It is the average mental state of the people living in the town that strikes the key-note. The stronger vibrations affect the average, and give a mental tone to the place. The best proof of this effect being caused by mental vibrations is found in the fact that two towns only a few miles from each other, each having the same atmospheric and geographical conditions, will manifest entirely different mental atmospheres. Think over this a little, and you will see the truth of the statement.

The Effect of the Mentative Vibrations.

People often ask: "If it be true that the ether is filled with Mentative Currents, why are we not affected more than we are?" The answer is that they are affected more than they imagine, but they are still affected much less than one would suppose at first thought, for the reason that the currents conflict with each other and rob each other of their force. And then again, Nature instinctively affords a safeguard and sets up additional powers of resistance. Just as Nature protects the hearing sense of those who are surrounded with many and constant noises, until they fail to hear anything but an unaccustomed noise—just as she operates upon the smelling sense of the chemist until he fails to notice the odors which are most apparent to the stranger entering his shop—so does she give additional unconscious resisting power to people situated within an active field of Mentative Induction.

Bring a person from a quiet place into a bustling, active city, and he is apt to be swept off his feet at first with the "spirit of the place"—he will either be swept into its prevailing life with an almost irresistible impulse, or else he will be repelled by reason of the inharmonious mentative currents. In either case, however, he will be intensely aware of the vibrations. But, the same man, after a time, will fail to be so affected—he will be better able to resist the vibrations and will manage to live with a greater peace and poise than at first, although he will, of course, alter his nature more or less in harmony with the prevailing tone of the place. He will "feel" the vibrations less as time goes on. Some people have so developed this resisting power that they are almost immune, while others have so little power of resistance that they are swept here and there by each strong wave of Mentative Energy that reaches them—they are always in some field of Induction and being swayed by its vibrations.

WAVES OF "FEELING."

This phase of Mentative Induction explains the phenomena attendant upon those great waves of feeling that sweep over a country, like the emotion that followed the sinking of the Maine in the harbor of Havana. You will remember the first shock that came to you when you read the account in the morning papers. Then there came upon you a growing sense of some impending event of great moment, mingled with a feeling of horror and indignation, followed by an almost irresistible desire to join in a movement to avenge the outrage. This latter feeling grew perceptibly as wave after wave of feeling passed over the country in Mentative Currents, setting up increased mental feeling by induction. Older people will remember many similar waves that swept over the land in past days.

MENTATIVE CYCLONES.

These things are common, and give you a clue to the apparent mystery of the forming of, and action of, mobs composed of a number of individuals who combine in numbers and then commit acts that no one man of the lot would think of perpetrating singly or individually. The conscience of the mob is apparently a thing apart from the individual consciences of the units composing it. After the excitement—the morning after—many, if not all, of the persons concerned, feel a sickening horror and wonder at their work. A mob is a cyclonic center of Mentative Currents, resembling a whirlpool or whirlwind, with an active center and a less active circumference.

Great waves of religious fervor noticeable in communities during the progress of "revivals" are accounted for in the same way. A few active revivalists start a whirlwind of fervid feeling and emotion, and it spreads out in constantly widening circles, increasing until a climax is reached, and then a diminishing strength is apparent, which gradually settles down into the accustomed mental state of the community.

These whirlwinds or whirlpools of emotional excitement, of whatever kind, are, of course, strengthened by the constantly repeated suggestions of those participating in it, which with the constantly growing volume of Mentative Energy being thrown forth serves to add fuel to the fire. This force would go on forever, steadily gaining in strength and volume, were it not for a provision of nature which causes the law of Rise and

Fall; Increase and Decrease; that Universal Law of Rhythm, to manifest in this as in all else in her domain. Everything has its rise, its Climax, and its Decline.

So far for these general waves of Mentative Energy, or Mentative Currents. But there is another phase to be considered—many phases, in fact. Let us examine them.

THE CENTRES OF THE MENTAL WHIRLPOOLS.

First there are Mentative Currents, arising from the strong centered Desire of some person, who forming a strong Mental Image, by means of Visualization, creates for himself a Center of Desire-Force, which guided by his Will-Power attracts to himself all that will fit into his plans. He constitutes himself a Mentative Center, around his Visualized Idea, and constantly sends out strong Mentative Currents charged with the strongest, most ardent Thought-Force, guided, directed, and projected by his developed Will-Power. He thus sets into operation the great mental Law of Attraction, of which the early writers on Mental Science talked so much. These Mentative Currents, charged with Desire, spread out, and soon begin a rotary movement like a whirlpool, sweeping around and around, always drawing in toward its center persons and things tending to fit in with the plans of the Center.

The original Desire in the man's mind is reproduced in kind in the minds of thousands of people by the law of Mentative Induction, and they all fall in with the plan, the degree, of course, depending upon the degree of positivity or negativity of the receptive mind, multiplied by the degree of positivity of the Mentator. The great plans of the so-called "Captains of Industry" are carried out by reason of this law.

Many of these great centers of Desire-Force—these successful men, who attract to them that which they want, and those whom they need—do not realize the nature of the force that they are using, but there is a constantly increasing number who do know it, and they are "working it for all it is worth." Many of these steady, cool business leaders are really deeply versed in occult laws. If the true facts of the case were to creep out, there would be the greatest sensation that the country has ever known.

MENTATIVE INFLUENCE.

Then there is still another phase of the matter. I allude to the cases of men who (generally consciously, but sometimes unconsciously) are focusing their Mentative Currents directly upon some person or persons who are necessary to their plans and desires. They are filled with Desire to have these persons do thus and so, or not do thus and so, as the case may be. These men, according to their degree of concentration and Will-Power, direct to the other person or persons strong Mentative Currents of Desire-Force, and by Mentative Induction set up vibrations of a corresponding rate in the minds of these others, the degree of effect produced, of course, depending upon the degree of negativity of the recipient. This effect is produced in two ways, both according to the law of Mental Induction.

The first way is to set up corresponding Desire vibrations in the mind of the other, so that it will in turn cause his Will to carry out the Desire. A variation of this is to direct the Desire-Force toward the Will of the other, and thus "entice" or "charm" the other's Will into compliance with the Desire of the sender. This will be understood if you will remember what I have said about the resemblance of the Desire Pole to the Feminine, and the Will Pole to the Masculine. You will see an illustration of this at every point of Mentative Influence.

MORE ABOUT MENTATIVE INFLUENCE.

The second way is for the Will of the sender to force its way past the Will of the other and boldly "make love" to the Desire of the other, and endeavor to "seduce" it by mere strength and persistency until it accedes to his wishes. The variation of this is seen in the case where the attacking Will boldly "tackles" the

Will of the other, and by sheer superiority of power overcomes it and makes it captive and obedient. This latter is very rare, except in cases of personal interviews between the two persons, aided by Telementation between interviews.

You will notice that the phase in which the Desire Pole of file Mentator does the work is along the lines of Feminine action, the force being of a charming, fascinating, drawing, coaxing nature; and where the Will is employed, the action is decidedly Masculine, the attack being made boldly, and with a show of strength, the subtlety of the Desire attraction being absent. The giants in the art of Mentative Attraction combine Poles in their attacks and work, and thus in the words of "Uncle Remus": "Dey cotch 'em comin', and dey cotch 'em goin'," like "Brer Fox."

PERSONAL INFLUENCE.

Then again, there is the use of Mentative Induction, in what is known as "Personal Influence," which we will see in another lesson of this series—the Fourth Lesson in this book. In this phase the Mentator pours forth his Mentative Currents, either in a general way, or else in a concentrated, directed manner, toward the other, in a personal interview. This is the secret of what is called "Personal Magnetism," and also of that unaccountable (to the uninformed) manner which some people have of overpowering others by sheer "strength of character." The "Personal Magnetism" phase of Personal Influence is the Desire phase—the Feminine activity; and the "Force of Character" phase is the operation of Will—the Masculine activity.

MENTAL SUGGESTION.

Then there is that form of Mentative Induction called "Mental Suggestion," which I take up in the lesson following immediately after the present one. Although Suggestion has to do with words, etc., rather than with Mentative Currents, still the principle is the same—the Mental State is "induced" by words or physical things which are the result of Feeling and

Mental states, just as is the phonographic record the result of the original speech which it is able to reproduce when the diaphragm is brought in contact with it by means of the needle. And then there is very little Mental Suggestion that is not accomplished with Mentative Currents—very little, indeed, if any, as we shall see in the next lesson.

NATURE'S PROTECTIVE ARMOR.

Now, in closing this lesson I wish to caution my readers to refrain from manifesting or feeling anything like Fear at what I have said about the use of Mentative Energy by other people. Remember, that Fear in itself is the most negative influence and most weakening mental state known. It renders negative the most positive man if freely indulged in. No matter how potent may be these Mentative Currents, there are none that may not be rendered impotent and ineffectual by your own Will-Power set in motion by your own Desire-Force. Each and every one of you have within you, and under your own control, a force that will render you perfectly and absolutely immune from undesirable Mentative Influence, no matter who may use it against you.

Nature has blessed all of us in this respect—it makes no bane without its antidote, and does not depart from its rule in this phase any more than in any other. It supplies the means of Self-Protection to everyone, and always furnishes the defensive weapon to match the offensive one. As a matter of fact, you are defending yourself constantly, although you may not know it. Much of this defensive work is done along subconscious lines, but you are doing much of it consciously by the use of your Will and spirit of Individuality. You are using the mental "No!" all the time—that is, unless you are some poor creature who is afraid to say "No!" even mentally, and if you are that then this book is doubly needed by you.

The Underlying Force.

Self-Protection.

I shall instruct every student of these lessons, in many different ways, as we proceed with the lessons in this Art of Self-Protection. No one who studies these lessons need ever again fear any undue influence on the part of others. I purpose to make Mental Masters of you, and to teach you to throw off the bonds and shackles of Mental Slavery. I intend to make you Strong, Positive Individuals, instead of Weak, Negative Personalities.

There is nothing to be afraid of except Fear—so the sooner you cast off Fear the better you will be, and the more advanced on the road to Mastery. While this is not the place for Exercises, still I want each and every one of you to start right in Now and form a Mental Attitude of Fearlessness and Strength, that you may begin at once to send forth Mentative Currents of that rate of vibration. If you do so—and you Will, I know—then you will begin to notice an improvement at once. You will begin to realize your increasing Power, and you will also see that others are beginning to feel it. Begin today—this moment—to radiate Mentative Currents of Strength and Power in all directions. Stimulate the currents by arousing a strong, intense, burning Desire to be Strong and to radiate Strength vibrations—then back this up by the application of a strong, steady, masterful and dominant Will—and then "the trick will be done."

Learn How to "Feel" and Will.

But right here remember, first, last, and all the time, that it is not a mere matter of Thinking—but a matter of Feeling. Thoughts are cold, but Feelings are warm, alive and vital. Therefore you must not merely think "I Am Strong," or say it like a parrot—but you must stir up your nature to its depths, until you can really Feel that you are indeed Strong and possessed of Radiant Energy of Mentative Force. Feeling is Living Thought. Everything that is worth while was produced by this Feeling Thought. Feeling—Desire—Emotion—Passion—Wanting—

Willing—these are the things that have Creative Power, not mere clear, cool thinking. So do not deceive yourself with this "holding the thought," or any such nonsense of which you have heard so much until you get sick at the mention of the words. It is not simply "holding the thought," it is "holding the Desire," and backing it up with the Will, that does the work. To create a thing you must Want It with a burning, eager want that brooks no denial—backed up by a Will that knows no such word as "Can't" or "No."

Now, get to work!

Lesson III.

Mental Suggestion.

What Is Mental Suggestion?—The Phases of Suggestion—Suggestion Entirely Emotional—The Meaning of the Term—My Own Definition—The Power of Words—The Subtle Insinuation—Impression and Induction—Degrees of Suggestibility—Ideas Induced by Feeling—Feelings vs. Reason—The Four Lines of Action—The First Line of Action—Man, An Obedient Animal—The Origin of Obedience to Suggestion—The "Confidence Men"—Extreme Instances—The Keynote—Those Easily Affected—The Degree of Power—The Second Line of Action—Human Sheep and Apes—Imitative Mental Contagion—The Third Line of Action—Words but Symbols—Associated Feeling—The Art of the Suggestor—The Master-Key—The Spell of Oratory—The Power of Words—The Actor—How to Protect Yourself—The Fourth Line of Action—The Secret of this Form—Cuckoo Feelings—Mental Impressions—The Force of Repeated Statements—A Warning—The Three Forms of Application—The First Form—Children and Suggestion—The Rule of Involuntary Suggestion—The Second Form—Suggestive Treatment—Hypnotic Suggestion—The Third Form—Feelings vs. Reason—The Psychology of Salesmanship—Agents' Suggestions—Advertising Suggestions—Illustrative Examples—The Psychology of Advertising—A Striking Example—Suggestion Accepted—Suggestion Among Lawyers—A Dangerous Use—The Suggestive Question—The Suggestive Position—Different Degrees—Suggestion and Personal Influence—The Importance of Suggestion.

Lesson III.

Mental Suggestion.

Every student of psychology and mental science has heard and read much of that phase of mental phenomena called "Mental Suggestion." Much has been written and taught about it, and the term has been claimed by some teachers to cover all phases of Mental Influence. I do not entirely agree with these extreme advocates of Suggestion, however, for I find much in the subject that calls for a further explanation. But, nevertheless, I feel certain that Mental Suggestion plays a most important part in almost every instance of this class of phenomena and must be seriously considered by all careful students of the subject. Combined with Mentative Induction by means of Mentative Currents, it accounts for nearly every phase of the phenomena of Mental Influence. Therefore I shall devote an entire lesson to the consideration of its underlying principles, laws and method of application. I feel that no one can be a successful practitioner of Telementative Influence or Personal Magnetism who is not a good Suggestionist, because the very "knack" of projecting strong Suggestions is necessary for the forceful projection of Mentative Energy and Mental Currents.

The Secret of Mental Magic

What is Mental Suggestion?

While all who have examined the subject are aware of the force and effects of Mental Suggestion, few have found it possible to correctly define or describe the term, or to explain it to others. And so in this lesson I shall have to undertake a task that many other writers on the subject have "dodged." But I feel assured that my theory of Mentative Induction, and the two Poles of the Mind, will enable you to form a very clear and comprehensive knowledge of the underlying laws of the subject, so that, understanding it "from the ground up," you will be able to apply its method of application to the best advantage.

The term "mental suggestion," used in the sense of personal influence, means that influencing or controlling of the mental states of others by means of words, actions, appearances, etc.

The Phases of Suggestion.

I divide the phenomena of Mental Suggestion into two general classes or phases, i. e., (1) Active Suggestion, and (2) Passive Suggestion, as follows:

By Active Suggestion I mean the induction of mental states in others by means of positive command, affirmation, statements, etc., bearing directly upon the desired mental state. By Passive Suggestion I mean the induction of mental states by the subtle insinuation, introduction, or insertion of ideas into the minds of others, which insinuated ideas act in the direction of inducing the desired mental state. Active Suggestions are associated with the use of the Motive Pole of the Mind of the Suggestor; and Passive Suggestions are associated with the Emotive Pole of the Suggestor. One is the Masculine method and the other the Feminine.

Suggestion Entirely Emotional.

And right here is a good place in which to direct your attention to a very important face concerning the operation of Suggestion in inducing mental states in others. I allude to the fact that Suggestion operates along the line of "emotional mentality" or "feeling," and has nothing to do with judgment, reason, argument, proof, etc. It belongs clearly to the "feeling" side of the mind, rather than to the "thinking" side. One's reason may be appealed to by clever reasoning, argument, logic, proof, etc., and an effect gained—but this belongs to an entirely different phase of mental action. The induction of mental states in others by means of Suggestion has to do entirely with the "feeling" phase of the mind. It deals with the production of "emotional mentality" rather than with "rational mentality." This is a most important point, and one that should be thoroughly understood by all students of the subject.

It is true that Suggestion may accompany an appeal to the reason or judgment of the person influenced, and, indeed, is generally so used; but, strictly speaking, it constitutes an appeal to a part of the mind entirely removed from reasoning and judgment. It is emotional, first, last, and all the time. And it operates along the same lines as the Mental Induction produced by Mentative Currents, as we shall see.

THE MEANING OF THE TERM.

And now, with this preliminary understanding, let us pass on to a considering of the meaning of the terms used. There is nothing like a clear understanding of the terms employed in treating of a subject. If one understands the "exact" meaning of the terms, he has progressed very far to an "exact" understanding of the subject itself, for the terms are the crystallized ideas involved in the subject. To understand the full and complete meaning of the terms of any subject is to know the whole subject thoroughly, for no one can understand a term thoroughly until he knows it in all of its relations—all that pertains to it.

Let us start with the word "Suggestion" as used by the writers on Mental Suggestion. Some authorities give the broad, general definition of "anything that is impressed upon the mind through the senses," but this I consider entirely too sweeping, for this definition would make the term cover knowledge of all sort, no matter to what part of the mind it appealed, for all knowledge of the outward world is obtained through the senses.

Other authorities define the term as "anything insinuated into the mind, subtly, cautiously, and indirectly," this definition fitting nearly the one favored by the dictionaries in defining the word "suggestion" in its general sense, which is as follows: "a hint; a guarded mention; an intimation; something presented to the mind directly; an insinuation; etc." But this last definition of Mental Suggestion does not fit all the phases of the subject. It fits admirably into the phase known as Passive Suggestion, as above described; but it leaves undefined the phase of Active Suggestion, which operates by direct, forceful command, statement, etc.

My Own Definition.

And so I must give my own definition of the term to fit my conception of and understanding of its meaning. I, therefore, here define my use of the term "Mental Suggestion" as follows: "A physical agent inducing mental states." This is a broad definition, which, I think, will cover all the observable phenomena of Mental Suggestion.

I use the word "physical" to distinguish Suggestive agent from the "mental" agents inducing mental states by the operation of Mentative Energy, Mentative Currents, Telementation, etc. Of course this distinction will not please those who would claim all "mental" action as a form of the "physical," or vice versa. But as I have to draw the line somewhere, I prefer to draw it between the "physical" agent and the "mental," and I think that the majority of my readers will approve of this position. The word "agent" means, of course, "an acting power or cause," etc.

Mental Suggestion.

The word "inducing," as I have used it, has been defined in the previous lesson.

So again here is my definition of a "Mental Suggestion"—"A PHYSICAL AGENT INDUCING MENTAL STATES." Better commit it to memory.

The Power of Words.

In my use of the term "physical" in the above definition I include all words, spoken, written, or printed; mannerisms; physical actions of all kinds; physical characteristics and appearances, etc., etc. All of these physical manifestations act as "agents" inducing mental states under favorable circumstances. By "Mental States" I mean states of "Feeling or Emotion," not abstract ideas or manifestations of Reason, Intellect, or Judgment.

It may be urged that the use of "words, spoken, written or printed," may be employed, and are employed, in every appeal to the mind of another, whether the appeal be along the lines of Suggestion or Argument, Reason, etc. Certainly! But these are not all "agents inducing mental states, i. e., feeling or emotion." Arguments appeal to judgment and reason—but not feeling and emotion, which are, on the contrary, excited or induced by Suggestions or other forms of Emotional Induction. One may present an idea to the mind of another, in a bold, forcible, logical manner, accompanied by argument or proof, but this is an appeal to reason and judgment, not to "feeling or emotion," which belong to an entirely different field of the mind. Then again, many personal appeals, which are apparently made to reason, are really made to the emotional side. One may subtly insinuate into an argument or conversation an appeal to the feelings or emotion of the hearer, in the shape of an idea in the nature of a hint or indirect mention. Such idea will be "felt" by the listener, who will accept it into his mind, and before long he will regard it as one of his own thoughts—he will make it his own. He will think that he "thought" it, whereas, really, he simply "feels" it, and the "feeling" is induced. This is a case of "suggestion."

THE SUBTLE INSINUATION.

In ordinary social intercourse you will find that women are adepts in this subtle form of insinuative suggestion, as compared to men. Men will blurt out statements and ideas, and attempt to "prove" them, but the woman will gently "insinuate" the idea into the mind of the other person, so that, without having proven a fact, she will have managed to create a definite idea of feeling in the mind of the other by "suggestion." I think I need not give examples of this fact—it is apparent to all who have mingled with people.

And really this "suggestion" resembles the Mental Suggestion of the psychologists very much. It is true that the practitioner of Mental Suggestion, in his "treatments," often makes use of direct, forceful statements, such as "You are strong, cheerful, well and happy," but you will notice even here that he does not "argue the point," or attempt to "prove" his statements. He simply affirms and asserts the fact, and by constantly repeated suggestions he finally causes the mind of the other person to accept the statement. So you see a "suggestion" may be either a subtle insinuation or a bold, positive statement—but it is never an argument, or process of proof.

IMPRESSION AND INDUCTION.

The word "Impression" is good, as applied to the effect of a suggestion, but I prefer to stick to my own terms, and therefore I shall consider that the effect of Mental Suggestion is caused by Induction. "What," you may say, "I thought that Induction was a term used when a Mental State was set up in one by Mentative Currents from the mind of another?" Yes, this is true, but my last statement is true also. An Induced Mental State is one set up by outside influence of some kind, whether that outside influence be a Mentative Current or by Suggestion through a word, a book, a sight, or anything else. The word "Induce," you know, means: "to lead; to influence; to prevail on; to effect; to cause; etc." And any Mental State that is induced by an outside influence comes clearly under the term.

Any physical agent that tends to induce a feeling in the mind of another may be called a Suggestion. Even the well-known instance mentioned in the text-books on psychology comes under this rule. In that instance it is related that a soldier was carrying some bundles and a pail to his barracks, when some practical joker yelled to him in an authoritative voice, "Attention!" Following the suggestion, which induced in him the "feeling" preceding certain habitual actions, he dropped his pail and bundles with a crash and stood at "attention," with eyes front, chin out, protruding breast, stomach drawn in, and hands at his sides with little fingers touching the seams of his trousers. That was a suggestion! Do you see the point?

The lives of all of us have been moulded largely by induction through suggestion. We accepted this suggestion, or that one, and it changed the whole current of our lives. Certain things induced certain feelings—called into activity certain mental states—and action followed close upon the heels of feeling.

DEGREES OF SUGGESTIBILITY.

There are varying degrees of suggestive power, just as there are varying degrees of what is called the "suggestibility" of persons—that is the tendency to accept suggestions. There are people who scarcely ever act from motives originating within themselves, but whose entire lives are lived out in obedience to the suggested ideas and feelings of others. The development of the Will Pole of Mentation regulates the degree of suggestibility. The man of the strong Will is not so easily affected by a suggestion as is one whose Will is weak, and who accepts without resistance the suggestions coming from all sides. But note the apparent paradox, persons of weak will may have their wills so developed and strengthened by scientific suggestive treatment that they may become veritable giants of Will.

IDEAS INDUCED BY FEELING.

The careful student may feel inclined to ask me, at this point, why I speak of suggested "ideas," when I have said that Suggestion has to do with "mental states of feeling and emotion." Are not "ideas," he asks, something connected with Thought rather than with feeling? The question is a proper one, and I must meet it. The word "idea" comes from the Greek word, meaning "to see." In its general use it means "a mental image, or a general notion or conception held in the mind." An idea is "symbolic image held in the mind." It is a symbol of something Thought or Felt.

Ideas are not formed by Thought alone—Feeling contributes its share of these mental images. To tell the truth, the majority of people scarcely "think" at all, in the highest sense of the word. Their reasoning and logical faculties are by rudimentary. They accept their ideas at second hand or second-hundred hand—their thoughts must be predigested for them by others, and the handed-down "idea" is the result. The majority of ideas held in the mind of the race arise from Feeling and Emotion. People may not understand things, but they have experienced feelings or emotions regarding them, and have consequently formed many ideas and "ideals" therefrom. They do not know "just why" an idea is held by them—they know only that they "feel" it that way. And the majority of people are moved, swayed and act by reasons of induced "feelings," rather than by results of reasoning. I am not speaking of intuitional feelings now, but of the plain, everyday, emotional feeling of people.

FEELINGS VS. REASON.

Do you know what a feeling is? The word, used in this sense, means: "a mental state; emotion; passion; sympathy; sentiment; susceptibility; etc." And "Emotion" means an excitement of the feelings. "Feelings" belong to the Instinctive side of our mind, rather than to the Rational or Reasoning side. They spring up from the subconscious strata of the mind, in response to the exciting cause coming from without. The Instinctive part of our minds are stored with the experience, feelings, emotions and mental states of our long line of ancestors, reaching away back to the early beginnings of life. In that part of the mind are sleeping instincts, emotions and feelings, our inheritance from the past, which await but the inducing cause to call them into activity. The Reason or Judgment, by means of the Will, act as a Restrainer, of course, according to the degree of development of the individual. And these outward agents, if of a "physical" nature, are Suggestions of all kinds.

Look around you at the world of men and women. Then tell me whether they seem to be moved principally by Reason or Feeling. Are their actions based upon good Judgment and correct and careful Reasoning? Or are they the results of Feeling and Emotion? Do people do things because the things are considered right in the light of Reason, or do they do them "because they feel like it?" Which produces the greatest motive force—an appeal to the Reason of a number of people, or an appeal to their Feelings and Emotion? Which sways a gathering of people; the votes of a people; the actions of a mob—Reason or Feeling? Which moves even You, good student, Reason or Feeling? Answer these questions honestly, and you will have the Key of Suggestive Influence!

THE FOUR LINES OF ACTION.

Mental Suggestion produces its effect upon the minds of people along one or more of four general lines or paths of action. All the phenomena coming under this head can be placed in one or more of the four classes. These four paths, or lines of action, along which Mental Suggestion operates, are as follows:

1. Obedience.
2. Imitation;

3. Association;
4. Repetition.

I shall now proceed to consider these four paths, or lines of action, separately, in order, and in detail. Beginning with the first mentioned line of action, let us consider:

The First Line of Action.

Suggestion Through Obedience.—Suggestion operating along these lines consists of the induction of Mental States, etc., by the agency of a positive statement, assertion, assumption, authoritative attitude, etc., which so impresses itself upon the mind of the person suggested to that he sets up no opposition or resistance, but acquiesces quietly to the suggestion made to him.

The most common form of this first form of Suggestion is seen in the very general acquiescence to real or pretended "authority" on the part of the majority of people. Such people hearing a statement made, positively and in a tone of conviction, by some person in authority, they accept the statement, and the feelings arising from the accepted statement, without resistance, and without any attempt to submit the matter to the exercise of their reason. And this is true not only when the person speaking has really a right to speak authoritatively, by virtue of his knowledge, experience, wisdom, etc., but also when some pretender sets up an appearance of authority, and speaking in a positive style, along the "Thus saith the Lord" manner, impresses his hearers with the idea he wishes to suggest to them. And then the good folk meekly acquiesce without question and allow their feelings to be aroused accordingly, for the feelings are generally followed by actions in accord therewith.

Man, an Obedient Animal.

It is astonishing, from one point of view, to see how obedient to this form of Suggestion the masses of people are. They will allow their Mental States, Feelings and Emotion to be induced by the impudent statements and claims of cunning, shrewd and designing men, as well as by ignorant, self-deluded fanatics, who thus influence and sway them. These self-constituted authorities utter their oracular statements and opinions in a tone of absolute certainty, and the crowd takes them at their own valuation. It seems to be only necessary for some positive man to attract the attention of the people and then make some bold claim or statement, in the proper manner and tone, and with their appearance of authority, and lo! some of the people, at least, fall into line.

Did you ever think that people as a rule are "obedient animals?" Well, they are, providing you can manage to impress them with your authority. It is much easier for them to acquiesce than to refuse to do so. They find it easier to say and think "Yes" rather than "No." Their Will is not often called into action by their Reason and Judgment, it being too often entirely under the control of the Feeling and Emotional side of them.

THE ORIGIN OF OBEDIENCE TO SUGGESTION.

There is a fundamental law under this phase of Suggestive action, and in order to find it we must go back to the beginning of the race, perhaps further. In the earlier days, among animals and men, there were natural leaders, who ruled by force of might of body or mind. These natural leaders were implicitly obeyed by the masses, who had learned by experience that it was better for the tribe, or herd, as a whole, to be governed by their strongest and sharpest-witted members. And so gradually this dominant idea of acquiescence and obedience to authority developed and became a fixture in the race-mind. And it is firmly planted in the mind of the race today, so much so that only the strongest minds are able to free themselves from it to any great extent. It is authority here, and authority there, in law, letters, religion, politics, and every other field of human endeavor. People do not begin by asking themselves, "What do I think about this matter?" but instead start off by saying, "What does So-and-So think of it?" Their "So-and-So" is their authority, who does their thinking for them, and they take their key-note from him or her. The authority induces their mental states for them.

If these leaders and authorities were really the wisest of the race, it would not matter so very much, although even then it might prevent the development of Individuality in the masses. But the worst feature is that the majority of these "authorities" don't know, and know that they don't know, but the people haven't found them out. They assume the manners, air, appearance, etc., of "the real thing," and the people being accustomed to these symbols of authority, and mistaking the imitation article for the real, are impressed by the authoritative utterance and accept the suggestion.

THE "CONFIDENCE MEN."

This fact is well known to the classes that prey upon the public. The "confidence men" (in and out of the criminal class) assume this air of authority, and their suggestions are accepted by the people. They are good actors—that is one of the requisites of the Suggestionist, and these people understand the law. They proceed upon the theory accredited to Aaron Burr—that remark, you may remember, was that "the Law is that which is boldly asserted and plausibly maintained." And so these folk keep on "boldly asserting," and "plausibly maintaining," and find that "it generally goes."

EXTREME INSTANCES.

To see a principle in its naked simplicity one should look for its operation in extreme instances. And the extreme instance in this case is the hypnotic somnambule who has surrendered his judgment entirely to the mind of the operator. The somnambule will acquiesce in the most absurd suggestions from the operator and proceed to carry them into effect. And Suggestion, you know, is the active factor in hypnotism, the hypnotic condition being only a psychological condition in which the effect of Suggestion is heightened.

But one does not have to go to the ranks of the somnambules for striking illustrations, for such are to be found in all walks of life among people who have no individuality of their own, but who seem to live and act entirely upon the "say so" of others. They have no quality of Initiative, but must always be told just what to do, and how to do it, by others. These people will accept almost any kind of Suggestion, if made by others in an authoritative tone and manner. They do not have to be persuaded by argument, but are fairly driven and ordered to do things by stronger-willed persons. They are impressionable and "sensitive," and seem to have no wills of their own. These people are very suggestible, and every day's history records many startling cases of the effect of Suggestion through Acquiescence on the part of such people.

THE KEYNOTE.

The Key-note of this form of Suggestion is a positive statement or command, given with the air and appearance of authority. The secret of the effect is the tendency upon the part of the majority of people to acquiesce in an Authoritative Statement or Command, rather than to dispute it; and the tendency toward thinking "Yes" rather than "No!"

THOSE EASILY AFFECTED.

This form of Suggestion is to be observed in the highest degree among those who have always depended upon others for orders, or instruction, and who have not had to "use their own wits" and resources in life. Unskilled laborers and the sons of rich men belong to this class as a rule. These people seem to need someone to do their thinking for them, even in the smallest events of their lives, and are most suggestible along these lines. Then the degree of suggestibility along these lines decreases as we ascend among people who have had to "do things" for themselves, and who have not depended upon others so much. It is the slightest among people who have had the ordering of others to do, or who have had to depend upon their own wits in getting through life—the men of marked degree of Initiative have scarcely a trace of this form of Suggestibility. "Initiative," you know, is a term for "doing things without being told"—using one's own wits and resources—the true "American Spirit" (which so many Americans lack).

The Degree of Power.

The degree of power in giving this form of Suggestion depends materially upon the development of Will on the part of the Suggestor, and also upon his assumption of the appearance; manners, air and tone of authority, the latter requisites being the outward symbols. If one has the Will-Power strongly developed, the symbols will appear of themselves as a natural consequence. But to those who have not the developed Will-Power, and whose authority is more or less "counterfeit," the assumption of the outward symbols becomes a matter of great importance, and these people devote much study to the cultivation of these outward forms. And these "counterfeit" symbols—the art of the actor—serve their purpose to impress and suggest to the crowd, and their assumers set up a very brave front and obtain a very fair degree of success in the part they are acting—that is, until they come in contact with a man of real Will-Power, when they gracefully retire after the first clash of Mentative swords.

To those who are negative and who are too susceptible to this form of Suggestion, I advise the Cultivation of Will-Power, which will be fully taught in the concluding lesson of this series, called "Character Architecture." Nothing but the cultivation of the Will will render them positive and impervious to suggestive influences of this sort.

Mental Suggestion.

The Second Line of Action.

The second line of action of Mental Suggestion is that called:

Suggestion Through Imitation.—This form of Mental Suggestion is very common—perhaps the most common of all the forms. Man is essentially an Imitative Animal. He is always copying the actions, appearances and ideas of others, thereby going to prove his descent from the monkey-like ancestors, in whom this trait of character was largely developed. Personally, I believe that this trait of Imitation may be traced back to the early days of the race, or before, when animal and man were in a wild state and exposed to constant danger of attack of enemies. Then a motion of fright on the part of one would be communicated to the others of the tribe, and gradually the trait of instinctive Imitation was developed, the traces of which are still strongly with the race, even to this day. We may find instances of this trait all around us. When we watch a tight-rope walker, our bodies instinctively sway in imitative motion. When we watch the faces of actors on the stage, our own faces work in sympathy, more or less. And so it goes on all around us, and in us—ever the tendency toward Imitation. Children manifest a great degree of this trait and copy and acquire the mannerisms of those around to a surprising degree of detail.

Human Sheep and Apes.

This form of Mental Suggestion is very common. People are constantly taking up the suggestion of the Mental States, Feelings, and Emotions of those around them, and reproducing them in their own acts. The majority of people are like human sheep, who will follow a leader everywhere and along all sorts of paths. Let the old bell-wether jump over a rail, and every sheep in the flock will do likewise—and they will keep on jumping over the same place, at the same height, even if the rail be removed before the whole flock gets over. We are constantly doing things simply because other people do them. We are constantly aping after others. In our fashions, styles, forms, etc., we are servile imitators. Larry Hehr shows a vest button hung by a thread and all the young apes in the land follow suit. Funny! isn't it?

Imitative Mental Contagion. This law of Imitation plays an important part in the phenomena of Mental Suggestion along these lines. Somebody does a certain thing and at once other people take up the Suggestion and copy the original actor. Let the newspapers record a certain crime and many others of the same type follow closely after. Let there be a suicide, and many others follow, usually adopting the same methods. Let there be a number of cases of some kind of folly and dissipation, and immediately there is "an epidemic" of the same thing. Let the papers say much about the appearance of a new disease, and at once a number of people manifest symptoms of it. Diseases get to be quite the fashion in this way. The Feelings and Emotions of the Instinctive part of the mind are called into sympathetic action along the lines of Imitative Suggestion, and physical effects follow shortly after.

Shrewd men take advantage of this tendency of the human mind, and, by getting a few people interested in certain things, they manage to set the fashion, and the crowd follows like sheep. Get people talking about a thing, and the contagion spreads until everybody is interested in the matter. The majority of people are more or less susceptible to this form of Suggestion, the degree depending upon their habit of thinking, judging and acting for themselves. The man or woman who has ideas of his, or her, own, is not so apt to be impressed by every wave of popular fashion, style and thought as those who maintain a more negative attitude toward the minds of others. The method of curing an undue tendency toward Imitative action is to start in to build up your Individuality, and to develop Postivity, along the lines mentioned in the concluding lesson of this series.

The Third Line of Action.

The third line of action of Mental Suggestion is:

Mental Suggestion.

Suggestion Through Association.—This form of Mental Suggestion is very common. It is based upon the acquired impressions of the race, by which certain words, actions, manners, tones, appearances, etc., are associated with certain previously experienced Mental States. Mental States take form in physical action and expression, as we know. A man feeling in a certain way is apt to express himself by certain actions or in certain words. These actions and words thus become symbols of the Mental State producing them, and consequently they produce upon the mind of the person seeing or hearing them the mental image connected with that Mental State. And this mental image is calculated to induce a similar or corresponding state in the mind of the person seeing and hearing. So that these symbols are really Mental Suggestions, since they tend to induce mental states.

Words But Symbols.

Right here I wish to remind you that every written, printed or spoken word, or words, is the outward and physical expression of some inner mental state of the person uttering or writing the words. The words are the "outward and visible signs" of an "inward feeling"—remember this always. Mere words, in themselves, have no suggestive value—the value depends upon the meaning impressed upon them by the mind of the person using them, accompanied by an understanding of their meaning by the person hearing or reading them. The word "horror," for instance, or "uncanny," has a definite meaning to persons familiar with it. It bears a direct relation to a mental feeling, or emotion, and is the physical and outward expression of the same. One may say the word over and over again to a person who has never heard it, or to one of another race who does not understand the term, and no suggestive effect follows. But speak the word to one who is accustomed to connect and associate it with a definite feeling that they have experienced, and the feeling will be reproduced, or "induced," if the circumstances of the use of the word be favorable. The word "Love," used properly, will awaken in the mind of its hearers feelings corresponding with the term. And these feelings must have been experienced before, either directly or indirectly, before they may be induced by suggestion. Feelings experienced by one's ancestors leave a record in one's subconscious mentality, which may also be induced by the appropriate suggestion.

Personally, words seem to me to be like the wax record of a phonograph. The record is covered with minute impressions produced by the sound-waves entering the phonograph. Place this record in its place in the phonograph and start the latter in motion, and lo! the minute impressions on the record will reproduce or "induce" in the diaphragm the same kind of sound-waves that originally caused the impressions. In this way a word, which is the physical symbolic record of a feeling, will produce its associated feeling in the mind of the person hearing or reading it.

Associated Feeling.

And, as I have said, the feeling produced will depend largely upon the understanding of the meaning of the word held by the person receiving the impression. For instance, in the case of the word "Love," let us suppose that the term is strongly and feelingly suggested to a number of persons at the same time, and in the same way. You will find that the feeling induced in the one person will be that of Love of Parents; in another Love of Children; in another Love of Husband or Wife; in another Love of God; in another an exalted affection for some person of the opposite sex; in another the low animal passion for one of the other sex; and so on, each experiencing a feeling occasioned by his or her association of the word with some feeling previously entertained. The same word may induce a feeling of the greatest pleasure in one person, and the greatest horror or disgust in another—the difference depending upon the association of the word in the mind of the two persons. As an illustration of this last statement, take the word "Passionate," for example, or the word "Pious."

I have dwelt upon these facts in order to make clear to you that there is no magic power in words in themselves, and that all their force and effect depends upon the associated feeling of which they are the crystallized physical and outward former symbol. The word is the body—the feeling is its soul.

THE ART OF THE SUGGESTOR.

And so it is with the Suggestion of appearance, manner, surrounding, etc. Each of these depends for force and effect upon some accustomed association with some inner feeling, which feeling is reproduced or induced by the outward symbol of the thing. We associate certain things with certain feelings, and when we see these things we are apt to experience the feeling indicated. People have been overcome by the sight of a picture, or a scene in a play—a song—a poem—or suggestive music.

And here is where the art of the Suggestionist comes into play. He watches closely and discovers that certain words, tones, manners, appearances, actions, motions, etc., are associated in the minds of people with certain feelings and ideas. And so when he wishes to reproduce, produce, or induce in others these ideas or feelings, he simply reproduces the associated physical symbols, in words, manner, motion, or appearance, and the effect is produced. The conjurer makes certain motions with his hands which you have always associated with certain actions, and you feel that the action itself has been performed—but the conjurer omits the action, and you are fooled. The "confidence man" assumes the appearance, manners and actions which you have always associated with certain qualities of character and you feel that he is what he seems to be—but he isn't, and you are fooled. This "play-acting" of people is all a form of suggestion, and you are fooled because you accept the symbol for the reality, unless you understand the game. The actor assumes the actions, tones, dress and words of certain characters, and if he is a good actor you forget the reality and laugh and weep, and otherwise feel that what you see is reality, although you really know underneath it all that it is only a play. And all this is Mental Suggestion, remember.

THE MASTER-KEY.

Remember, now and always, that a Mental Suggestion operates by the presentation of the outward symbol associated with the feeling to be induced. Put the right record in the phonograph and the corresponding sound is produced or induced. Do you see? This law underlies all the phenomena of Mental Suggestion—understand the Law of Suggestion and you have the master-key to the phenomena.

THE SPELL OF ORATORY.

Oratory, and other forms of appeal to the feeling by spoken words, gives us a typical example of the operation of this form of Mental Suggestion. The orator; the lawyer; the preacher; each uses words calculated to induce mental states, feelings and emotions, in the minds of his hearers. Such a one soon begins to learn the suggestive value of words, tones, and expression. He avoids the use of cold, abstract words, and drifts into the use of those which are symbols for deep feeling and emotion, knowing that these word symbols uttered with the proper tone and expression, will induce the feelings, for which they stand, in the minds of the hearers. The hearers' emotions and feelings are played upon, in this way, like an instrument. The emotion or passion, whether it be love, fear, hate, greed, patriotism, courage, jealousy, sympathy, etc., etc., is awakened by the skillful use of the words, tones, and expression which stand as symbols for these feelings.

If you will remember how you were touched by an address, that afterward seemed trivial and flamboyant to you—without argument, proof or sense—then you will realize how you were made the subject of Mental Suggestion through Association. The skilful salesman operates upon you in the same way. So does his twin brother, the advertising man. The revivalist has this art reduced to a perfect science.

THE POWER OF WORDS.

Words—words—words—inciters to action; inducers of feeling; symbols of mental states, and reproducers of mental states—despise them not; sneer not at them, for they have brought down low the mightiest of minds, when properly used. Even when written, their potency is great. Countries have often been made captive by a clever phrase, which when analyzed meant nothing in reason—merely an awakener of feeling. Let me make the catch-phrases of a country, and I care not who makes its laws!

THE ACTOR.

The man best adapted to employ this form of Suggestion is he who is more or less of an Actor—that is, who possesses the faculty of throwing "expression" and "feeling" into his words, actions and manner. Good orators, pleaders, salesmen, and others have this faculty largely developed. It belongs to the Feminine side of the phenomena, for it has the "charming" drawing, leading aspect, and works by the employment of the Emotive Pole of Mentation, rather the Will or Motive Pole, as in the case of the first mentioned phase of Suggestion—that of Authoritative Statement or Command. It operates not by beating down the Will of the other person, but rather by inducing a sympathetic rhythm of feeling and emotion, which overpowers his own Will, and causes it to act accordingly.

HOW TO PROTECT YOURSELF.

One should ever be on guard against this kind of influence. The best way to escape it, is to adopt the policy of never acting immediately in response to an appeal of this kind. Rather wait until the effect has worn off, and then submit the matter to the consideration of your reason and judgment. Of course, the cultivation of Will-power will act as a shield or armor, protecting you from the subtle vibrations of this kind, for this form of suggestion is usually accompanied by strong Mentative Currents from the mind of the speaker. Fence yourself off from a too ready response to sympathetic appeals along the emotional lines. Let the head stand by the heart, ready to prevent its running away with you.

Men should have the Reason in the ascendant, not the Emotional nature. When you feel yourself being carried off of your feet, by some emotional excitement, steady yourself and ask your mind this question: "Is this not a mental suggestion?" The question will tend to bring you to your state of equilibrium. When you know what a Mental Suggestion is, then you will learn to recognize them, and be on the lookout for them. This state of mind will act as a strong neutralizing agent for the most skilfully put suggestion. Have your Torpedo-nets out, no matter how secure you may imagine yourself to be. One caution more—be especially cautious, and slow to accept a suggestion when you are worn-out, tired, or in a passive, pleasurable state—that is, whenever your Will is resting, or else exhausted. On these occasions, "when in doubt, say No!" You will save yourself much regret by remembering this bit of advice. It is based on a proven psychological law. I have learned this law by bitter personal experience. Remember it!

The Fourth Line Of Action.

Let us now consider the fourth line of action of Mental Suggestion:

Suggestion Through Repetition. This form of Mental Suggestion is quite common, and the study of its manifestations is quite interesting, for it brings into operation a well known psychological principle, which has its correspondences in the physical world—"constant dripping will wear away the hardest stone."

You know the story of the man who told his favorite lie so often that he believed it himself? Well, this is a psychological fact. People have started in to make a certain appearance of truth, in words, or manner, by assuming something to be true that was not so. Then they kept on repeating the thing, adding a little here, and a little there, until the thing got to be "a fixed idea" with them, and they actually believed it. And if a person can suggest himself into accepting a false belief in this way, you can see how it will operate on others.

THE SECRET OF THIS FORM.

The secret of the operation of this form of suggestion lies in the psychological facts of "weakened resistance through repetition of the attack," and the "force of habit." The first time an unaccustomed suggestion is made, the mind sets up an active resistance; but the next time it is presented, the suggestion is not quite so unfamiliar as before, and a lessened resistance is set up; and so on, until at last no resistance is interposed, and the Suggestion is accepted. You know the old verse:

> "Vice is a monster of so frightful mien,
> That to be hated, needs but to be seen.
> But seen too oft, familiar with her face,
> We first endure, then pity, and then embrace."

And this rule holds good with Suggestions. We first resist them; then endure them; then accept them—unless we understand the game.

CUCKOO FEELINGS.

The psychological fact involved in this form of suggestion is that impressions upon the brain-cells become deepened by constant repetition. It is like sinking a die into a cake of wax—it goes deeper at each pressure. The mind is very apt to accept as true, anything that it finds deeply impressed upon its records. It has become accustomed to finding these deep impressions only when they have been made by repeated efforts of its own intellect, or judgment, or experience, and so when it finds these deep impressions that have been placed there by repeated Suggestions of others, it is not apt to discriminate. It finds itself "feeling" these things that have been repeatedly impressed upon it. Like the cuckoo's egg in the robin's nest, these illegitimate mental impressions are nurtured as one's "very own."

Mental Impressions.

There is a constant struggle for existence upon the part of the ideas, or mental images impressed upon one. The strong crowd out the weak. And in the majority of cases, the strongest ones are those which have either been impressed in a vivid manner, or else by repetition. The second time you meet a man, you may have trouble in remembering him; but the third time it is easier; and so on, until at last you forget that he ever was a stranger. And so it is with these suggested ideas—you grow familiar with them through repetition; they lose their strangeness to you; and at last you cease to concern yourself about them. A strange thing is generally inspected, examined, viewed suspiciously, etc., but after the strangeness has worn off, you cease to exercise the former caution. "Familiarity breeds Contempt"—and also Lack of Caution. Suggestion gains force by each repetition. This is one of the fundamental laws of Suggestion, and one that all should remember.

The Force of Repeated Statements.

If you would take mental stock of yourself, you would find that you entertain a vast number of feelings, ideas, and opinions, which you possess simply through this law of Repeated Suggestion. You have heard certain things affirmed, over and over again, until you have come to accept them as veritable facts, notwithstanding that you possess not the slightest personal knowledge of, or any logical proof concerning them. Shrewd moulders of public opinion employ this law, and constantly repeat a certain thing, in varying words and style, until at last the public accepts it as a proven and unquestioned fact.

Many a man has gained a reputation for wisdom, merely because his friends repeatedly affirmed it, and the public accepted the suggestion. Many a statesmen has had a reputation built up for him by friendly newspaper correspondents, whose constantly repeated suggestions have caused the idea to crystallize into a material form in the public mind. And many a reputation has been destroyed by the repeated shrugs, sneers, and insinuations of gossips and evil-wishers.

Advertisers understand this law, and keep the repeated suggestion of the merit of their wares constantly before the public mind, until it becomes gospel with the people. "If at first you don't succeed," and "Never take No! for an answer," are two axioms very dear to the heart of the man who uses Suggestion "in his business."

A WARNING.

Do not be deceived by this subtle form of Suggestion. Do not imagine that an untrue thing becomes true because it is repeated often. Do not allow your judgment to be lulled to sleep by this drowsy repetition of the slumber-song. Keep awake—keep awake! An understanding of this Law of Suggestion will throw light on many things that have puzzled you heretofore. Think over it a bit, when you have time.

THE THREE FORMS OF APPLICATION.

Let us now consider the various Forms of Application of Suggestion in everyday life. They are several, and for convenience I separate them into three forms, or groups, *i. e.*, (1) Involuntary Suggestion; (2) Voluntary Suggestion; and (3) Auto-Suggestion. Let us now consider the first form:

The First Form.

Involuntary Suggestion. By this term I mean the use of Suggestion involuntarily; without a particular purpose; or unconsciously. We are all giving Suggestions of words, manner, action, etc., every moment of our lives. And these Suggestions are constantly being accepted by those around us. We are constantly influencing those with whom we come in contact, the greater part of the work being performed unconsciously to us. We are acting as living Inspiration for some, and living Discouragement for others, according to circumstances. Our moods, actions, words, appearance, manners, etc., act as Suggestions to those around us. I am not now speaking of the effect of Mentative Currents, etc., but of Mental Suggestion, pure and simple.

A business house is permeated by the personality of its head, and his personal characteristics impress themselves upon those under him, by the means of Suggestion. He sets the gait of the place. If he is active, and enterprising, so are the workers employed by him; and if he is careless and shiftless, so will they be apt to be. We affect those around us by our Mental Attitudes, manifested in action, and they affect us—if we allow them to do so.

Children and Suggestion.

Children are quite amenable to Suggestion of this sort, being natural imitators, and they soon take on the mental attitude of the parents toward them. If the parent treats the child as being beyond control, the child will respond; if the child be considered obstinate, etc., he will take on the suggestion, and the original trouble will be magnified. People talk before their children, little realizing that the little minds are very Suggestible, and are constantly taking Suggestive color from those around them. One should endeavor to present to their children only the best, positive, helpful, uplifting, and encouraging mental states. One should avoid giving the child the impression that it is "bad," or "mean," or "deceitful," or "shy," or anything of that sort. The child will be apt to accept the Suggestion coming from a source that it naturally looks to for information, and it will be very apt to proceed to act upon the Suggestion and make the words of the parent come true. I have heard of children who had become so impressed with their parents' suggestion that they "would come to some bad end, yet," that they had to fight against it the balance of their lives. Sow the Suggestive Seeds that you desire to sprout into Reality—be careful to select the right kind. This subject of Suggestion to Children can be merely alluded to here, for it would fill a book of itself. I felt impelled to say a few words about it in this lesson, because my experience has taught me its extreme importance.

THE RULE OF INVOLUNTARY SUGGESTION.

This is the rule of Involuntary Suggestion: OUR WORDS, ACTIONS, MANNER, TONES, APPEARANCE, AND GENERAL PERSONALITY CONVEY SUGGESTIONS TO THOSE AROUND US, INDUCING MENTAL STATES IN ACCORDANCE THEREWITH.

Therefore, act out only the character that you wish to impress upon the world—and act it the best you know how. The world will connect you with the part you are playing, according to the suggestions thus made—sometimes you will get a better verdict than you really deserve; sometimes a worse one, but in either event, your Mental Attitude, reflected by your Involuntary Suggestions, will have caused the verdict, whatever it may be. Therefore, form a correct Mental Attitude, based upon some Ideal of the part you wish to play—and then play it out to the best of your ability. Observe the Outward Appearance of the part you are playing, for this is what the world sees first, last and all the time—and you are judged by your Suggestive "make-up," and stage action. Act well your part, for thereupon rests the verdict of the audience.

THE SECOND FORM.

The second form of the application of Suggestion is:

VOLUNTARY SUGGESTION. This form of the application of Suggestion, is manifested in cases in which the Suggestion is deliberately and purposely made with the end of impressing other persons. Its manifestations may be grouped into three classes, as follows: (a) Suggestive Treatment; (b) Hypnotic Suggestion; (c) Suggestion in the form of Personal Influence.

SUGGESTIVE TREATMENT.

By (a) Suggestive Treatment I refer to the practice of Mental Suggestion used as a form of "treatment" for physical ills, or mental deficiencies, etc. The treatments for physical ills come under the term of "Suggestive Therapeutics," and will be spoken of in my lesson of that title. Treatment by Suggestion for mental deficiencies, etc., is a branch of Science that is rapidly coming to the fore. For some time it was clouded by its mistaken connection with Hypnotism, but now that it has been divorced therefrom it is being used to a much greater degree by scientists in all parts of the world. Its principle rests on the fact that Brain-Centers, and Brain-Cells may be "grown," developed, and increased by properly directed Suggestions, so that one may be practically "made over" mentally. New qualities may be induced, and objectionable ones decreased. Objectionable habits and traits may be eliminated, and desirable ones substituted or newly induced.

The wonders of this form of practical psychology are being unfolded rapidly, and a great era is before us in this branch of Science. I have conducted many experiments along these lines, with a surprising degree of success, during the past seven years, and I purpose making the results of this work public at no distant date. The broad principle of the "treatment" lies in the fact that the Mental States induced by the proper Suggestions, tend to exercise and develop the portion of the brain in which they are manifested. Hence the theory once understood, and the best method adopted, the rest of the treatment becomes as simple as developing any muscle of the body by the appropriate exercise. I call this form of treatment "Brain Building," by Suggestion, etc.

Hypnotic Suggestion.

(b). Suggestion in Hypnotism is a subject that I shall merely refer to here, for this is not a manual of Hypnotism. Sufficient it is to say that Hypnotism is a combination of the use of Mentative Energy in a certain form, coupled with Suggestion. The Will of the hypnotic subject is overpowered by Mentation, and the Suggestions are then made him. It is a proven psychological fact that in the Hypnotic Condition, all Suggestions have a greatly exaggerated effect, and a Suggestion that would scarcely be noticed in the ordinary state, becomes a strong motive force to one in the state of hypnosis. In this state the most absurd suggestions are accepted, and acted upon—the most extraordinary delusions are entertained—and the Suggestions of future action, or post-hypnotic Suggestions, are made effective. I shall speak further of this subject in my next lesson, on Personal Influence, but I wish to caution my students against allowing themselves to be hypnotized for experimental or other purposes. It is conducive to a negative condition, and I heartily disapprove of its use. I would not allow anyone to hypnotize me, and I would urge upon my students a similar attitude toward "experimenters." The best effects of Suggestion may be obtained without Hypnosis—the latter is merely an abnormal and morbid state, most undesirable to normal people. Let it alone!

(c). Suggestion in Personal Influence is referred to in other parts of this lesson, and will appear more fully in my next lesson on Personal Influence, for it belongs to that phase of the general subject.

THE THIRD FORM.

The third form of application of Suggestion is what is known as:

AUTO-SUGGESTION. By this term is meant Self-Suggestion, or Suggestions given by one to his own mind. This is a most interesting and important phase of the subject, and will be dealt with fully in my last lesson on Mental Architecture, under which head it falls. It is by Auto-Suggestion that so many people have "made themselves over," mentally, and have become that which they willed to be. Its principles are precisely the same as in the other forms of Suggestion, except that the treatment is given by one's self instead of by another person.

The Vehicles of Suggestion, i. e., the Voice, the Manner, etc., have been alluded to in this lesson as we proceeded. But these points will be elaborated in the next lesson, on Personal Influence, as they form a part of that subject.

FEELINGS VS. REASON.

An eminent teacher of the use of Suggestion in Commercial Pursuits, in speaking of the effect of Suggestion in inducing Mental States, says: "You can make a man think with you if you work on his feelings or higher nature, even though you run counter to his ordinary judgment. If in this way you can dazzle his reason sufficiently, you can spur him to almost any action of which man is capable." And this teacher is perfectly right in his statement, although he follows the old "subjective mind" idea and identifies "feeling" with the "higher nature," instead of treating it as belonging to the Emotive Pole of Mentation as I do. And, if I may be pardoned, I would suggest that the above statement would be a little nearer the true state of affairs if he had said: "You can make a man FEEL with you if you work on his Emotive mentality," etc.

Mental Suggestion.

The Psychology of Salesmanship.

The teachers of Business Psychology very ably instruct their pupils in the art of Suggestion in the process of making sales. They instruct the salesmen to first gain the prospective customer's "attention," then "arouse his interest," then awaken "desire," and then—close the sale. These steps in the psychology of salesmanship apply equally well to the science of advertising, or any other appeal to the minds of people, and are logically correct. The attention once gained, the mind becomes more or less receptive; the mind once receptive, interest is aroused and a greater degree of receptivity is induced; interest is gradually led to Desire, induced by the subtle suggestion of words and the exhibition of the article to be sold; and at last, when the proper psychological state is aroused, the trained salesman gently but firmly gives the positive suggestion of authority, or demand, pointing to the place where the customer must sign his name, thus using Suggestion along both the lines of Acquiescence and Imitation—and the order is taken. Did you ever subscribe to a book at the solicitation of a good book agent? Well, if you did, and will let your mind run backward over the proceeding, you will see how the above rule works in practice. (1) Attention, (2) Interest, (3) Desire, (4) Sale—these are the steps of Salesmanship by Suggestion; and Advertising Sales as well. Great is Suggestion in Business!

I have known salesmen to gently suggest the closing of a sale by handing the customer a fountain pen, placed at the "suggestive slant," at the same time pointing to the space on the order blank, with the "take-it-for-granted" tone and utterance: "Sign right here, please!"—and it was signed.

Agents' Suggestions.

The largest employers of agents have regular training schools, in which the new agents are given the benefit of the experience of the old hands at the business—and some of these old hands could give a professional Suggestionist points on his own science. The agent is told how the different classes of people act, the objections they will be likely to raise, and how the trained agent may overcome these obstacles by clever work, including, of course, an intelligent use of Suggestion. I have talked with many successful men in this line, and it has always been a source of wonder to me at the detail of the use of suggestion manifested by them in their work. The average person would be surprised at the ideas advanced and the knowledge possessed by some of these men.

One of these agents once told me that one of the first things he learned when starting to work was that the agent should never permit the customer to take his "prospectus," or sample pages, in his own hands. He said to me: "I always keep the prospectus in my own hands, for if I let it get away from me I will have lost the power of controlling the attention and interest of the customer. He will then have the matter in his own hands, and will have gotten away from me—he will then do the leading, instead of my doing it. I always keep the upper hand of my man or woman. I do the leading, guiding, directing and influencing myself—I keep the controlling gear in my own hands, always."

I wish I could take the space and time to tell you other things I have learned in this way, of Suggestion in Business. But this is not a treatise of Suggestive Salesmanship, and so I must hasten on. I trust that I have said enough, however, to give you the proper cue in the matter.

Advertising Suggestions.

And, in the Science of Advertising, also, there is a constant use of Suggestion—usually conscious and premeditated. This is taught in the "courses" and "schools" of Advertising, and the Ad. men are well grounded on the subject. The use of the "Direct Command," as the ad. men call it, is very common. People are positively told to do certain things in these ads. They are told to "Take Home a Cake of Hinky-dink's Soap Tonight; your Wife

Needs It!" And they do it. Or they see a mammoth hand pointing down at them from a sign, and almost hear the corresponding mammoth voice, as it says (in painted words): "Say, you! Smoke Honey-Dope Cigars; They're the Best Ever!!!" And, if you manage to reject the command the first time, you will probably yield at the repeated Suggestion of the same thing" being hurled at you at every corner and high fence, and "Honey-Dope" will be your favorite brand until some other Suggestion catches you. Suggestion by Authority and Repetition, remember! That's what does the business for you! They call this "the Direct Command" in the Advertising Schools.

Illustrative Examples.

Then there are other subtle forms of Suggestion in Advertising. You see staring from every bit of space, on billboard and in newspapers and magazines: "Uwanta Cracker," or something of that sort—and you usually wind up by acquiescing. And then you are constantly told that "Babies Howl for Grandmother Hankin's Infantile Soother," and then when you hear some baby howling you think of what you have been told they are howling for, and then you run and buy a bottle of "Grandmother Hankins."

And then you are told that some Cigar is "Generously Liberal" in size and quality; or that some kind of Cocoa is "Grateful and Refreshing;" or that some brand of Soap is "99.999% Pure;" and that some Pickle Man makes "763 Varieties;" etc., etc., etc. Only last night I saw a new one—"Somebody's Whisky is Smooth," and every imbiber in the car was smacking his lips and thinking about the "smooth" feeling in his mouth and throat. It *was* Smooth—the idea, not the stuff, I mean. And some other Whisky Man shows a picture of a glass, a bottle, some ice and a siphon of seltzer, with simply these words: "Oldboy's Highball—That's All!" All of these things are Suggestions, and some of them very powerful ones, too, when constantly impressed upon the mind by Repetition. They "get in their work" on you.

THE PSYCHOLOGY OF ADVERTISING.

A writer on the Psychology of Advertising advises, among other things, that advertisements of articles to eat or drink should contain the words calculated to induce the feeling of "taste" in the minds, of the readers. "Sweet," "refreshing," "thirst-quenching," "nourishing," etc., etc.—how suggestive they are! And how effective! How do they act? you ask. How? Well, this way—just you read these words: "A NICE, BIG JUICY LEMON—TART AND STRONG—I CAN TASTE IT NOW!" Just imagine these words accompanied by a picture of a man squeezing the juice of a lemon into his mouth, and where are you? I'll tell you where—your mouth is filled with saliva, from the imagined taste of the tart lemon juice! Now, isn't it? Tell this to some of your friends and see how it works. I heard a story once of a bad little boy, who would stand in front of a German Band, with a lemon to his mouth, sucking away for all he was worth. Result: the mouths of the musicians became filled with so much moisture that they could not play on. Exit boy, with Professor Umpah, the bass-horn player, in full pursuit, the air being filled with "Dunner und Blitzen!" and worse. See!

BUSINESS PSYCHOLOGY.

I have known of dealers in Spring goods to force the season by filling their windows with the advance stock. I have seen hat dealers start up the straw hat season by putting on a straw themselves, their clerks ditto, and then a few friends. The sprinkling of "straws" gave the suggestion to the street, and the straw hat season was opened. Do business men understand Suggestion? Well, rather! Even the newsboys understand it. The best ones are above asking, as the green ones do, "Want a paper, mister?" or worse still, "You don't want a paper, mister, do you?" The good ones say, instead, boldly and confidently, "Here's your paper, mister!" sticking it under your nose—and you take it. Let me tell you a tale about a "barker" at a pleasure resort in

Chicago, several years ago. He was the best I ever heard. Here is the story—it's a true one:

A STRIKING EXAMPLE.

This man was the "barker" or "spieler" for one of the attractions of the place, the "pony ride" attraction. Many were the ponies lined up to carry the children around the ring, for a nickel a ride. The "spieler" would wait until a crowd of children, with or without their parents, would enter the place and then he would begin in the strongest, most strenuous, rasping, suggestive tones: "Ride, ride, ride! Have a ride, take a ride, have a ride, take a ride! Anybody, everybody; anybody, everybody! Ride, ride RIDE, R-R-R-R-R-R-RIDE!!!! Anybody rides, everybody rides—rides, rides, rides—rides, rides, RIDES—R-R-R-R-R-R-RIDES! Take a ride, have a ride, take a ride, have a ride, take a ride, have a ride! Anybody, everybody, anybody, everybody—RIDE, RIDE, R-R-R-R-R-R-R-R-RIDE! R-R-R-R-R-R-R-R-R-R-RIDE! R-R-R-R-R-R-R-R-R-R-R-R-R-RIDE!" He would keep this sort of thing up for several minutes, apparently without taking a fresh breath. The very air seemed to quiver and vibrate in the rhythm of his "r-r-r-r-r-ide, r-r-r-r-r-ide!" And every child within hearing who could raise a nickel would surely RIDE! The word "RIDE!" positively, authoritatively and constantly repeated, was one of the most startling exhibitions of this form of Suggestion that I have ever seen or heard. I have heard many imitators of this "spieler," but have never met his equal. Perhaps he has now passed on to some higher form of usefulness—he was worthy of it. He was "on to his job," surely.

SUGGESTION ACCEPTED.

I have seen men in bowling alleys caused to make false plays, by some bystander suggesting the false shot. The same thing is true in shooting galleries, etc. You have but to look around you and see these everyday instances of Suggestion, in some form or other. INDUCED FEELING, remember! That is the key of all manifestations of Suggestion. Look out for it! And, in conclusion, I know of a little boy who exemplified the law of Suggestion one April Fool's Day by placing a sign on the coat-tail of another boy. The sign read "KICK ME!" And they did!

SUGGESTION AMONG LAWYERS.

The skillful lawyer uses Suggestion in his work in examining or cross-examining witnesses. He suggests things to a suggestible witness, and coaxes and leads him on to admissions and statements that he did not intend making—sometimes statements that are not strictly correct. Such a one will say, "You DID so and so," or "You SAW so and so, didn't you?" etc., the direct statement made in an authoritative manner causing the suggestible witness to acquiesce. Look out for this Confident Authoritative Manner, in lawyer or anyone else. It is calculated to lead one into acquiescence, for man is "an obedient animal," and it is "so much easier to say Yes! than No! when you see that Yes! is expected."

A DANGEROUS USE.

It is charged that police detectives have worked false "confessions" out of suggestible criminals in this way, by keeping hammering away at them until their wills are worn out, and they would say "Yes!" to escape further questioning, like the girl who finally accepted the lover's repeated proposal in order to get rid of him. This Firm, Decided, Authoritative Statement or Demand, when allied to the law of Repetition, has caused much mischief in the world, and many have "given in" to it, to their sorrow. I trust that these warning words will save some others trouble of this kind. When the law is once understood it is comparatively easy to escape the suggestion. The strength in the Suggestor of this kind lies in the ignorance of the person suggested. Forewarned is Forearmed, in this case. You now begin to see my idea in "Turning on the Light," don't you?

The Suggestive Question.

I have heard of business men who would instruct their clerks to ask questions of their customers in this way: "You like this pattern, do you not?" or "This is a beautiful shade, is it not?" etc., etc., etc. Do you see the point? The statement is made first, and the question is asked right on top of it. Isn't it easier to say Yes! than No! to this kind of a question? (See there, now, I asked the question in that way, myself, although I had no intention of doing so. Took my own Suggestion.)

The Suggestive Position.

In this connection I may add that it is a well known psychological fact that, when two persons are conversing, the one standing, or sitting higher than the other, has the advantage of a certain Positive Attitude or Position. And the person seated below the speaker is forced into a relatively Passive or Negative condition, or position. That is, everything else being equal, the person elevated will be Positive to the other, and the one seated on a lower level will be Passive, relatively. The raised platform of the teacher, speaker, preacher, etc., has a good psychological basis. And the power that a lawyer feels when "talking on his feet" to the jury seated in front of him is a manifestation of a law that he may not be aware of—but the judge has one better than him, for the lawyer must look up to him when he talks.

Try the experiment of practicing the above position with some friend, first one being seated and then the other, and see how you can actually feel the difference between the two positions. The raised position of clerks in the large stores, and the low seats so accommodatingly placed for the customers, have good reasons. If you ever feel that some one is placing you in a Negative or Passive Condition, rise to your feet, and you will feel doubly strong and forceful. This is a little hint that may be worth many times the price of this book to you, some of these days. Look over the fool things that you have been talked or influenced into, and see if you were not seated and the other fellow standing, or seated higher than you. This is a little thing—but it works big results, sometimes. Better heed it.

Different Degrees.

There is a great difference in the suggestibility of persons, some being almost immune from Suggestion, while others are so suggestible that they have but to be told a thing in a positive, forceful, confident, authoritative tone and manner, to accept the suggestion, particularly if it be repeated several times. They will likewise readily absorb the Suggestions of Imitation and Association. But I have told you about this elsewhere in this lesson. Study those around you, and you will soon discover the different degrees. The hypnotic somnambule is at the extreme negative end of the scale.

Suggestion and Personal Influence.

And now, friends and students, we have come to the end of this lesson on Mental Suggestion. As you will have learned by this time, the subject of Suggestion overlaps the subjects of several of the lessons to follow, this being notably true in the case of the next lesson on Personal Influence. But it was necessary to make you acquainted with the general nature and effects of Suggestion, and with its laws, before taking you to the lesson on Personal Influence. Having now studied Suggestion, you will be the better prepared to understand the subject when you meet it in the instruction on Personal Influence.

Suggestion deals with the Physical Agents of Mentative Induction, while Personal Influence deals principally with the Mental Agents. But the two agents generally work together in Personal Influence, and therefore must be studied in connection with one another. You will see this more plainly as you proceed with the study.

Mental Suggestion.

The Importance of Suggestion.

But here a word of caution. If you desire to learn the MENTAL FORCES, do not ignore the Physical Agents employed in Suggestion. The Physical Agents appeal to the senses of man, while the Mental Forces reach another avenue of approach to the mind. And both are important. Of the two, Suggestive Influence is the most easily produced, and, in fact, is generally the first invoked by skilful users of Mental Influence, because of its simplicity, and its faculty of preparing a good foundation for the other influences. In your study of the subject of Personal Influence, you must first thoroughly post yourselves on the laws underlying the phenomena of Suggestive Influence. This is the first step toward the understanding of the whole Subject. A good Suggestionist is always a master of Mental Influence, because his very "knack" of Suggestion, brings the Mentative Influences into operation. Suggestion brings about the proper Mental Attitude for the higher phenomena.

Lesson IV.

Personal Influence.

Introductory—Mental Suggestion and Personal Magnetism—The "Sixth Sense"—Mental States and Physical Actions—Illustrative Examples—Acting Your Part—Things as They Are—Use vs. Abuse—The Inner Form—"Mental Magnetism"—A Bit of Occult History—Personal Magnetism—Its Use in Business—Its Use in Emotional Religion—Its Use in Politics—The Day After—Infectious Enthusiasm—Mental Epidemics—Cause and Effect—Self-Protection—Personal Force—The Mentative Struggle—Instances of Extreme Positivity—The Other Extreme—Impressionables—The "Magnetic Man"—Contact with the Universal Will—Universal vs. Personal Will—A Center of Forceful Will—The Magnetic "Air"—A Magnetic Mental Image—Magnetic Desire-Force—Creative Mentation—The Drawing Power of Desire—The Magic Flame—The Intense Desire—The Twin Forces—The Magnetic Voice—The Control of Tone—The Suggestive Voice—The Flexible Expression—The Vibrant, Resonant, Expressive Voice—The Walk of the Magnetic Man—The Expressive Eye—The Powerful Glance—The Secret of Influence—Review Work—Strange Occurrences Explained—Personal Atmospheres.

Lesson IV.

Personal Influence.

The preceding lesson on "Mental Suggestion"—the present lesson on "Personal Influence"—and the lesson next following, on "Telementation"—are closely connected, and their subject matter "laps." In order that you may understand this connection, let us suppose that the subject of "Personal Influence" is the central thought. This Central Thought deals with the Mentative Influence of the Person. This Mentative Influence consists in the Induction of Mental States in other persons. And this Induction operates along two lines, *i. e.*, (1) the line of Mental Suggestion, which requires a physical agent; and (2) the line of Mentative Currents, which do not require a physical agent, but which produce their effect directly upon the mind of the person without the operation of the physical senses, or the physical agents, necessary to reach such senses.

Well, then, the preceding lesson dealt with Mental Suggestion, that line of action of Personal Influence requiring a physical agent of induction or impression. And the present lesson will deal with Mental Suggestion in its method of application, as well as in the method of application of Mentative Currents along the lines of Personal Magnetism, etc. And the next lesson will take up the subject of Mentative Currents, in its phase of

Telementation, or "long distance" operation. So you see that while all these three lessons deal, in a way, with the general subject of "Personal Influence," yet each has its own special line. And in this present lesson, all the lines converge.

MENTAL SUGGESTION AND PERSONAL MAGNETISM.

But before proceeding with the general subject of the lesson, I would ask you to remember this distinction between Mental Suggestion and what is called "Personal Magnetism," or Personal Influence through the agency of Mentative Currents. The chief difference is this:

In Mental Suggestion a physical agent is necessary BECAUSE THE IMPRESSION IS MADE THROUGH THE PHYSICAL SENSES of Seeing, Hearing, Smelling, Tasting, Feeling—principally through Seeing and Hearing. But, in Personal Magnetism no physical agent is necessary, because there is no appeal to the physical senses—BECAUSE THE IMPRESSION IS MADE DIRECTLY UPON THE MIND OF THE OTHER PERSON THROUGH A SIXTH SENSE. This Sixth Sense cannot strictly be classed as a physical sense, because it is not affected by physical agents or objects, ITS IMPRESSIONS BEING OBTAINED FROM THE VIBRATIONS OF THE CURRENTS OF MENTATIVE ENERGY. Just as the five physical senses receive impressions from physical sense-objects, and transmit them to the brain and mind; so does this Sixth Sense receive impressions from the vibrations of the Mentative Energy of other minds, and then passes them on to the brain and mind. Kindly fix this idea in your mind, so that you may understand the distinction hereafter.

THE "SIXTH SENSE."

Regarding this Sixth Sense, which I shall call the "Telemental Sense," I would say that there have been a number of theories advanced to account for it, some of which endeavor to locate a physical organ for it. Some very good authorities hold that the "Pineal Gland" is the organ receiving the vibrations of the Mentative Energy. The "Pineal Gland" is a small gland of reddish-gray color, cone-shaped, and attached to the floor of the third ventrical of the brain, in front of the cerebellum. It is composed of a mass of nervous matter, containing tiny nerve-cells, or corpuscles, of a peculiar nature; and also containing small particles of a gritty, calcareous matter, known as "brain sand."

Physical Science gives no information regarding the use of the Pineal Gland, and its text-books content themselves with the statement that "its function is not known." I shall not attempt to prove that this gland plays any part in the phenomenon of the Sixth Sense, because, for the purpose of these lessons, it is not necessary for you to accept or reject the idea. Personally, I believe that it plays its part, but I also believe that there are many other cells which have to do with the subject—in fact, I believe that every cell, or cell-center in the body is capable of being impressed by vibrations of Mentative Energy, a fact that the latest investigations into Mentative Therapeutics go far toward proving. But, all this has no immediate bearing upon the subject before us, as interesting as it may be for myself, and many of you. I will have a little more to say to you upon the subject in my lesson on Mental Therapeutics.

MENTAL STATES AND PHYSICAL ACTIONS.

There is another point to which I would direct your attention at this stage. I refer to the well-known psychological fact that "Mental States express themselves in Physical Action." Every Mental State has its associated Physical Action. And these Actions when perceived by another person, are apt to induce a similar Mental State in that person, along the lines of Mental Suggestion. But there is another law, less understood by the public, and that is that "the manifestation of a Physical Action tends to induce in the mind of the person performing it, the Mental States generally associated with the production of the action."

Illustrative Examples.

Let us take a common example, to illustrate the operation of these two related laws. Let us suppose that you are holding a Mental State of Anger, Fight, Combativeness, etc. In that case you will find that your brows will frown; your jaws will be fixed in a savage "bite," and slightly protruded; and your hands will be clenched—the Mental State has taken form in Physical Action. Very well, then—you all recognize this fact.

But, there is the law reversed. If you will frown deeply; clench your fists savagely; fix your jaws in a fighting trim, etc., and will maintain that physical attitude for five minutes, at the same time allowing it to manifest in your walk, etc. (as it surely will) without interference, you will find yourself growing into a Mental State of annoyance, combativeness, etc., and if you keep it up long enough, you will be "mad in earnest." So true is this that if you carry the thing far enough, and run into someone else, you will be very apt to "get into a row" with him. And, still more remarkable is the fact, the person that you "run into" will be very apt to take up the Mental Suggestion of your manner, and will also "feel fighty." It would not take much to stir up trouble between the two of you.

And, still more remarkable, if you continue this physical attitude until it produces the Mental State, you will find that you are inducing similar Mental States in those around you, by the agency of Mentative Currents. So you see the close connection between Physical Action, Mental States, Suggestion, and Telementation! They act, and re-act upon each other. What has been said of the Mental State of Anger applies equally to any intense Feeling or Mental State. Like begets Like, along all the lines mentioned.

Acting Your Part.

Now, all this means that the man who is possessed of a strong Mental State will manifest, unconsciously, the physical actions which will affect others, along the lines of Mental Suggestion—

he will not have to study the question of what suggestions to use, providing he "feels" sufficiently strong to automatically manifest the actions. But when a man does not "feel" sufficiently strong to manifest the suggestive actions, he may produce the same effect by "acting the part" (without being actually involved in it) by first reproducing the physical actions, which will thus induce a sufficiently strong Mental State to manifest itself both along the line of Suggestion, and also along the line of Personal Magnetism. Every good actor induces feeling in you in this way, along both these lines. And you may do the same if you want to—plenty of "magnetic" people are doing it every day.

In this lesson, so far as I have gone, I have given you a most important secret of psychological influence, in a plain, practical way—so simple in fact that there is a risk of many of you entirely overlooking its importance. Better go back over this part of the lesson again—many times—until you are able to catch its inner meaning, and are able to read between its lines. It's quite worth while, I assure you.

THINGS AS THEY ARE.

Of course, some of my kind critics will take me to task for teaching this "acting out" idea. They will call it "inculcating principles of deceit," etc., etc.—and will then go on their way admiring "magnetic" personalities, and regretting the absence of "tact" in other persons who have rubbed them the wrong way. I have noticed that these hyper-critical people are generally hypocritical as well.

But, be this as it may, I purpose going right on to the end, and telling about things as they are in this world of ours; and, so far as possible "why" they are, and "how" they are. This is a lesson on "Personal Magnetism," and not a treatise on social ethics, or a discussion regarding the dividing line between "politeness" and "sincerity."

I have known many good men who were not "magnetic," and the world "turned them down," and often "jumped all over them." And I have known quite a number, not quite so good, who possessed quite a goodly degree of "magnetism," and the world received them with open arms, and showered its praises and rewards upon them. But this does not mean that one cannot be "good" and "magnetic" at the same time. There are plenty of "good" men who are highly "magnetic"—and there are plenty of "bad" men equally so. And there are plenty both good and bad, who lack "magnetism." But, note this fact, please—that the good men, and the bad men, who are highly "magnetic," generally manage to "get there," along their own line of life. And both the good and bad who lack "magnetism" are generally stranded along the wayside. "Magnetism" is neither good nor bad—it is a natural law—and is used by all. In this respect it is like any other natural law.

USE VERSUS ABUSE.

And, then again, these lessons are not for the purpose of teaching the "bad" use of "magnetism," rather than the "good." They state the principles and the law, as they are. It is true that the bad man may take advantage of the law and use it for bad purposes; but so may the good man take advantage of it and make himself a greater power for good. "Personal Magnetism" is just as effective in the "Preacher" as it is in the "Confidence Man"—and just as effective in the salesman and business man, and everyday person, as it is in either the preacher or the confidence man. It is a natural quality, and has nothing to do with "good and bad"—any more than has elocution, oratorical ability, or personal appearance.

If the good folk prefer to leave this important subject for the bad folk, that is their own concern, not mine. Personally, I feel like the old preacher, who when remonstrated to by some hide-bound old parishioner regarding certain musical innovations that had been introduced in the church service. The old preacher looked kindly at the old veteran "conservative" of the flock, and said: "Well, brother, it may strike you in a different way, but to me it seems wrong to allow the Devil to monopolize all the good music—I believe in giving the Lord his share of it." And I say "Amen I" to this idea.

If "Personal Magnetism" was as much used to further the interests of Right, as it has been to further the interests of Wrong, the old world would get down to a little easier motion. If the Preacher would make his talks as "magnetic" as the actor does his plays, and the lawyer does his appeals to the jury, there would surely be "something doing" in church work, and the prevailing emptiness of the pews would be cured. If "goodness" was made as ATTRACTIVE as "badness," the Devil would be placed on the retired list.

THE INNER FORM.

And, now, let us consider this phase of "Personal Influence" that we call "Personal Magnetism." Remember that "Mental Suggestion" is the outward form of Personal Influence, and "Personal Magnetism" the inner form. We have considered the former—now let us consider the latter.

"MENTAL MAGNETISM."

Perhaps the best way would be to look into the word "Magnetism" as used in connection with Mental Influence, etc. We often hear the term used, as "Personal Magnetism;" "Mental Magnetism;" "Magnetic Personality;" "Magnetic Attraction;" "Magnetic Influence," etc., etc., used in the sense of Mental Attraction; Personal Influence; Fascination; Charming; Psychological Influence, etc. Let us see just why the term is used. The explanation involves an interesting bit of little known Occult history.

The word "Magnetism," of course, arises from the word "Magnet." Now here is an interesting bit of history. You will see in the dictionaries that the term "Magnet" was given the Lodestone, or natural magnet, because it was first discovered near Magnesia, a town in Asia Minor. This explanation is most amusing to those familiar with the records of the old occult brotherhoods, for the latter know that the Lodestone was the Lodestone being named after the town, the town was named after known centuries before the town of Magnesia was named, and, instead of the Lodestone, or Magnet.

A BIT OF OCCULT HISTORY.

The natural Magnet was known in China, India, and Persia thousands of years ago. Its name, "Magnet," arose from the same Persian word as "Magic," namely "Mag," signifying the esoteric priesthood or Magians. The name was given because the power of the Lodestone resembled the mental power exerted by the Magians, and the stone was called literally "the Magian Stone," or the "Magic Stone," hence the words "Magnet" and "Magnetism." So you see we come by our use of the word in a perfectly natural way.

An interesting fact (and one that goes to prove that minds work in accustomed channels) is to be noted in the circumstance that the mysterious phenomena of Mesmerism, etc., noticed in Europe and America during the past century or so, came to be naturally called "Animal Magnetism"; "Personal Magnetism," etc., the mind of the public intuitively connecting the phenomena with that of the Magnet, which it very much resembles. And, in our day, we speak of people being "very magnetic," "lacking magnetism," having a "magnetic presence," etc., etc. And so history repeats itself. The Magnet which was originally called the "Magian or Magic Stone," because its force resembled the Mentative Force manifested by the Magi or Magians, serves to give a name to similar manifestation of mental force centuries after. The "Magnet" gives back to the Twentieth Century Magians, the name it borrowed from the Magians of Ancient Persia. It has repaid the debt.

Personal Influence.
Personal Magnetism.

While the phase of Mentative Energy which has to do with the operation of the force upon distant minds and objects is perhaps the most startling, still that phase which is called "Personal Magnetism" is one of the most important and remarkable. Its very frequent occurrence often causes us to overlook it, but it is the phase which is effectively used by those who understand it, and the one which it behooves us to guard ourselves against. This phase is known by many names, the favorite terms being Mental Magnetism; Personal Magnetism; Suggestion; Fascination; Charming; Mesmeric Influence, etc. But these terms are merely names for Personal Magnetism, which itself is merely a manifestation of Mentative Energy.

All have noticed that some individuals seem to have a "winning way" about them, and are able to induce others to fall into their way of thinking or desires, and to do what they wished done. The so-called "magnetic" man is able to sway audiences or individuals by his mystic power, and one often fails to realize just how it was done when he recalls the words spoken, or reads them in cold type the morning after. The secret lies not alone in what is said, or even in how it is said, but rather in how great a degree Personal Magnetism was emanated by the speaker.

Its Use in Business.

Many persons who have dealings with the public in the direction of selling goods; securing subscriptions; selling life-insurance, etc., etc., have acquired a degree of the art of using Personal Magnetism often unconscious of the force they are employing. And many large employers of agents have schools wherein the agents are taught the psychology of suggestion, personal influence, etc., and where more or less of Personal Magnetism is taught, although under some other name. And, more than this, every person who is in earnest, when talking to another person manifests more or less Personal Magnetism, unconsciously, or consciously.

Its Use in Emotional Religion.

While the statement may bring down upon my head the wrath of those who believe that the phenomena of the "old-fashioned revival" is due to the "workings of the Spirit," I do not hesitate to affirm that all students of psychology know that the greater part of the fervor is due to emotional excitement produced by Personal Magnetism, manifesting along both the lines of Mentative Currents and Suggestion. Anyone who has ever attended a negro revival or camp-meeting has carried away with him a memory of the effects of a certain kind of Personal Magnetism upon a certain type of emotional minds.

Its Use in Politics.

And not alone in the field of "emotional religion" does this force manifest itself so strongly—it is just as plainly demonstrated in the case of "emotional politics." Let any man sit down and sanely consider the performances of the average man of the rank and file of either of the political parties during a campaign. See how men are swayed by emotional appeals to their prejudices and party spirit. See how they allow themselves to be blinded by glittering promises and statements, without a shred of reasonable argument, until they become fanatics.

Their emotions are skillfully played upon by the leaders and speakers, and the current of Personal Magnetism, and Suggestion, spreads over the body of the party until they become a mob possessed of certain fixed ideas that have taken possession of them. Families are split by factional differences, and hatred reigns when love formerly had its abode. The excitement grows fiercer and fiercer, until at last the day of the election is at hand, and the country goes into a paroxysm of emotional excitement. Then the result is announced. The next day every one suffers from a relapse, and the country begins to laugh over what has happened.

The Day After.

After the sting of defeat has worn off, and the elation of victory has melted away, it is found that the country is moving along about as usual—not going to the dogs because some man is defeated, nor taking great leaps forward because some other man has been elected Town Supervisor, or President, as the case may be. The people play their parts year after year—that is the majority of them—being swayed by emotional excitement rather than by reason, thought, or intelligence. And the men who pull the mental strings grin to themselves as they think over "what fools these mortals be," and prepare themselves to pull the same strings again upon the next occasion, and to make their sheep-like followers again dance to the tune of "My Party, right or wrong, My Party."

And in both revival and political campaign the moving spirit is the same: Our old friend Personal Magnetism, operates through the force of a few fixed "feelings" conveyed from the minds of the few to the minds of the many, aided and abetted in its subtle influence by its mate, Mental Suggestion. Gaining force under the force of the Desire and Will of each person who adds his force to the original impulse it swells in volume until, like the rolling snow-ball, it grows to mammoth proportions and sweeps all before it.

Infectious Enthusiasm.

You have often heard that "enthusiasm is infectious." Did you ever wonder why? Have you ever wondered why you enjoyed a theatrical performance more when the house was filled than when only half its seating capacity was used? Have you ever understood the cause of the wave of enthusiasm that has swept over the large audience, including yourself, until you felt all in a mental glow? Have you ever realized that what is known as "the psychology of the crowd," by which term is meant the influence that can be gained over a crowd, whereas the separate individuals composing the crowd cannot be so affected is due to Personal Magnetism and Mental Suggestion, started into operation and then spread from mind to mind by the added Desire and Will manifested in Mental States and their associated physical actions?

And there is another fact to be remembered while we are considering audiences and crowds. I allude to the fact that the speaker is affected by the Personal Magnetism of the audience which flows back upon him, giving him increased power to send again to them his own ideas, awakening fresh emotional excitement in them. It is Action and Reaction always.

Mental Epidemics.

It is of the greatest importance that one understands the causes of these "mental epidemics," for when the cause is once understood one is far less liable to be carried away by emotional excitement spread in this way. Many sober, sensible people have been swept off their feet by these waves of Personal Magnetism, and have done and said things that would otherwise have been impossible for them. They have allowed the Personal Magnetism to reach their minds through the Emotive Pole, arousing ideas and Desires that otherwise would have been impossible.

We have seen, or heard, of respectable citizens, including the members of the so-called learned professions, lawyers, doctors, teachers, preachers, joining in mobs and allowing themselves to be carried away by the Personal Magnetism and Suggestion of the more excitable members thereof, and participating in acts that afterwards seemed like horrible nightmares to them. The emotional nature is always very near the surface, in the majority of men, and it should be ever guarded from outside arousing influences. The Motive-Pole of the Mind—the Will-Power, should ever be on guard to resist this invasion of the Emotive-Pole of Mind.

And so should the Will ever be on guard to prevent the Personal Magnetism of others who in personal interviews seek to bend the minds of their hearers to their ideas, and by thus arousing Desire mould them so as to work their Wills upon them.

Cause and Effect.

In all of these cases of Personal Magnetism, and Mental Suggestion, whether along the lines of personal influencing, appeals, artful suggestion, etc., as well as in cases of "mental epidemics," the effect is produced by the Mentator, or Suggestor, obtaining the voluntary attention of the other or others, and thus holding his Will engaged, and his Emotive Pole of mind thus unguarded, while he pours in his Mentative Currents, or Suggestions (usually both), into the Emotive Pole of his hearers. He thus induces in them the desires, emotions and feelings which act as motive forces, causing them to act according to his wishes and Will.

The person affected is rendered unable to reason correctly, or intelligently, for his Will is "on a vacation," and his Reason is swayed by his Desires, Emotions and Feelings thus induced, the necessary support of the Will being lacking. The Will of the man sending the Mentative Currents, or Mental Suggestions, is in control, instead of the Wills of the hearers and persons influenced. In the cases of widespread "mental contagion" the influence spreads from mind to mind, along the same lines, and according to the same laws.

Self-Protection.

I trust that what I have said along these lines will appeal to the student in the direction of causing him to interpose a resistance to these Currents and Suggestions, in cases such as I have mentioned. The remedy is in his own hands—simply the interposition of the Will, in the manner of which I shall speak as we proceed. Surround yourself with an armor of Will-Power which will act as a shield against influences of this sort, and which will beat them back upon their senders. If people but understood this law they would cause these selfish Mentative

Currents to be reflected back upon the sender until he was swept away in the whirlwind of his own raising.

PERSONAL FORCE.

It is apparent to all students of human nature that there is a wonderful difference in the degrees of what is called "Personal Force" observable in different persons with whom we come in contact. Some are very "forceful," and others are quite "forceless," and others form varying degrees between these two extremes. This difference in "personal force" depends upon the degree of "Positivity" or "Negativity" in the "Magnetism" of each person.

The man who is able to manifest a strong degree of Mentative Energy along the lines of Motive Polarity, or Will-Power, becomes magnetically "Positive." I use the word "positive" in this connection in the sense of Webster's definition: "having the power to direct action or influence." Passing down the scale, through varying and lessening degrees of "positivity," we reach the case of the man who is almost devoid of this power of manifesting Mentative Energy—and his condition we call that of Magnetic "Negativity." By "Negative," as I use it here, I mean: "not-positive; lacking the power of direct action or influence."

THE MENTATIVE STRUGGLE.

Now, every person has his own degree of Magnetic "Positivity." Each one is Magnetically Positive to some others, and Magnetically Negative to others still—unless indeed one have reached the limit of Positivity or Negativity, which limit cannot be definitely fixed. Two persons meet each other. At once there ensues a silent, quiet struggle between their Mentative Magnetism, depending for its intensity upon the importance of the meeting. Still, in any and all events, the struggle ensues, usually unconsciously. It may be over in a moment, or it may last a long time, but from that struggle, sooner or later, one or the other must emerge a victor, unless, as is rarely the case, they are of equal degrees of Positivity. And there is no mistake about the result—each one recognizes himself as the victor, or the defeated, and adjusts himself to his relative position.

I do not mean by this that the degree of Magnetic Positivity is fixed permanently in either person. For the contrary is the case. One of the persons who is really stronger, usually, may be weaker at that particular time, owing to his Will being fatigued, or by reason of his having relaxed his Will-Power, as is often the case. And in such a case, the defeated one may be the victor at the next encounter, or may even rally his energies in a moment later and turn the tables. One may have a strong Will, in moments of activity, and yet in moments of passivity he may relax it very much. And, a still more important fact: One may so increase his Will-Power that he will be able to completely dominate those who formerly over-mastered, and even over-awed him. All of us know of instances of this kind in our own personal experiences.

Instances of Extreme Positivity.

At the extreme Positive Pole of Personal Force are to be found those wonderfully forceful men who seem to dominate all with whom they come in contact. These people fairly paralyze the Wills of those around them, and induce Emotive States almost at will. When in deep, earnest, mentative effort, they seem to actually "plunge" their Will into the mind of the other persons, and set themselves up as the Dominant Force therein, taking the others' Wills captive and holding them obedient to the Master Will of the Positive Man. Such men are of course rare, and whenever they exist they make a strong mark on the history of their times, local or general. I do not like to quote Napoleon Bonaparte as an example, for he has been used to illustrate almost everything. But still, the mind intuitively flies to him in thinking of the Dominant Will. Napoleon had a marvelous Will—an almost superhuman Will. It was manifested not only on the world at large, but also upon those closest to him in the way of personal contact. This man worked his Will on those around him, and forced his Desires upon them, also. He dominated everything and everybody, and his contemporaries, even his enemies, testify to this marvelous personal power. He is a very good example of this extreme Positive type.

THE OTHER EXTREME.

Passing down the scale, we see men of strong Personal Force in all walks of life. These men formerly played the part of warriors or rulers of kingdoms, but the increasing importance of commercial life in the world's affairs has developed and brought forth a new type of these Positive men, who now show themselves as "captains of industry," prominent figures in "frenzied finance," makers and rulers of the great "trusts" of this country, and others. A little lower in the scale of Personal Force we find men of marked power, but still a little less strong than those above them. And so we pass down, through the varying degrees of the scale, meeting the average man and woman, and then on to the "weaklings" of the race. At the extreme Negative end of the scale we find those impressionable creatures, known to students of hypnotism and psychology as "somnambules," or "impressionables," who have merely to be told to do a thing, in an authoritative manner, in order to have them attempt to do it, or at least to feel impelled to do so.

"IMPRESSIONABLES."

Now, about this subject of Hypnotism, I want to say right here that the actions of the hypnotic subject are caused not so much by sleep having been produced as by the existence of an exaggerated state of suggestibility developed in the subject. The best authorities now know that it is not necessary to induce sleep in order to have these "impressionables" obey the suggestions. They will act upon them without sleep. In fact, the sleep itself is now known to be induced by Suggestion, mingled with the induction of the "feeling" of sleep, by Mentative Currents.

Personal Influence.

There are many people in whom the phenomena of Hypnotism may be produced while they are wide awake. They will feel the "burn" on their hands, caused by your finger, if you but suggest it to them in the right way. They will be unable to draw apart their hands, which have been fastened together by your strong suggestion. They will be drawn backward, or forward, by your suggestion. There are many people of this kind, some more impressionable than others, but all quite impressionable, who will be driven this way or that way by those who understand the subject. Fortunately, this fact is not generally recognized, or else we should hear of still mote cases of "strange influence," etc., in the newspapers. But the subject is becoming more widely discussed and known now, and it is only a question of time when the law will be compelled to take cognizance of it.

Fortunately, however, the extreme Negative condition may be overcome by one, by developing his Will and learning the principles underlying the subject. Knowledge of the nature of the subject robs the force of much of its effect, the latter depending largely upon the passive ignorance of the subject. Give him the proper instruction, and he will be able to interpose a resistance. Every man has his present place on the scale, but he may improve his position!

The "Magnetic Man."

Now, for the purpose of illustrating the personal qualities of the Magnetically Positive man, along the lines of Personal Influence, in this lesson, I shall proceed to illustrate these qualities as existing in a suppositional individual whom I will call "the Magnetic Man." We will consider this "Magnetic Man" as an actually existent individual, in our treatment of him. You must endeavor to imagine him in this way, that you may understand his qualities. He is a very Positive man, magnetically—one of the examples of a strong, forceful man of affairs, who is constantly meeting people, and having relations with them. How does such a man act, talk, look, move, and conduct himself. Let us see!

In the first place, let us consider the appearance of the Magnetic Man. Well, he may be tall or short; dark or fair; stout or slender—these things do not count. But, notice this, that no matter which of the characteristics just mentioned he may possess or lack, he has a certain "air about him" that all may recognize, once they have seen it in any one. Let us notice this "air" carefully, for it may give us a clue.

Well, the principal feature about this "air" of the Magnetic Man is its suggestion of Self Confidence and Fearlessness. Our man seems to have a certainty of an inward Power and Force about him. Not the blustering, self-important air manifested by the pinchbeck imitators of our man, but a calm, contained, poised, consciousness of Strength and Self Confidence. Our man seems to feel that there is "something in him" that gives him a strength and firmness unknown to the majority of people. Every Magnetic Man has this inner consciousness, and I shall tell you what it is.

Contact with the "Universal Will."

As I have said in the Second Lesson, entitled "The Underlying Force," there exists under all the manifestations of Life and Mind an "Infinite and Eternal Mentative Energy," of which, and in which, all personal manifestations of Mind are but Centers of Consciousness. Now, this "Infinite and Eternal Mentative Energy," in its outward manifestations of one Pole of its Energy, at least, resembles an Universal Will. That is, while its inner nature cannot be known, yet in the outer aspect of one of its Poles of Energy it resembles an Infinite Will in operation everywhere. And, so, we are justified in thinking of it as Universal Will Power.

Now, the more Positive a man becomes, in Mentative Magnetism, the closer does he become in contact with this Universal Will. And the closer he is to this Universal Will, the more Positive does he become. It is a case of action and re-action. "To him that hath shall be given" applies in this case. The quality of Magnetic Positivity draws one to the Universal Will, and the nearness to this Will renders one more and more Positive.

UNIVERSAL VS. PERSONAL WILL.

But there is this to be noted in connection with this truth. When a man feels the sense of Power that comes from a mental relation with the Universal Will, and allows the Energy to flow through him, and manifest in his acts, he has a reservoir of Will Power back of him which is inexhaustible and never failing. But if, in his conceit arising from some successful action, he begins to think that the Power is due to some "personal strength," then he becomes "conceited" and "the pride of personality" grows upon him. This is where he makes his mistake. By this personal view of the matter he fences himself off from the Universal Will and limits his force to that portion which is locked up within his own mind, induced there by the Will of the Universe. Such a one separates himself from the source of Power and puts up a barrier between himself and the Universal Supply.

Now, do not jump at the conclusion that I am trying to "preach" to you, or to force metaphysical teaching upon you—I am not doing anything of the kind. I am giving you the Inner Teachings of the great schools of Occultism, and which teachings agree perfectly with the latest theories of modern Science. There is a great ocean of Universal Will, in which we are but Centers of Activity, and if we will but open ourselves to the Power and Will contained therein, we will have an unfailing store of Power upon which to draw.

A CENTER OF FORCEFUL WILL.

And so our Magnetic Man places himself in a Magnetically Passive attitude only toward this great Will, and in a magnetically Positive one toward all else. In this way he really becomes a most active Center of Force and Will, which becomes manifest to all with whom he comes in contact. He may not realize just what he is doing, and may know nothing of the truth herein stated, but, still he feels that he is "in touch with Something" that aids and assists him and which gives him strength and "Magnetism." He may talk about his "luck," or his "lucky star," or he may secretly believe himself specially favored by Providence (this is a secret belief of the majority of successful men)—but the fact remains that every Positive and successful man feels, underneath it all, that he has SOMETHING back of him. And this belief takes form in action and causes him to manifest that "air" of calm, positive Power and Self Confidence noticeable in such men in every instance.

THE MAGNETIC "AIR."

I cannot very well describe this "air" to you, for unless you have met a man of this kind you will not understand it. But it is a very different thing from the pompous, self-sufficient, self-important, fussy air and demeanor manifested by the "cheap" imitators of these great men. The Magnetic Man does not tell you how great, or smart, or important, he is—that folly he leaves for his cheap imitators—he makes you feel his strength by his very manner and atmosphere, without saying a word. He has that "something about him" the people notice and wonder at. And that "Something" comes from his conscious, or unconscious, relation to the Universal Will.

A MAGNETIC MENTAL IMAGE.

I would advise all who wish to become like the Magnetic Man to cultivate the Mental Image of the Universal Will—think of it as a great ocean of Will Power, in which you live, and move, and have your being. Feel yourself in touch with it. Think about your relation to it, constantly, and you will find that your mind will gradually open out to admit of the inflow of its Power. And when you learn to know the real source of Power, and Will, then you will no longer deceive yourself and attempt to shut off the flow of the Universal Will by erecting petty personal barriers of Conceit.

This inner consciousness of the Magnetic Man, especially if he understands its true nature, will react on a man's personal manner and appearance and cause to manifest in him that calm, serene, positive "air" of Power, Will and Strength, that the great leaders of men always possess. And that "air" is in itself a mighty Suggestion to others, for the world has learned to associate it with Power and Ability. And, just as the Feeling manifests itself in Action, so will the outward Action tend to induce the inward Feeling, as I have told you. And, so, if you will endeavor to imitate and reproduce the outward carriage, manner, "air" and demeanor of this Positive Man, you will have taken a step toward inducing a corresponding Mental State in yourself. But do not remain satisfied with this—go right to the fountain-head and receive your Power direct from the Universal Will.

Magnetic Desire-Force.

But there is something else about the Magnetic Man which is different from Will Power. The Will is a cold, keen, powerful force, devoid of color—it is like a great natural force devoid of feeling or emotion, although acting in response thereto. What other great force is manifesting strongly in our Magnetic Man? Desire-Force! Yes, that is the other great force within him—Desire Force. No matter how strong a Will a man may have, even though he gets in the closest touch with the Universal Will, he will accomplish nothing unless he be possessed of a developed Desire. One must "want" to do things, before he Wills to do them. I have explained this to you in a previous lesson. Let us see what this Desire Force is.

The Universal Mentative Energy seems to be a strong Something, containing within it all the Force and Energy there is in existence. It does not seem to have the attributes of Personality about it, except when it becomes manifested in

Personal Minds, or Centers of Consciousness. When a Personal Center, or Personal Mind, is established in the Universal Energy, then there seems to spring into manifestation a Creative Desire, which constantly urges toward outward expression.

This Desire Force is seen all through Nature, in all of her forms, and is manifested by all that we call Life Energy—that is, the Energy which prompts the building up of form and shape. This Desire Force is evidently identical with the Life Force as we know it. It causes the seed to sprout and the plant to grow—the cell to multiply, and the higher forms to evolve from the lower. It is the great Creative Life Energy ever manifest in Nature. It is essentially a Feminine Principle, and is constantly desiring to "give birth," "bring forth," "create." It stirs the Will into action, and never satisfied unless it is performing creative work, mental or physical.

Creative Mentation.

Now, there are persons who seem to possess but very little of this Desire Force, except on the physical plane. Their mental plane manifests very little of this force, and consequently they accomplish little or nothing of the world's work, and merely carry out the desires of others. But there are others who have this force manifested most strongly within them. They are possessed of a craving, longing, desiring force that impels them to "do things." That is, it fills them with ardent desires, along mentative lines of creation, which are ever crying out for satisfaction. The strong men and women of the world have this Desire Force highly developed, and its effort toward expression is what causes these people to accomplish things. Now do not mistake me. This Desire is not always in the direction of "owning things," but rather in the direction of "doing things." It is true that when one's Desires are along the line of accumulation, the force will be bent in that direction; but it may be less along these lines, and in that case the accumulation will be a mere incident of the "doing."

Personal Influence.

Our Magnetic Man has a great deal of Desire Force within him. He "wants" to do certain things, and he wants to do them very much. He wishes to accomplish certain ends, and the Desire becomes an ardent, glowing force that stirs up the desires in those around him, and at the same time incites his own Will into action. His Desire Force combines with his Will, and wonderful things are accomplished.

The Drawing Power of Desire.

When you come into contact with a man of intense desire, you can fairly feel the force emanating from him. Our Magnetic Man has learned to concentrate his Desire Force. When he wants some particular thing, he forgets about the minor things, and focuses his desire upon the particular thing craved by him, and thus draws it toward him with intense energy. The Will drives, forces, impels, and compels, with a "push"—the Desire Force draws, induces, pulls toward one, with an irresistible "pull." When our Magnetic Man meets you, and wants you to do something, you can feel the pull of his Desire Force, drawing, coaxing, inducing, alluring, and attracting you toward him and his objects.

The Magic Flame.

One who wishes to "do things" should keep the flame of his Desire burning bright. He should continually pour upon it the oil of Suggestion, and place before it the lantern-slides of the Mental Images of the thing desired. If you will study the man of strong Desire, you will see that he draws everything toward him that he wants. He has a "pull" upon things and leaves nothing undone in the direction of his want. He is hungry and thirsty with Desire, and he seeks satisfaction wherever it may be found, his wits being sharpened by the intensity of the desire. And he draws people to him by the very strength of his Desire Force. You will find that people will instinctively fall in with the suggestions and urgings of the strong Desire man. People, as a rule, are "drawn" rather than "pushed" or forced into a thing. The seductive, drawing, charming, fascinating force of men is that of Desire Force, not of Will Power. Yes, again I say to you that he who would succeed must, of necessity, keep his fire of Desire burning bright and fierce, else it will not awaken into action his own Will, nor stir the Desire in others.

The Intense Desire.

We talk much about Will Power, and its possession, but the majority of men fail because they do not Desire things hard enough. They must want things "the worst way," and then they will bend everything toward getting them. This is true in the case of both good and evil desires—the law is the same in both cases, and operates along the same line. We are acquainted with the disastrous consequences attendant upon the possession of evil desires, and have seen many instances of the harm wrought upon others by reason thereof. But did you ever stop to think that the same degree and intensity of Desire, turned in the right direction, would accomplish wonders of good works? If you will put into your plans of proper attainment and aspiration the same degree of energy that the evil man puts into his schemes of selfish gratification, you will be able to move mountains of difficulties.

The Twin Forces.

This Desire Force in the Magnetic Man is that which causes us to feel that "he wants this thing, and is going to have it" You know the feeling, if you have come into contact with strong men. And they draw their own to them by the exercise of this elementary force of Nature. They learn that by mentally drawing to themselves a supply of the Universal Energy they are enabled to transform it into Desire Force, as well as Will Power—the Emotive Pole is charged, as well as the Motive Pole. Both draw from the same source, and both have a constant source of supply. And both may manifest a wonderful degree of this transformed Energy, in the shape of Will Power and Desire Force. In our Magnetic Man, both Poles are fully charged, and in active operation.

THE MAGNETIC VOICE.

So much for the "air" of our Magnetic Man. Now, how does he speak?

Well, the voice is a mighty indicator of the Mental State within. Excepting the Eye, no outward form of expression of character responds so quickly and fully to the inner Mental State than the voice. The voice and eye are the two principal outward avenues of expression of the Mental States within, and both register the subtle changes and degrees of the inner state. If you will stop to think for a moment and consider the different voices of the people you know, you will see that the voice in nearly every case gives one a clue to the character or prevailing mental states of the speaker. Not alone the quality of the voice but the Tone. Every reader knows the difference between the tones of the hesitating, timid, self-doubting person, and that of the confident, self-reliant individual. There is a subtle vibration about the tone of the latter that causes one to feel confidence and respect, and which exacts obedience in a quiet, calm way, devoid of bluster or rant. Let us listen to the tones of our Positive Man.

THE CONTROL OF TONE.

Well, first, it is under the control of his Will. It is loud or soft, as he wills it to be—it never runs away from him. If the person to whom he is talking raises his voice to a strident pitch. our Positive Man does not follow suit. On the contrary he puts a little more force into his tone, but keeps the pitch the same, and before long, by his Will, in his evenly pitched tone, will actually force down the pitch of the other to a normal degree. I have seen many instances of this fact, and have noticed that the temper of the other person is toned down in accord with his decreasing pitch of voice. A calm, even, positive tone, in which the Will is apparent in self-control and in forceful effect, will master the tones of others pitched in a fiercer key; and in the mastery of the voice of the other you will often effect a mastery of his Will. By making captive the Outer Expression you often capture the Inner Man.

There are two very good reasons for one studying the voice of the Magnetic Man, as follows: (1) Because it is by his voice that he manages to make one of the most powerful Suggestions upon others; and (2) because by the expression in his voice, or rather the inner impulse causing the vocal expression, he causes to flow out strong Mentative Currents which affect and influence the other person. So in its Inner, and Outer, aspects the cultivation of the voice of the Magnetic Man is quite desirable.

THE SUGGESTIVE VOICE.

You will find that the Magnetic Man, particularly if he is engaged in an occupation necessitating his giving orders, and directions, or advice, to others, has developed a voice resembling in many details the "Suggestive Voice" habitual to the practitioner of Mental Suggestive treatments. The reason is plain. Both the man of business affairs and force, and the Suggestionist, have accustomed themselves to speaking in a forceful, firm, positive manner, and thus fairly "driving home" their ideas expressed in words. The man of affairs does not know just why he does this, but his tone is the outward expression of his forceful mental states. And this is likewise true of the Suggestionist, although he may have deliberately cultivated the Suggestive Tone at the beginning of his practice.

It is somewhat difficult to correctly define and explain the Suggestive Tone, although if one once hears it he will never forget it. But I will try my best to make it plain to you here.

In the first place, the Suggestive Tone is fairly charged with the mental idea back of the words. Each word has an inner meaning, and the Suggestive Tone carries this idea with it, so that the hearer gets the full Mentative benefit and influence of it. Do not imagine that this tone is theatrical, or tragic, or unnatural. It is none of these. It is a forceful, natural tone. Its expression is that of "being in earnest" and meaning just what you are saying. You know how you would speak if you were earnestly telling some one to do some important thing, upon which much depended. Well, that's the tone, modified of course by the particular circumstances and necessities of each case. It must be in earnest—must be more or less "intense"—must have focused in it the "feeling" behind it, in such a way as to awaken in the mind of the hearer the feeling back of the words.

The Flexible Expression.

The voice of the Magnetic Man is flexible, and adaptable to any mood or phase of feeling that he wishes to induce in his hearers. It may be positive and masterful, along the lines of Suggestion by direct command, or authority. Or it may be subtle and insinuating, along the lines of Suggestion by Association or Imitation. Or it may assume a teacher-like tone, along the lines of Suggestion by Repetition, in which the statement is made in a quiet, convincing way, as a teacher makes his statements to his class, the repetition of which brings conviction to the mind of the hearer. Or it may take on that peculiar caressing tone which is noticed in Magnetic men of a certain type, who allure, charm, fascinate and draw to them other people by reason of their subtle power of "charming." This power, which finds its expression largely in the voice, always reminds me of a female leopard or tiger, for the feline is mingled with the feminine in a peculiar way: This tone of the voice can be best described as "caressing"—when it is exhibited by one well versed in its use every word seems to be a soft caress, and has a peculiar soothing effect upon the hearer, lulling his Will to sleep and opening his

Emotive mentality to the suggestions and Mentative Currents of the speaker.

The Vibrant, Resonant, Expressive Voice.

In short, the Magnetic Man, in his use of the voice, has acquired to a certain degree the art of the actor and orator. He is able to express "feeling," real or assumed, by his voice, so that a corresponding mental state is set up in the minds of his hearers. And one may acquire this art. By practice a vibrant, resonant, expressive voice may be cultivated, and used, too, with the greatest effect in Personal Magnetism. As an instance of this let me cite you the case of Nathan Sheppard, the well-known lecturer and authority on public speaking. Mr. Sheppard relates that when he first made up his mind to devote himself to public speaking he was told by his tutors that he would be a perfect failure in such a profession, because, as he says, "My articulation was feeble; my organs of speech were inadequate; if I would screw up my little mouth it could be put into my mother's thimble." These facts were enough to discourage any man, but Sheppard rose above them, and determined to apply his Will to the task of conquering these disadvantages, and mastering the subject of public speaking. And he succeeded marvelously. By pure Will Power he, as he says, "increased my voice tenfold; doubled my chest, and brought my unoratorical organs somewhat in subjection to my will." He became one of the best public speakers of his time. So there is hope for all of you, if you will but manifest persistency and earnestness in your application of the Will. In my last lesson I will give you some exercises and directions along this line.

The Walk of the Magnetic Man.

And how does our Magnetic Man walk? How would you suppose—like a shambling, feet-scraping, wilt-less person; or firmly, deliberately, masterfully, like a true Individual? Which of these walks do you think better represents and expresses the

Mental States of such a man? Answer this, and you will know how the Magnetic Man walks. I tell you, the inner Mental State always expresses itself in the outer physical action.

THE EXPRESSIVE EYE.

And what kind of an Eye has our Magnetic Man? Need you ask this question? What would you expect? Of all the physical avenues of expression of the Mental State within, the Eye is the most potent and nearest to the "soul within." The eyes have well been called "the windows of the soul," and they give a clearer idea of the Inner Man than all else combined. And, therefore, we may expect our Magnetic Man to have an eye that reflects the Power within him. And we are not disappointed, for even a hasty glance will show that he has what people call "an expressive eye." It manifests every Mental State, at the Will of its owner. Now stern, now tender, now commanding, now loving, now masterful, now caressing—it is an obedient instrument of the Will operating it. And it produces the most wonderful suggestive effect upon those coming under its spell. As an inducer of Mental States, the Eye has no equal among the physical agents—even the Voice, wonderfully potent though it be, must yield precedence to it. It is more than a physical agent—it is a direct avenue for the passage of Mentative Currents.

Very Magnetic people, when aroused by deep interest, emotion or desire—combined with Will—seem to have a constant stream of Mentative Magnetism flowing from their eyes, which is felt by those within their field of influence. I need not call your attention to the wonderful power of eye, for you are fully acquainted with it from personal experience. You know how Power shows itself in the eyes of people. In cases where the Will has been developed to a very high degree, it is true that the Mentative Energy can be so concentrated by a very earnest and powerful glance that an actual physical effect may be produced.

THE POWERFUL GLANCE.

I have known, and heard of, cases in which a powerful glance halted people in their tracks. Cases of this kind are told of Napoleon, and others of developed Will Power. Andrew Jackson is said to have so paralyzed the will of a noted desperado by his glance that he surrendered meekly and accompanied his captor, although fully armed and heretofore deemed absolutely fearless and dangerous. The desperado afterward said that he could not understand just why he did not kill Jackson where he stood. It is related in some of the ancient histories, or tales, that one of the old Greeks paralyzed an enemy by a single burning glance. You have all seen people flinch and quail before the masterful glance of one possessed of a developed Will Power. You, yourself, know how this feels.

THE SECRET OF INFLUENCE.

But, after all, the Secret of Influence in onr Magnetic Man lies in his Mental States. The outer forms are but reflections of the Inner. If you will cultivate the connection between your mind and the Great Universal Will—the Universal Mentative Energy—then your Will becomes so strong that the outward expressions will come of themselves. But in mounting the first steps of Attainment, it becomes important for the student to pay attention to the outward characteristics, because by so doing he makes a dearer mental path for the acquisition of the desired mental states. By the very laws of Mental Suggestion he is able to imitate these outward expressions, and thus induce in himself the Mental States, which, in time, become habitual. I do not mean that one should allow the Suggestion of the others' appearance to move him in this way—this is not the idea. What I mean is that one may by Auto-Suggestion so reproduce the outward characteristics associated with a Mental State or quality, and by acting them out actually materialize into reality the Mental States themselves. Remember the rule—Mental States take form in action—and action reproduces their associated Mental States! It is a rule that works both ways. The voice makes the phonographic record—and the latter reproduces the sound! Remember this illustration, for it will help you to get the right conception of the psychological law underlying the phenomenon.

REVIEW WORK.

Concluding this lesson, let us take another glance at the first principles underlying Personal Influence, in both of its forms of Mental Suggestion, and Mentative Currents. Nothing like reviewing the fundamental principles. Here they are:

The Underlying Principle is Mentative Energy.

Mental States are exhibitions of Mentative Energy.

Mental States are Original or Induced.

Induced Mental States are caused by the Suggestions, or Mentative Currents, of others.

Suggestion induces Mental States, by reproducing the Original Mental States of others; or one's own previously experienced Mental States, including the experience of the race-ancestors, inherited and recorded in the sub-conscious minds of their descendants.

Suggestion operates along the lines of Acquiescence, Imitation, Association, and Repetition (as described in the previous lesson), always acting through physical agents for inducing Mental States, like the phonographic record.

Mentative Currents are waves or streams of vibrant Mentative Energy, emanating from the minds of people, and carrying with them the vibrations of Mental States; the vibrations tending to induce similar Mental States in the minds of people within the Field of Induction.

There are Two Poles of Mentative Energy, i. e., the Emotive Pole, manifesting Desire, Feeling, Emotion, etc.; and the Motive Pole, manifesting Will, etc.; the acting force, affecting other minds, manifested by these Two Poles being called Desire-Force and Will-Power, respectively.

Desire-Force tends to awaken similar vibrations in the minds of others, thus producing similar desires—or it charms the Wills of others and causes them to carry out its desires—its action and nature bear a strong resemblance to feminine mental power.

Will-Power tends to awaken Desire in the minds of others by sheer mastery and forcefulness—it also acts in the direction of combating and overpowering the Wills of others, and taking them captive—it also directs, masters, concentrates, or restrains one's own Desire-Force, on occasions—its action bears a strong resemblance to masculine mental power.

In Personal Influence, along the lines of Personal Magnetism, the Mentator pours out his Mentative Currents, generated by his Will or Desire, or both; either in a general way, or in a concentrated, directed manner; in a personal intervtew, and thus Influences the mind of others by Induction—this is usually, or always, accompanied by Mental Suggestion, using physical agents, such as the voice, eye, manner, etc., which heighten the effect produced.

So, you see, by reference to these Underlying Principles, just why and how Personal Influence, or Personal Magnetism, operates.

STRANGE OCCURRENCES EXPLAINED.

And now, as we pass on to the next lesson, on "Telementation," it will be well for us to glance over the pages of ancient history and see how the many strange occurrences of Personal Influence therein recorded may be understood in the light of our knowledge of Mental Magic. Cases of Dominant Individuality, extraordinary Will Power, Burning Desire, Fascination, Charming, Suggestion of all kinds, Personal Mastery, and many other forms and instances of the Mental Domination and Influence of Man over Man, may be understood clearly and divorced from the mystery and glamour of their local surroundings. It may be seen that one law underlies them all. And coming down to the present time, do we not now have a clearer idea of the strange personal atmospheres, or influence, surrounding some people, which so strongly attract or repel others? Can we not now better understand the remarkable influence of those men of mighty Wills and ardent Desires, who seem to either compel all things to bow to their Will-Power, or else draw to them all that they really want, by the strength of their developed Desire-Force? I think that even so far as we have gone, many things now seem clearer and plainer to us. Is it not so with you?

PERSONAL ATMOSPHERES.

You will readily see, from what has been said, that the "Personal Atmospheres" of persons depend upon the character of their Mental States, and are the result of the Mental Currents emanating from them. Every person has his or her own Mentative Aura, or body of Radiant Mentative Energy, which flows from them in all directions. These Mentative Atmospheres affect the people with whom one comes in contact. You all know cases of people who seem to carry with them an atmosphere of "feeling" which affects a roomful of people, or even a building. This atmosphere may be Positive or Negative in its effect—that is, stimulating or depressing. All of these things arise in the way which I have mentioned. It is related of Rachel, the great French actress, that although she was not beautiful in form or face, still she had that indescribable charm of personality about her that caused everyone to consider her a beautiful woman, so great was her fascinating charm.

That which so many call "Personal Magnetism," as distinguished from Personal Force, consists of this Mentative Atmosphere, or Radiant Mentative Energy, which induces in all within its field a feeling of similar emotion or vibration. The charm of the "fascinating person" is accounted for in the same way. It is all a matter of the Mentative Force inducing feeling in others.

The power called "Fascination," which has been known in all times and countries, arises from the same cause. It operates by the strong Mentative Currents pouring from one's mind, and inducing Mental States in others. The phenomena of Hypnotism, Mesmerism, etc., etc., are all forms of the same force, the phase of Mental Suggestion, of course, playing its part in all of them. Hypnotism and Mesmerism are only "exaggerated" forms of Personal Influence, depending upon Mentative Currents and Mental Suggestion for their effect.

But, you may complain, we have not yet been told about those mysterious mental influences that have swayed people, and things, in bodies and numbers, and at long distance! No, that is quite true—you haven't! But what you have been told has cleared a way for your more comprehensive understanding of such more remarkable forms of Mental Magic—you are now the better prepared for it, are you not? And this being so, there is no use in keeping you waiting longer. So I shall proceed to the consideration of the subject of the Fifth Lesson—"The Science of Telementation"—the most remarkable and wonderful lesson of all, for it combines all the principles within its field. But carry with you that which has already been told you. It will all fit into its place in the course.

Lesson V.

The Science of Telementation.

The Universal Mentative Energy—The Mentative Currents—The Conversion of Energy—The Nature of Mental States—Vibrational Excitement—How Vibrations Are Transmitted—Currents and Waves—The Law of Wave-Motion—Experimental Proof—Mentative Waves and Currents—Important Principles—A Mental Picture—The Sea of Energy—The Formation of Currents—The Essence of Energy—The Degrees of Power—The Centres in Action—Rotary Currents—A Great Moving Picture—The Second Plane—The Second and Third Planes—The Four Higher Planes—Second Plane Sights—Tinted Thought Clouds—Emotional Colors-The Meaning of Blue, Yellow, Orange, Brown, Red, Green, Grey, and Black Thought Colors—Desire and Will Appearances—Vitality Vibrations—The Human Aura—How People Affect Each Other—Suggestions in Action-A Positive Exhibition—Will-Power Lightning—Desire-Force Induction—A Combined Attack—Charming, Alluring Attraction—Repelling Attacks—The Force in Churches, Theaters, etc.—Mental Atmosphere of Towns and Places—Unlucky and Haunted Places—Positive Atmospheres—The Various Appearances of Thought-Forms—The Mentative Wire—Rotary Forms—Thought Forms Like Living Forces—Telementation Explained—Long-Range Influence—White Magic, and Black—The Mental Image—The Evil Effects of Fear—Adverse Treatments—How to Neutralize Them—Black Magicians in Disguise—The Secret of Charms—How Witchcraft Operated—Startling Examples—Good Employment of the Force—How Schemers Use It—Valuable Rules for Self-Protection—Illustrative Examples—Generalized Telementation—How Strong, Positive Men Use the Force—How to Repel the Waves—The Law of Attraction—Illustrations of the Law—The Key of Telementation—Visualization, and the Laws and Principles of Its Operation—Full Directions—A Caution—The Working Principles Explained Fully—Concluding Advice.

Lesson V.

The Science of Telementation.

You will see by reference to Lesson II, that the term "Telementation" is used by me in the sense of "Mentative Influence at a distance," the word being derived from the Greek word *Tele*, meaning "afar off;" and the word "Mentation," which I use in the sense of "Mental Activity."

The Terms of the Subject.

You will also remember that the word "Mentation" implies activity of the Mentative Energy, which I hold to be Universal in its character. You will also remember that the action of Telementation depends upon the production of Induced Mental States by Mentative Currents in and of the Mentative Energy. Mentative Induction, you remember, operates along the same lines as Magnetic or Electrical Induction in Physical Science, that is, an Original Mental State (being an exhibition of Mentative Energy) may reproduce itself in another mind by Mentative Induction operating by means of Mentative Currents.

TECHNICAL TERMS NECESSARY.

I have explained how Mental States may be Induced by Suggestion, as well as by Mentative Currents, and shall not allude to this phase at this place, but shall consider Mentative Induction in its phase of manifestation by means of Mentative Currents. This mention of technical terms may seem somewhat "dry" to you, but you should acquaint yourself with the intelligent use and meaning of the terms, for thereby you will be enabled to hold the ideas firmly in your mind. Terms are "pegs" upon which you may hang thoughts and ideas, so that you may find them when you need them. Otherwise they are scattered around in confusion.

THE UNIVERSAL MENTATIVE ENERGY.

In order that you may more fully understand the wonderful phenomena of Telementation, I think we had better take another look at the Fundamental Principle, or Mentative Energy itself. By understanding the nature of the Force employed, you may better understand its effects and laws of operation. You will remember that I have postulated, claimed and assumed the existence of an Universal Mentative Energy or Force, which is imminent in, and manifested in, all forms of Life, Energy and Mind. I have also held that all personal manifestations of Mind, in ourselves and others, are but Centers of Mentative Energy in the great Ocean of the Universal Mentative Energy. You will remember also, that I have claimed that the Brain was not a "creator" of Mentative Energy, but rather in the nature of a "converter" or "transformer" of the Universal Mentative Energy into usable forms and phases. Well, so far, we understand the matter. Now let us pass on to the consideration of the Mentative Currents.

THE MENTATIVE CURRENTS.

Well, in the first place, the Currents must be set into motion somewhere and somehow. Where and How? Let us see! Well, we must see that the Mentative Currents have their origin, or rather, their initial impulse, in and from the Mind of some Individual. How? Well, in and from his Brain, of course. Why? Well, the Brain is the "transformer" or "converter" of the Mentative Energy into usable shapes and phases. What is the nature of the Brain's action? Well, Science, as well as the Occult Teachings, inform us that in all brain-processes there is a "burning-up" of brain substance and nervous matter, just as there is a corresponding "burning-up" of the elements in an Electric Battery. The process is very similar in both cases.

THE CONVERSION OF ENERGY.

Both Brain and Battery "convert" or "transform" an Energy already existing in an universal form, which energy cannot be created, added to, nor taken away from. And both use up material in the process. And both generate "currents" of force which are capable of effecting changes in other substances, etc. Science shows us that there is a production or generation of "heat" in the manifestation of "Mind-Energy" in the Brain. The temperature of the Brain rises when it is employed in active thought-work, or other forms of mental activity or excitement. And, even the temperature of a tiny nerve increases when it is used. There is no use in disputing this fact—it has been fully demonstrated by Science.

THE NATURE OF "MENTAL STATES."

What causes the Brain to manifest this Energy? Mental States! What is a Mental State? Well, you know what "Mental" means—and "State" means "a condition." So a Mental State is "a mental condition" then? Yes! Then upon what do Mental States, or "conditions," depend, and why do they vary? Well, upon the degrees of Vibration of Excitement of the Mental Apparatus! Mental Apparatus? Then, has a thing to have a Mental Apparatus, before it can manifest Mental States, original or induced? Yes! but remember this, *everything* has its

Mental Apparatus, even down to the Atom, and the particles that compose Atoms; everything "feels" and "responds to feeling," even among the most material forms—Science states this emphatically; and everything that "feels" and "responds," must manifest Desire and Will, if only in an elementary way, and must have Mental Apparatus in order to do this; there is Mind, and the machinery of Mind, in every Atom, and all that is evolved therefrom. This is not my personal statement, alone, but is the last word of Modern Science, as voiced by her most advanced advocates.

VIBRATIONAL EXCITEMENT.

"Vibration of Excitement," I have said. What is a Vibration? Well, it is a state of intense, rapid movement of a particle. Science informs us that everything is in vibration, always; and that the differing nature of things depends upon their respective rate of vibrations. And what is "Excitement" as I use the term? Well, it means "aroused Activity." So, then, there is to be found a condition of "aroused vibrational activity" underlying all Mental States? Yes. that's just it! And this aroused vibrational activity communicates motion to the Mentative Currents, and starts them toward others in whom they induce similar Mental States. That is the story in full.

HOW THE VIBRATIONS ARE TRANSMITTED.

Well, then, we have a Mental State of "aroused vibrational activity" of al' individual. How is this passed on to other individuals without direct contact? By Mentative Currents or Waves I What are Mentative Currents or Waves, and how do they operate? Well, now we are right up the question, with a full understanding of what it means. Then let us answer it in the light of Modem Science.

The Science of Telementation.

About "Currents" and "Waves."

There is a great misapprehension in the minds of the majority of people about "currents" and "waves" of Light, Magnetism, Electricity, Heat, etc. They are aware that Heat and Light, for instance, travel over millions and millions of miles from the Sun to the Earth, and are then felt here, although originating there millions of miles away. They know this fully, but they seem to think that the Heat and Light actually "travel" in waves over the distance. But this is not the teaching of Science, which, on the contrary, holds that Light and Heat do not so travel, but that the original Heat and Light vibrations (for that is what Light and Heat is—a matter of vibrations) set up "waves in the ether." The ether is a suppositious fine form of matter, filling all space, even between the atoms, as swell as between the worlds—nobody knows anything "actually" about the ether, but Science has been forced to postulate its existence, in order to account for certain phenomena.

Ethereal Waves.

Well, then, Science holds that these "waves in the ether," once set into motion, travel on until they come in contact with matter capable of taking up their vibrations. When this kind of matter is found, it takes up the ethereal vibrations, and reproduces them in the shape of Heat and Light. In other words, the original Light and Heat of the Sun does not "travel" to the earth to be then experienced by the latter, but, on the contrary, the original Solar Heat and Light set up the "waves in the ether," which travel along until the earth is reached, when meeting with the proper material they are reproduced or "transformed" into Heat and Light vibrations similar to those of the original impulse, and we of the Earth feel the Heat and see the Light. Electricity and Magnetism are reproduced in the same way. Do you see? It is just like the Voice vibrations setting up electrical vibration in the telephone, which travel along and then are re-transformed into Voice vibrations again at the other end of the line. Do you understand it now? And when you think of this, please remember that the receiving-end vibrations are "Induced." Now you begin to see what I am driving at, don't you?

THE LAW OF "WAVE MOTION."

And there is something else just as much generally misunderstood. People think that these "waves" actually travel. But they don't! No waves travel! But, you may say, waves in water travel, when we drop a stone in the pond! No they don't! What really happens is that the motion of the stone produces an elevation of the water, that you call a wave. Then the motion is passed on and another wave is formed. Then another, and another, until you have a series of waves that apparently travel toward the shore. But the waves don't travel. They merely communicate their motion to the particles of the water next to them and a continuous moving effort is exhibited.

EXPERIMENTAL PROOF.

The real motion of a wave is "up and down" only. Place a cork in the water and then create waves and you will see that while the wave motion travels outward, the cork merely bobs up and down and does not move with the waves. Here is how Science illustrates the motion: It bids you take a rope and tie one end of it to a post or wall, etc., the loose end being retained in your hand. Now slack the rope a little and begin to agitate it up and down. What happens? You will see a wave motion generated, and a series of waves passing over the rope from your hand to the post or wall. And yet you know that the rope itself has not traveled, but has merely moved up and down. It is not a matter of *travel*, but of communicated and induced motion. Try the experiment yourself! Do you see it now? Well, all waves are alike in this respect—Light-waves, Heat-waves, Electrical-waves, Magnetic-waves and Mind-waves. All communicate vibrations, which move on in a wave motion.

Waves in the Ocean of Mind.

But these Heat and Light waves are "waves in the ether" which ether is a material thing. Do I hold that Mind-waves are the same? Not exactly. I hold that the Universal Mentative Energy is higher even than the finest Ethereal matter, and that it pervades the latter. And I hold that we are all Centers of Mentative Activity in a great Ocean of Mentative Energy. We are like bubbles in the ocean, so use a crude figure of speech. And, therefore, I claim that the Mentative Currents and Waves are really Currents and Waves in that Great Ocean of Mentative Energy. And the Vibrational Activity set up in your mind, my mind, or the minds of thousands, pass on their vibrations to the great Ocean of Mentative Energy, and produce "waves" or "currents" of Energy, which travel on until they reach the Mental Apparatus of other Individuals, in which they tend to reproduce the original Vibrations or Mental States—by Induction, remember.

Mentative Waves and Currents.

In other words, I hold that these "waves" and "currents" are like the ocean's waves and currents—not only *of* the ocean, but also *in* it. My idea of the Mentative Currents or Waves are that they are not only manifestations of the Universal Mentative Energy, but also that they travel *in the Ocean* of that Universal Principle. And that great Mentative Ocean is full of currents, and waves, and eddies, and swirls, and whirlpools, and gulf-streams, and other forms of Activity.

Important Principles.

I must ask every student to acquaint himself with the principles of these Mentative Currents as I have stated them from the beginning of this lesson up to this page, that he may get an idea of the laws and operation of Telementation. The analogy between the two Oceans—of water and Mentative Energy, respectively—is so close that an understanding of one will throw much light on the other. "As above—so below; as below—so above," says the old occult aphorism. Each plane of life has its corresponding manifestations. Study the physical world and you will understand the metaphysical.

A MENTAL PICTURE.

And now, having familiarized you with the idea of the Ocean of Mentative Energy, and the Currents, Waves, Whirlpools, etc., contained therein, I must ask you to use your imagination to the full in order to form a Mental Picture of this Great Mentative Ocean, that you may fully understand the laws in operation in its manifestations. This Mental Picture, if firmly fixed in your mind, will give you always a "key" to any manifestation of Mentative Energy, along the lines of Telementation, that you may be called upon to consider, examine or study. If one can form this Mental Picture clearly and distinctly, he will always be able to grasp the Secret of Mental Magic, besides which the very clearness of the picture will enable him to more intelligently apply the Mentative Energy when he sees fit, without the resistance ordinarily set up in the average mind, because of the inability to "see" just what is needed. Here is this mystical Mental Picture.

THE SEA OF ENERGY.

Picture to yourself a great Ocean of Mind. If you are unable to grasp the abstract idea of Mind as a Principle, then do the next best thing, and think of this Mental Ocean as a great Sea of Electrical Energy. Or, if you prefer, think of it as a great Ether of Force, filling all space. At any rate, the picture must show this Mind Energy as filling all space, even in between the atoms, and even *in* the atoms themselves. Perhaps you had better commence, by forming the picture of all Space as being empty of all forms and shapes, and containing nothing but this Pure Mental Energy—Mind Principle—an Ocean of Mind, with nothing else in it—All Mind, remember. And this Mind must be thought of as an Energy or Force, capable of setting into operation all kinds of manifestations when started.

THE FORMATION OF CENTERS.

Then think of a tiny Center of Energy being formed in this great Mind Ocean—a little Whirlpool, so tiny that the strongest microscopes could scarcely distinguish it. Then see countless numbers of similar whirlpools being formed in this Ocean of Mind. These little whirlpools, we will call Centers of Energy. They combine and shapes begin to appear. Atoms of Matter appear, being composed of combination of these tiny Centers, which thus become larger and greater Centers. Then come combinations of these Atoms, and the various forms of matter result, for all substances you know are composed of Atoms, in various combinations; all the Atoms, seemingly being composed of little particles called Electrons, which seem to be like tiny Units of Force, but which are attracted and repelled by each other, and seem to have their "likes" and "dislikes," thus showing the elements of Mind within them.

FROM SIMPLE TO COMPLEX.

And then these shapes and forms of Matter become more and more complex, and the Centers of Energy more potent. And the forms of living things begin to appear, mounting from the lowly microscopic cell on to combinations of cells, in plant life, then animal life, and then human life. And each form, as it mounts higher, displays more and more Power of Mind. Until at last we see Man with his wonderful Mind, as a great Center of Energy in this Great Ocean of Mind.

THE ESSENCE OF ENERGY.

But, remember this, always, that all these shapes and forms, and cells, and plants, and animals and men, have as their inner essential substance this same Mind principle, of which the Ocean itself is composed. They are Centers of Activity in this

Mind Ocean, but are composed of the same substance as the Ocean itself. You may think of them as Vibratory Whirlpools of Mind, if you like—and you will not be very far out of the way if you do. You see that, at the last, and underneath all, ALL IS MIND, and All is IN MIND. I shall not go into the metaphysical side of the question, although I have studied deeply that phase of the matter. But I shall confine myself to the Scientific side of the question in these lessons. But this idea of ALL IS MIND—that is All things are Centers of Mental Activity and Energy, in the Great Universal Ocean of Mind Energy, is scientifically correct. And it is correct from the Advanced Occult position, also. There is no con•flict between True Occultism and True Science, when each understands each other's terms.

The Degrees of Power.

Now, then, these Centers of Energy are of varying degrees of Force and Activity. We will call the strong ones "Positive," and the weak ones "Negative." So according to their varying degrees of Power and Vibration, each Center is Positive to some others, and Negative to others still. Each has its degree of Positivity. Now think of these Centers as Human Minds, and you will be able to fill out your picture in detail.

The Centers in Action.

And then picture each one of these Centers manifesting Vibrational Activity, and thus converting and transforming the Mentative Energy from the Ocean of Mind. And then see them sending out Waves, and Currents of Mentative Energy, which induce similar Vibrations or Mental States in other Centers. Then see some of the strong, positive Centers, setting up great rotating currents, resembling whirlpools in the body of the Mind Ocean, which extend further and further out from the Center, and affect other Centers far away from it.

Rotary Currents.

And, if you will examine your picture more closely, you will see that these rotary currents are continually drawing to these Centers the things, and persons, and ideas that they are attracting by reason of their particular rate of vibration, while things of different vibrations seem to be comparatively unaffected by the currents. This and other things you may see in your picture as it grows clearer to you. And, in addition to these currents you see great Waves traveling out in certain directions, toward certain objects to which they have been directed. In short, you see all the phenomena of the Ocean of Water reproduced in this Ocean of Mind. You see the picture of The Circulation of Mind. You see the forming and growing and evolution of Centers of Activity and Mentative Energy.

The Two Poles of Activity.

And when you come to look a little closer at your picture, you will see that each one of these Centers of Energy seems to have Two Poles of Activity, one of which acts in the direction of impelling, driving, pushing, forcing, urging, directing, etc., the action being always "outward;" and the other acting in the direction of drawing, pulling, attracting, coaxing, alluring, charming, leading, etc., the action always being "inward." One seems to be a Masculine force, the other a Feminine force. One seems to act as Will-Power; the other as Desire Force.

Motive Power and Emotive Force.

These Two Poles of Mentative Energy, possessed by each Center, are called the Motive Pole, and the Emotive Pole, respectively. I have described their characteristics several times as we have proceeded in these lessons. But, once more, let me call your attention to the meaning of the terms applied to them. "Motive" means, of course, "that which moves; that which incites to action." "E-motive" means "that which moves or excites the feelings." You will remember that "excitement" means "aroused activity." So, then, "Emotive" means "that which arouses the feelings into activity." And the Emotive side of the mind always has to do with "Feelings," and the "Motive" with Willing. And the best results always arise from a combination of both Feeling and Willing—Desiring and Acting. As in all other things, a combination of the Masculine and Feminine qualities and characteristics produces the best results. Each has its strong and weak points—but together they are irresistible along all lines of work, physical, mental and spiritual.

A Great Moving Picture.

And now the broad outlines of our Mental Picture have been drawn, and the general details filled in. But our Picture is more than this. It is a Moving Picture in vivid action and spirited motion. It will show us the varied phenomena of Telementation in a series of moving, acting, realistic, thrilling scenes. And yet all will occur right on and in the picture itself, without going outside of it for material. The Mental Picture contains the material for an infinite variety of action and combination—it is a world within itself. And now, good students, we will set the machinery into operation and show you your Mental Picture of this Mind Ocean and its Centers of Energy in full motion and activity. Kindly give me your full attention while I describe the moving scenes to you!

Phenomena of the Second Plane.

In describing the action of this Magic Mental Picture I will suppose that you are a highly developed Occultist and consequently are able to see on what Occultists call the "Second Plane." Without going into the subject in detail here (for it forms no part of this present work) I will say that Occultists recognize Seven Planes of Life, all of which have their own laws and phenomena. The First Plane is our ordinary Material Plane, the phenomena of which may be observed by all having their physical senses. This First Plane is the Plane of Matter, and all of its phenomena is that of Matter. All that can be seen on that Plane is the movement or presence of Matter. Even when we say that we see the manifestation of some Force (on this Plane), we really mean that we see that Force as it produces a movement or change in Matter–we do not see the Force at all; all that we see is the Matter moved by the Force. Do you see what I mean?

THE PLANE OF FORCES.

The Second Plane is the Plane of Forces, on which operate Energy or Force in all of its forms. Occultists who have reached the Second Degree of Unfoldment, are able to sense the phenomena on this Second Plane—that is, they are able to witness the phenomena of the Forces on their own Plane and independent of the presence of Matter. To illustrate this I would say that on the First Plane (the Plane of the majority of the race) the phenomena attaching to Electricity can be sensed only through the agency of the Matter in which the Electricity operates—you can see Material objects moved by Electricity, but you cannot see the Electricity itself. The same is true of Magnetism—you may see the needle drawn to the magnet, but you cannot see the current of Magnetic vibrations themselves. You cannot see the vibratory Light-waves, but you can see the manifestation of Light when these waves strike upon a material object.

DIRECT "SENSING" OF THE FORCES.

But, on the Second Plane, those who have attained the Second Degree, report that the "vibratory-waves" of Electricity, Magnetism, Light, Heat, etc., are capable of being sensed by them without the presence of the Material Agent. They report that they are able to see the Vibrations themselves—for instance, they can see the waves of Electricity or Magnetism as they pass through the ether and before they reach the Material objects which they affect in a way visible to the ordinary eye. They report that even the vibratory-waves of the X-Ray are visible to them, without the agency of the fluorescent screen used by scientific men before the X-Rays become apparent to them. You know, of course, that these X-Rays, and in fact also the higher rays of ordinary Light, are invisible to the human eye, although capable of being recorded by instruments, photographic plates, etc.

THE SECOND AND THIRD PLANES.

And these Second Plane people report that the vibrations of the Mentative Waves, or Currents, are plainly perceptible to them. But, mark you this, notwithstanding that some of these Second Plane people believe and will tell you that they "can see Thought," or can "see Mind-waves themselves," they are mistaken. All that they can see is the Force of Energy of these Waves or Currents, but Mind in itself they cannot see at all—this last is reserved for the Third Plane, or Mental Plane. To make this plainer, these Second Plane people seeing the Force or Energy, and mistaking it for Mind itself, are just like the First Plane people who see the Material motions and phenomena, and think that they are seeing Electricity, Magnetism, etc., in themselves. The Third Plane phenomena is purely Mental, and those who have reached the Third Degree of Occult Unfoldment, report that they are able to see Mind in itself. They are unable to tell us "just what it looks like," for the reason that it is different from anything that we know on either the Material Plane or even the Plane of Forces—it is "Something Different"—it is the "Essence of Energy."

THE FOUR HIGHER PLANES.

The remaining Four Planes, that is the Fourth, Fifth, Sixth and Seventh Planes, respectively, are subjects that belong to the higher degrees of Occultism, and form no part of these lessons or subject. I merely mention them so that advanced students may recognize that I am aware of their existente and importance, and am not misled by any erroneous belief in their being only Three Planes, which some of the teachers have fallen into. These lessons belong to the Second Plane teachings, and do not deal with the Third Plane, except incidentally. They deal with the "Energy" phase of Mind—that is Mind in its aspect of Mentative Energy. Some day I may write of the "Higher Planes"—but not now.

SECOND PLANE SIGHTS.

So, to return to our Magic Mental Picture, I will assume that you are able to sense the Second Plane phenomena, and thus actually see the passage and existence of the Mentative Waves and Currents. By giving you the teachings in this way, I will be able to picture the phenomena much clearer than if I held to the First Plane method. I want to show you the Forces, themselves, as well as their effect upon Material Forms. You Understand just what I mean, now, don't you?

THE TINTED THOUGHT CLOUDS.

Well, the first thing that you will see in our Magic Mental Picture, is the presence of great clouds of vapory substance, somewhat resembling the fleecy clouds of a summer day, although some of the clouds are much heavier and darker looking. And, you will note the presence of color in these clouds, some of them being a dull grey, and others being tinted like the clouds at sunset or sunrise. It is a beautiful sight, this ever changing mass of colored clouds of all kinds, shapes, forms, and degrees of density. Let us consider just what these various colors mean—for each has its own meaning, the color being dependent upon the degree of vibration and the degree of vibration depending upon the FEELING which started the waves into motion. I had not intended to mention this in these lessons, but I now see that I cannot omit it without causing a loss to my students. When one gets talking about Second Plane phenomena, it is hard to refrain from telling the story through to the finish.

THE "EMOTIONAL COLORS."

Let me give you the "Emotional Colors," that you may recognize them as you see them in the Picture. Here they are:

SPIRITUAL BLUE.

Blue, is the vibrational color pertaining to Spiritual Feeling, and represents the various religious feelings, and emotions, the shade growing lighter as the religious concept rises toward true spirituality. Light Blue represents a high unselfish spiritual feeling; a beautiful violet representing the highest religious feeling; and a peculiar shade which may be called "ultra-violet" representing a Spiritual Unfoldment of a very high order.

INTELLECTUAL YELLOW.

Yellow is the vibrational color appertaining to the feelings and emotions associated with Intellectual Power, the shade growing clearer as the intellect mounts to higher conceptions. A dull, dark yellow is the color of the ordinary intellectual state, while the brilliant intellect shows itself in a beautiful golden hue. There is a shade still higher than this, although most rare among the race. I allude to that shade of true Primary Yellow, which belongs to those who have attained a high degree of True Occult Unfoldment–the spiritually illumined. The highest Occult Teachings inform us that the vibrational shade belonging to "Spirit" of the "Essence of Being," is a pure white light, of an unusual brilliancy.

ORANGE AND BROWN.

Orange, this shade which is a combination of Yellow and Red, pertains to those possessing the Pride of Intellectuality, or Intellectual Ambition, of a marked degree.

Brown is the vibrational color of Avarice and Greed.

PASSIONAL RED.

Red is the vibrational color of Passion, in all of its phases. Dull, deep Red betokens the Animal Passions, and Sensuality. A Dark Bright Red betokens Anger and Hate—when mingled with Black it is Anger or Hate arising from Malice, or Envy; when mingled with Green it relates to Anger arising from Jealousy or Envy; when shown without the mingling color it denotes "Fight" for some supposed right, or ordinary cause. When this color is seen in the shade of *Crimson*, it betokens a higher form of Love, the shade becoming lighter and clearer as the degree of the feeling advances in the scale of character. A gross, selfish love shows as a dull crimson, while a higher form of love displays a clearer shade, terminating in a shade approaching a soft rose-color when the character of the attachment is on a high plane.

DECEITFUL GREEN.

Green is a peculiar vibrational color, and betokens a number of odd phases of feeling and emotion. A peculiar dull, dirty Green betokens Jealousy or Envy. A Greyish-Green indicates Deceit, which shade becomes clearer and brighter as the quality of the "Deceit" rises in the scale. A bright clear shade of Green is seen when there is a manifestation of "tact"; "diplomacy"; "politeness"; "adaptability," etc., etc.

NEGATIVE GREY.

Grey is a negative vibrational color, which in its dark shades indicates Gloom, Depression, or Melancholy, etc.; and in a bright clear shade indicates Selfishness; and in a certain pallid shade indicates Fear or Terror.

HATEFUL BLACK.

Black is the vibrational color of Hate, Malice, Revenge, and similar states of feeling.

These vibrational Emotional Colors, of course combine, and blend into each other in countless combinations, but the above will give you a key to the same.

THE APPEARANCE OF DESIRE AND WILL.

The Vibrational Colors of the Two Mental Poles, can scarcely be called colors at all, for their colors and shades are derived from the character of the Feeling inspiring them, which gives to them the degree of vibration and color indicating the motive or emotive impulse. But there may be seen a difference even in these two; that is, the Emotive Pole, in its currents of Desire-Force, shows a scintillating effect, as if there were a multitude of minute sparks, or stars in the current; and the Motive Pole, in its currents of Will-Power shows an effect something like a multitude of tiny and minute lightning-fiashes, playing in the stream or current.

VITALITY VIBRATIONS.

In addition to the shades mentioned above, there is another that should be mentioned while we are considering the subject. I allude to what might be called the "Vitality Vibrations," which radiate from the living body, and which are caused by the "Vital Force" which permeates the body during life, and makes possible the running of the physical machinery—some prefer to call it Nerve Force. These vibrations show no special color, although when near, or in the body, they manifest a faint reddish tint. But when seen away from the body they show a lack of color, like clear water, and resemble the heated air arising from a stove, lamp, or heated ground—that is, to say, they look like a colorless, vibrating body of air. The degree and strength of these vibrations depend upon the state of physical health of the person manifesting them.

The Science of Telementation.

The Human Aura.

Now, as we gaze upon our Magic Mental Picture, and see moving thereon the shapes and forms of human beings, we may see that each being is surrounded with an "aura" or egg-shaped "atmosphere" of these Emotional Vibrations–radiations emanated from his Mental States. This Aura extends out from the body for a distance of about one yard, and gradually fades away as the distance from the body is increased. And the Aura of each person is seen to be colored according to the vibrations belonging to his prevailing Mental States.

The Colors of the Mental States.

Each Mental State shows itself in its appropriate shade, in the proper combinations, blendings, etc., and therefore, the trained Occultist is able to read a person's character like an open book, from these Emotional Colors. And even though one may not be manifesting any special Mental State at the moment, his Aura will still be colored because of his prevailing Mental State—his "Character," as it were. And of course, these vibrations composing the Aura of a person will affect those coming in contact with, or near him, or her. That is the reason why we feel the "personal atmospheres" of people when we come near them. Even beyond the visible aura, the vibrations continue in a fainter degree. And so, on our picture we can tell just what kind of people are passing before us—their Mental States are revealed by the Emotional Colors.

How People Affect Each Other.

And now we shall see how people affect others. We see one man approach another. The degree of Magnetic Positivity of the first man is superior to that of the second, and we see, as we watch, that the coloring of his Aura gradually interpenetrates that of the weaker man, and the coloring of the latter's aura gradually grows to more closely resemble that of the first man. We may watch the process, and thus become aware that the following things are happening, *viz.*, the Mental States of the first man are inducing similar feelings and emotions in the second man, by means of the Currents of Mentative Energy that are flowing toward him. The first man is making no effort to impress the second man, but being the more Positive his "magnetism" affects that of the other man and induces similar states. The second man "takes on the states" of the first man, as we may see by the change in coloring. This is the way that people unconsciously affect other people, and the latter are unconsciously affected. Simply a case of unconscious Mentative Induction, you see.

SUGGESTION VIEWED.

The second man moves on, feeling more depressed, or elated, as the case may be, by reason of his contact with the first man, and also carrying away with him a little of the other man's general feelings, and "character." This second man, a little later on, meets another man, and we may see bow this new man affects the "second man" by the Sugges•tion of his manner and words. He does not seem to be sending out such strong turrents as the man first spoken of, but his outward symbols of voice, words, manner, etc., are well aded out, and we soon see our "second man" having mental states induced in him by Suggestion. You have now seen two stages or phases of Mentative Indu~tion.

A POSITIVE EXHIBITION.

Our Positive Man has gone on his way, and soon he spies another man whom he wishes to influence in certain matters. Watch him now, and you will see something interesting. The Positive Man's Aura seems to be disturbed, and great tongues of color seem to leap from it, and lap around the other man, the whole process resembling the action of tongues of flame at a fire. These tongues of Mentative Currents, wrap themselves all around the other man, and some seem to scintillate as they manifest the action of fairly "pulling" him toward the Positive Man, while others seem to be beating upon him like a rain of tiny flashes of lightning—the one is the play of Desire-Force, and the other the action of Will-Power. This gives us a good illustration of Personal Influence in an interview, or a phase of Personal Magnetism.

WILL-POWER LIGHTNING.

As the action grows more spirited, you may see the Will-Power of the Positive Man darting out in straight, sharp flashes, like great sparks from an electric battery, and you may see the process by which he beats down, and neutralizes the Will-Power of the weaker man, until he seems to exhaust it and take it captive, and the man acquiesces in the statements and demands of the stronger Willed man.

DESIRE-FORCE INDUCTION.

This process is hastened by the fact that the Desire-Force of the weaker man has become so impressed by the stronger Will that it becomes dazed, or fascinated; the effect being strongly increased by the Desire-Force of the stronger man setting up Mentative Induction a corresponding vibration in the Desire-Pole of the weaker man. And a fourth element in the attack is that the strong Desire-Force of the strong man also tends to "pull" the Will of the weaker one toward it, and away from its natural mate, its own Desire-Pole.

A COMBINED ATTACK.

This is a case of a combined, determined attack. It is true that the Positive Man may not know a single fact regarding Mental Magic—but he has learned the process of affecting and influencing others, and bending them to his Will and Desire, although he is ignorant of the scientific explanation of the process. Every Positive Magnetic Man understands this, instinctively, and his knowledge increases as practice gives him more confidence in himself.

Charming, Alluring Attraction.

These people pass from the scene, and we may see in their place men and women "charming," "alluring," and "drawing" others by reason of their Desire-Force operating along the lines of so-called "Love," but which is but little more than selfish animal passion, in some cases grosser than that manifested by the animals, because it is abnormal in its manifestations, and inordinate in its demands.

Repelling Attacks.

We see much of this in our picture, but we notice here and there that some man or woman seems able to repel these attractions easily, and are not affected by the Currents of Desire. Why? Because their general Mental State is so dissimilar that too much resistance is interposed, and the attacking current is deflected and defeated, even without the use of a great effort of the Will. You see many instances of this in all forms of Mentative Influence. "Like attracts like" in this Mentative work, and those who are attracted are generally those whose Mental States correspond to a great extent with those of the person affecting them. There are, of course, exceptions to this rule, owing to ignorance and lack of experience, coupled with confidence and trust—but the rule is true in general.

The Force in Churches, Etc.

Passing before you in the Picture, you see preachers influencing their congregations. You see the great currents of Mentative Energy rolling over the hall, or church. The congregations being in a receptive and passive attitude, with Wills relaxed, they actually draw out the force of the preacher. You may judge just what grade of religious feeling the preacher is pouring out, by examining the shade of his "blue Emotional

Color." You will be apt to see a better shade among the poorer churches and denominations, and a very repulsive dark purplish blue among the "fashionable" churches, as a rule. You will notice also the waves and currents arising from the congregation, which establishes the "atmosphere" of the church, and which will be immediately felt by a stranger entering its doors. You will see similar things at the theatres, and political meetings, and all gatherings of people, the color always giving you the key to the character of the meeting, and the people attending it.

The Hypnotist's Force.

Next you see the Hypnotist and his "subject" in a public hall. You will notice that the hypnotist's Emotional Color is not attractive. You will notice the neutral grey color of the aura of the subject, who seems to have squeezed every bit of his own Mental States out of him—he is a "professional subject," and is a slave of the "Professor." You will see the Professor's magnetism pouring into the subject, and filling his mind completely. You will see how the Will of the Professor supplants the Will of the subject, and dominates him absolutely. You will notice that both the Desire Pole and the Will Pole of the subject seem to show no energy of their own, but are moved entirely by the personality and mind of the operator. This is an extreme case, of course, but it better illustrates the phenomenon. And, by its effect upon the audience, you may determine just how far advanced mentally they are, the color giving you the cue.

The Part Played by Suggestion.

Of course, Mental Suggestion is playing its part in all of these cases but we cannot see that because it is not a current or wave, but is merely the operation of outward symbols in the direction of inducing mental states in others—we may see the induced mental states, but can learn the nature of the Suggestion only by watching and listening at what is said and done. I am mentioning only a few of the many cases that you are witnessing in the Picture, but these few cases will illustrate the different phases of the principle and operation of the Force. But all of these cases have given you merely an illustration of Telementation at "short range"—now let us proceed to examine the instances of the operation of the same force at "long range," in all of its many and wonderful phases.

"Mental Atmospheres" of Towns and Places.

Before doing so, however, let us take a quick look at the "mental atmospheres" of the towns, cities, and villages, as well as of the buildings, localities, etc., passing before us on the Picture. This is most interesting and instructive. In the first place, you will notice the great clouds of Mentative Energy permeating every place, and every corner, each showing its own shade of vibrational color, indicating the vibrations arising from the prevalence of certain Mental States. I have spoken of the causes of this in a previous lesson, and shall not repeat the details here. You will remember that I have explained to you how the various currents of Mentative Energy, of all kinds and degrees, come in contact with each other, and often blend, combine, or else act in the direction of neutralizing each other's force. Currents of a similar degree of vibration harmonize, and form combinations, or blendings. Opposing vibrations in currents tend to antagonize each other, and neutralize each other's force. I have explained this at length in Lesson II. In this way are the "mental atmospheres" of places formed. You may see them in the Picture.

Mental Vibrations Persist.

But, you may ask, why do these clouds persist after the person has sent them forth? The answer is that force once set into motion persists for a greater or lesser time, depending upon the intensity of the original impulse. Just as the light of a star, or rather, its light-waves, exist and move on centuries after the star has ceased to be; just as the heat vibrations continue in a room, when the producing cause has been removed; just as odors remain when the cause moves away; so do the Mentative vibrations, and their corresponding Thought Forms, continue long after the original feeling has passed away—yes, for years afterwards, in some cases.

WHY PLACES ARE "UNLUCKY," "HAUNTED," ETC.

In this way places, houses, stores, etc., maintain "atmospheres" imparted by the vibrations of people long since moved away, or passed away. Stores are "unlucky" because of the negative mental states of some people who have occupied them. Houses are "haunted" by reason of the vibrations arising from intense desire or feelings, or horror and fear of some one participating in a crime, either as criminal or victim. The "atmospheres" of prisons are quite noticeable even to the ordinary visitor, who feels the vibrations with which the place is saturated. The atmosphere of places of low pleasures is equally noticeable. I know of a place of this kind in which the vibrations continued for years after the original tenants had departed and the building had been used for business purposes. Hospitals have a very depressing influence upon the majority of people. Of course these negative effects can be removed by mentally "treating" the place or room, and send forth streams of Mentative Energy of a Positive stimulating character.

POSITIVE ATMOSPHERES.

On the other hand, the presence of an active, energetic, successful man, or set of men, in a place, will permeate the place with Positive vibrations that will stimulate all who abide there. I have in mind a certain large office building in a large city, which is filled with these vibrations, originally arising from a few leading men who built and occupied it, and then attracted to themselves others of the same kind, the result being that the combined influence now renders the place an "inspiration" for those having offices in it. I have heard people say that after moving in that building their business doubled itself, and their energy increased in the same proportion. There is a Law underlying these things, and if people understood it they would take advantage of its Positive sides, and avoid its negative phases. I think that I have given you a good strong hint in this direction. Better heed it?

"Thought-Forms."

These great clouds of vapory manifested Mentative Energy, often constitute what are called "Thought Forms," which I shall proceed to describe to you. Follow my explanations of these things as they appear on the Picture, please. These Thought Forms are really "Feeling Forms" remember, although I use the more familiar term. These Thought Forms although all generated or "created" in the same manner differ very materially in their characteristics, and details. Let us consider some of these details and characteristics, and "appearances."

The Appearances of "Thought-Forms."

By "appearances," I mean of course, their appearance to those who can sense on the Second Plane. But whether one can so sense, or not, the effect of these Thought Forms manifest upon them just the same. It is not necessary to "see" a thing in order to "feel" its influence. But, you understand this, of course, from what has been said already. The most common form is that of a series of undulating waves, or ripples of a vapory cloud-like substance, passing out from the mind of the person experiencing the Mental State originating them, the waves manifesting a ring-like form, moving out in every direction from the common centre, just as do the rings caused by a stone having been dropped into a pond. The distance traveled, and the rate of speed manifested, depends upon the intensity of the emotional impulse. The speed diminishes according to the distance traveled, but long after the actual motion seems to have ceased, there exists an almost imperceptible motion that causes the outer wave to drift on, in a lazy, listless manner.

SMOKE-LIKE FORMS.

Another variety of Thought Forms manifest like a volume of smoke being blown from the lips of a ~igar smoker. Such forms pour out in long streams, then spread out and broaden, although maintaining the direction originally imparted to them. This form arises when the Mental State arises directly in connection with some other person or thing, and when the attention of the Mentator is centered, consciously or uncon•sciously, upon that person or thing. In this case, the motion of Thought Form is in the direction of the person or thing being directly consid•ered by the Mentator. Akin to this form, is a series of forms resembling and puffing forth of smoke from a huge smokestack, great "puffs" of Mentative Thought Forms being sent out in a certain direction, as the jerky repeated Mentative impulses are originated and manifested in the mind of the Mentator.

INTERESTING FORMS.

Other kinds of Thought Forms pour forth steadily, but lazily, in the direction of the object thought of. Others still, are ejected in all directions from the Mentator, like the steam escaping from the lid of a tea-kettle which is being lifted by the force of the steam within. Still another form appears like a "streak" of light flashing from a mirror held in the sun. Certain particular forms of Will-Power manifest as vivid lightning flashes. Other forms travel and seem to enfold the object thought of, and which being impelled by the strong Desire of the Mentator act as if they were trying to "draw" back to him the objects desired. In fact, that is exactly the nature of the action of this class of Thought Forms, the effect produced depending, of course, upon the positiveness of the Mentator, and the strength of the Desire. The effect of course also is materially inftuenced by the degree of positiveness of the person affected, and other attractions which prevent the yielding to the "pull" of Desire Force.

A Strong Desire Force.

In the case of a strong Desire on the part of the Mentator, providing that the "ruling passion" is being manifested day after day, there appears a combination of Thought Forms which resembles a huge octopus of dense structure, with enormous vapory tentacles or arms reaching out in all directions seeking the thing desired, and endeavoring to draw it back to its centre. In the case of a high aspiration, backed by a strong and active Will, this combination will appear tinted with a color and shade of Vibrational Color corresponding with the character of the Mental State, while in the case of a low character of Desire the darker colors will likewise manifest themselves.

Peculiar Forms.

Still another kind of Thought Form acts as if it were trying to push back the object in some particular direction, while others seem to hold back the object. In both of these cases, the action and direction of the Thought Form depends upon the nature and character of the Desire or Will of the Mentator at the time of the conception of the Mentative Current. A most peculiar kind of Thought Form appears when the Mentator is desirous of obtaining information regarding some certain subject, and is earnestly sending his Desire Force in all directions in order to draw it to him, the Mentator generally being unconscious or at least in ignorance of the nature of the actual process. In this case the Thought Form maintains a thin connection with the mind of the Mentator, and darting here and there it attracts to itself the Thought Forms emanating from the minds of others, which may happen to contain the desired vibrations. It even reaches out to the presence of other Mentators, and absorbs the mentative vibrations emanating from them, and literally "steals their ideas," if they have not properly guarded the same by their Will.

THE "MENTATIVE WIRE."

In this connection, I may call to your attention the well known fact that persons thinking along the same lines, although in different parts of the world, are often brought in close *rapport* with each other in this way, as many people know by their own experience. In this case, the Thought Forms seems to act as a sort of Mentative Wire conveying the vibrations from one mind to another. Very much akin to this last mentioned kind of Thought Form, is another which occurs in instances of direct Telemental communication between persons. In this case the Thought Form proceeds in a long straight line, from the one mind to the other, and then acts as a "direct wire" conveying the Mentative currents, or vibrations, from one to the other.

ROTARY FORMS.

There is another variety of Thought Form that spreads out in gradually widening sweeps, the Thought Form having a rotary motion. The sweeps are in a constantly widening circle, and reach out further and further each day, according to the impulse imparted to them by the Mentator. But the most peculiar feature of this Thought Form is a strange movement towards its own centre, by which it "sucks in" all that it attracts to its vortex. This phase is manifested by men of strong Positivity whose enterprise and schemes are spread over large areas, and who set themselves up as a centre of this Mentative "Whirlpool," and draw to themselves all that come within the sweep of their influence. They make things "come their way," in fact.

THOUGHT FORMS LIKE LIVING FORCES.

I have described but a few of the manifold appearances and varieties of the Thought Forms that you see before you on the Picture. But we shall consider a few more in detail as we proceed with the lesson. In thinking of these Thought Forms always picture them as having shape and form, like any material substance, for by so doing you will better realize the nature of their workings. Some Thought Forms indeed are not only "things," but become so infused by the intense Desire and Will of the Mentator that they become almost like "living forces." Such Thought Forms carry the characteristics of the Mentator to such an extent—are infused with his "nature" to such a degree—that when they are felt they seem almost like the actual presence of the Mentator himself, that is as if he were present urging his claims or statements in person.

Rare Cases.

Such cases are of course rare, so far as conscious production is concerned. They may be good or bad. A strong Desire on the part of a dying person has often caused an actual "appearance" by a loved one or friend, although the soul had not yet left the body. And in cases of dire distress or need, people often so "draw" upon those who care for them, that the latter will send to them a powerful Thought Form of help, advice, and assistance. Trained Occultists can do this voluntarily, and consciously, but very few others have reached this stage.

The Operation of Telementation.

And now let us return to the consideration of the various forms of the practical operation of Telementation. You will of course realize that even in case of Mentative Influence in Personal Interviews (with the exception of Suggestion) there is a passage of Mentative Currents and a manifestation of Telementation. The distance between the two minds is slight, but the principle in operation is precisely the same as when the distance is hundreds of miles—and the process is identical.

TWO FORMS OF ONE FORCE.

And you will also remember that when I speak of Desire Force, and Will Power, I am speaking of the Force of the respective Two Poles of Mentative Energy—both of these forms are but phases of the same energy or force—Mentative Energy. So do not imagine that there are three distinct Forces—there is but one Force, and that is Mentative Energy, of which Will Power and Desire Force, respectively, are but manifestations, the difference depending upon the two respective Poles of Force, the Motive and Emotive, respectively. I trust that you will remember this.

THE TWO MANIFESTATIONS.

I will divide the manifestations of Telementation into two general classes, *viz.* (1) Specialized Telementation, that is the use of the Force with the *direct purpose* of affecting a certain person or persons; (2) Generalized Telementation, that is the use of the Force with only a *general purpose* of effecting the desired result, without special attention to any particular person or persons. We will now consider these two classes of Telementation, in their different phases.

SPECIALIZED TELEMENTATION.

First, in considering the subject of Specialized Telementation, we see the cases of Personal Influence exerted in personal interviews, and under other circumstances in which the Mentator and the other person or persons are in close contact—that is within each other's sight. Under this sub-class falls the phenomenon of Fascination, Personal Magnetism, Hypnotism, Personal Influence, Persuasion, Charming, Inducing, etc., etc., in all of their many and varied phases. We have seen these several manifestations as we have proceeded in these lessons, and we need not stop to further consider them at length in this place. You understand that the effect is caused by the out-pouring of the Mentative Energy, in the forms of Will Power and Desire

Force, to the end that similar Mental States are induced in the minds of others, and the Desire or Will of the Mentator is satisfied, to a greater or lesser degree, or completeness, according to the circumstances of the case.

"Long-Range" Influence.

The Second sub-class includes those instances of Telementation at a "long-range," which produces the phenomena of Mental Influencing, Will Projection, Voodooism, Witchcraft, and other forms of influencing, under many names and disguises, including, of course, the employment of the Force for the benefit and advantage of the person "treated" or influenced, as well as the repulsive and deplorable uses alluded to as having been practiced by all peoples in all times, for the purpose of injury to others and selfish profit and advantage to the users.

White Magic and Black.

The one is what is known as White Magic, or use of the Force in an unselfish and justifiable way, and with worthy ends in view; and Black Magic, or the use of the same Force for unworthy ends, and in selfish and unjustifiable ways. But, as I have said in the early part of these lessons, this Force is like any other great natural force, and is capable of being used for good or for evil, according to the moral state of the user. It is true that the Black Magician is always entangled in his own web, sooner or later, and falls a victim to the forces he has aroused—but that does not alter the statement that I have made.

The Practical Workings.

In this form of Telementation, the Mentator usually concentrates upon the person or thing that he wishes to affect, and then consciously, and by the use of his Will, he sends to that person or thing a Current or Currents of Desire Force or Will Power, or both. It is known to Occultists that the degree of effect so produced depends largely upon the degree of concentration employed by the Mentator. The degree of concentration depends upon the Will, and is manifested in the form of Attention.

THE MENTAL IMAGE.

The usual plan is to use the Concentrated Will to form a clear Mental Image of the person or thing to be affected, and then proceed as if one were in the actual presence of the person. The clearer the image, the greater the degree of concentrated Will employed, and consequently the greater the degree of the projecting power of the Current. Underlying all the varied phenomena of "adverse treatments," witchcraft, etc., etc., is this same form of Telementation.

NO CAUSE FOR FEAR.

But, right here, I wish to say an important word, and that is that the generally claimed effect of these forms of adverse influence is greatly exaggerated, and all real Occultists know that the principal reason of the unquestioned instances of the effect of this power lies in the Mental State of Belief, Faith, and Fear of the persons affected. That is, if one "believes" or "fears" that another has the power of adversely influencing or affecting him, then the effect produced will depend largely upon that degree of faith or fear.

THE EVIL EFFECTS OF FEAR.

The persons who are affected by "adverse treatments" or "witchcraft," or similar forms of adverse influence, invariably "believe" and "fear" that these influences are effective against them. By their Mental States they render themselves negative, and receptive to the influences directed against them. This is an Occult Truth, and one that should be made widely known. It is the "Antidote" to the "Bane" of "Adverse Treatments" of which we hear so much, in modern times as well as in ancient history, under various names. If people would only "brace up" and assert their Individual Power as Centres of Energy, they would surround themselves with such a positive Protective Aura, that the waves of adverse vibrations would beat against them without ever reaching within their mental structure.

Adverse Treatments.

We hear of many cases of people being "treated" in this way, in these latter-day of pseudo-occultism. We hear of "treaters" making "denials" regarding people, and thus sending them adverse Telementation. These people will assert, and work themselves up, into a corresponding feeling of "I Deny that So-and-So is well; or prosperous, etc., etc.," some even going so far as to "deny" that the other person "*is*." You may imagine the effect of Currents of this feeling reaching a mind rendered negative by "belief" and "fear" that the other person can so affect them. The Suggestion of the "fear," or "belief" (and that is just what it is, "Suggestion") renders the mind of such a person a fit receptive agent for the adverse "treatment."

How to Neutralize Adverse Treatments.

I tell you, if you will but assert your Individuality, and assume the Fearless attitude, you will be able to laugh in the faces of these "adverse practitioners" of Black Magic, for that is just what it is, no matter how much they may try to disguise it by pious names.

Black Magicians in Disguise.

These modern "adverse treatments" are nothing less than forms of the old Witchcraft which so worried our great-grandfathers; nothing more than the Voodoo practices, or "conjure business" that so affrights the poor negro to-day. The principles are the same—the practice is the same—and the practitioners are the same at heart—Black-hearted Black Magicians, all of them, and subject to the same inevitable fate which overtakes all such people, no matter how high their pretenses.

The Secret of "Charms," Etc.

The physical and material agencies used by the Voodoo men, and the "witches" of old,—the wax images, and pith-balls, and all the rest of the Tom-foolery, were nothing but the agencies upon which the Will of the practitioner could concentrate—an aid to concentrated Will. Of course, besides, they served to terrify their victims by Suggestion. I do not deny that material objects "take up" and absorb the "magnetism" of people, good and bad—for that is a well established occult truth, and the efficacy of "charms," sacred relics, etc., etc., depends upon this fact, together with the aid of Suggestion. *But I do say that all the charms in the world—all the Witchcraft and Voodoo material agencies—can produce no other effect that is allowed them by the minds of the persons sought to be affected. Ferw and Belief determines the degree of receptivity to such influences.*

How Witchcraft Operated.

The "prayer-man" of the Sandwich Islands prays people to death, unless they buy him off—*but it is the fear and belief on the part of the people that render his work effective.* If they would say "Scat" to him, mentally, by asserting their Individuality as Mentative Centres, they would be absolutely immune. I need not recount the many instances of this kind of Telementation, for adverse purposes, for the pages of history are full of them, although the historians sneer at the whole Subject, deeming it a myth, and laughing over the credulity of our forefathers, notwithstanding the fact the "witches" and "conjurers" went to the scaffold and stake, confessing their guilt. It is all very well to attribute it all to the "Imagination" of the persons affected, but suppose they tell us a little about this strange "Imagination" that produced such real effects upon people. The cause many have been "imaginary" but the effects were certainly very "real."

AN EXAMPLE OF ADVERSE INFLUENCE.

I will relate but one instance, which will serve as a type of these forms of Telementation. It is cited by an old German physician. He relates that he was consulted by a farmer who complained of being disturbed at night by strange noises which sounded like someone striking iron. These noises occurred between the hours of ten and twelve every night. The physician asked him if he had any enemy he suspected of thus influencing and annoying him. He replied that there was no one but an old village blacksmith, an old enemy whose power he feared, and who lived several miles from the farmer. The physician bade him return the next day, and in the meantime visited the blacksmith, and asked him what he did between the hours of ten and twelve at night, accompanying the question with a glance of a strong Will and Power.

HOW THE BLACKSMIITH COLLECTED HIS BILL.

The blacksmith, now somewhat frightened, replied: "*I hammer a bar of iron every night at that time, and all the while I think intently of a bad enemy of mine, who once cheated me out of some money; and I will at the same time that the noise shall disturb his rest.*" The physician ordered him to desist, and at the same time made the farmer pay over the money due the blacksmith, and there was no more trouble. If you wish further instances of this sort, turn over the pages of any old book which treats upon the "Witchcraft Delusion," and note the similarity. But one instance is enough to illustrate the matter—they are all "cut out of the same cloth." You will note the two necessary elements present in every case, viz., (1) the use of the Force by one person; and (2) the belief or fear, or both, on the part of the second person. Now you have the whole story.

GOOD EMPLOYMENT OF THE FORCE.

And, also remember, this that I have told you—the same Force that is used in such cases for evil purposes, may also be used, and *is* used for the most beneficial and worthy purposes. The "treatments" for good things practiced by the "practitioners" of the various schools of Mental Science, and other New Thought people are along the lines of Specialized Telementation. People have been encouraged, helped, healed, reformed, and otherwise aided and benefited by Telementation. Do not lose the recollection of the Good in considering the Bad. The Good belongs to the phase of White Magic, and its use can result only in good to the practitioner of it; whereas the Black Magician must reap the whirlwind of the wind that he has sown. These things "come home to roost," always, according to their kind—and they bring their friends home with them.

HOW SCHEMERS USE THE FORCE.

In addition to the selfish and evil use above mentioned, there is another selfish use of Specialized Telementation that is quite common of these late years. I allude to the use of Mentative Influence, by Telementation for the purpose of influencing people to fall in with the schemes and plans and enterprises of the Mentator. The principle inivolved is the same as in all these "treatments" good and bad. And the practice is the same. The Mentator forms the Mental Image of the other person, and then floods him with Currents of Desire Force, or Will Power, or both, at the same time earnestly Willing and Desiring that he will do as the Mentator wishes him to do. The Mentator usually uses his Will to make the other do this in the Mental Picture—in Imagination—thus forming a Mental Matrix, to which he then tries to make the other conform. This is a form of "Visualization," of which I shall speak presently. Of course, this practice like any other of the kind, may be defeated by one asserting his Individuality, and Will. I give you here a few rules to use on occasions when you think that someone is trying to so "treat" or "influence" you. Better study them carefnlly. Here they are:

VALUABLE RULES.

1. In the first place, steady your mind, and calm your feelings. Then pause for a moment, and say the words, "I AM," calmly and forcibly, at the same time forming a mental picture of yourself as a Centre of Force and Power in the Great Ocean of Mind. See yourself as standing along and full of Power. Then mentally form a picture of your Aura, extending about a yard on all sides of you, in an egg-shaped form. See that this Aura is charged with your Will-Power, which is flowing outward repelling any adverse mental suggestions that are being sent to you, and causing them to fly back to the source from whence they came. A little practice will enable you to perfect this picture, which will greatly aid you in creating a strong Positive Aura of Will, which will prove to be a Magnetic Armor and shield.

A USEFUL AFFIRMATION.

The affirmation, "I AM" is the strongest known to Occult Science, for it is a positive statement of Actual Being. You may use the following Affirmation also, if you please—it has helped many: "I assert my Individuality as a Centre of Force, Power and Being. Nothing can adversely affect me. My Mind is mine own, and I refuse admittance to unwelcome suggestions or influences. My Desires are my own, and refuse to admit undesirable vibrations by Induction or otherwise. My Will is my own, and I charge it with Power to beat off and repel all undesirable influences. I am surrounded by an Aura of Positive Will, which protects me absolutely."

A USEFUL DENIAL.

The following Denial has proved of the greatest value to many: "I DENY, to all or any, the power to Influence me against my best interests—I Am my own Master." These words may seem simple, but if you will use them you will be surprised at their efficacy. You realize, of course, that it is the Mental State aroused by the words, that "does the work," rather than any special virtue in the words themselves.

GUARD AGAINST "IMPULSES."

2. Guard yourself from acting upon "impulses." When you feel a sudden or unaccountable "impulse" to do this thing, or that thing, stop and assert your Positive Individuality, and then drive out all outside influences, by repeating the Affirmations, etc., given above, and by creating the proper Mental Picture. Then, when you have recovered your balance, consider the impulse, and decide whether it is to your best interests, or otherwise. You will be able to see this clearly, by reason of your "mental house-cleaning" a moment before. Then, if the impulse seems to be against your best interests, drive it from you, saying: "I drive you away from me—you do not belong to me—return to those who sent you," or other words to that effect. This may be rendered more forceful if you will but create a Mental Picture of the discarded idea flying away from you in the shape of a tiny thought-wave. These Mental Pictures aid one very materially in such matters, both in the sending forth of an idea, as well as in the discarding of one.

THE POSITIVE AURA.

3. Cultivate the picture and idea of a Positive Aura, and always think of yourself as being encased in such a one. See yourself as a strong Positive "I"—a Centre of Power—encased in an Impregnable Sheath of Auric Force. You will thus be able to build up yourself into a mighty Centre. You will be surprised at the confused manner of people who try to influence you, when they come in contact with this Aura, and find their Suggestions and Mentative Currents being cast back upon themselves. Such people find themselves "all broken up" when

they meet a condition like this, which they do not understand for very few of them are practical occultists. The Mental Picture of yourself as a Centre of Power, surrounded with a Positive

Aura, will, if persisted in, render you extremely Positive, so that your influence is sure to be felt by the world with which you come in contact.

Amusing Sequels.

You will often be amused by occurrences following after the rejection of these "stray impulses," etc. You will find that if you have had an impulse to buy a certain thing, or sell a certain thing at a sacrifice, that in a day or so, perhaps an hour or so, you will be approached by some person who will advise you personally to do that same thing, the person being likely to be benefited by the scheme or plan. I do not mean that such person has necessarily tried to influence you by Mentative Currents, for he may not have consciously done so, but nevertheless that is just what has happened, and his Desire or Will has caused these Currents to flow in your direction, and you have felt them. Now that your eyes have been opened to this fact, you will be amused and surprised to see how many corroborative proofs you will receive. But always assert your Individuality as a Centre of Power, and all will be well with you in these matters.

Conscious and Unconscious Use.

In passing on to the other phases of Telementation, I would again remind you that in these instances of Specialized Telementation the Force may be used both consciously, or unconsciously. Those who know the laws of the use of the Force may direct these Telementative Currents direct to those whom they wish to influence, just as they may consciously give Mental Suggestions in a personal interview. But, even where these laws are not understood, the Currents or the Suggestions are sent forth by the strong Desire or Will animating the person. Of course the person who understands the subject will be able to direct his Force with greater precision and effect, but in any event the effect is produced in the same way.

THE SCIENCE OF TELEMENTATION.

GENERALIZED TELEMENTATION.

We now pass on to a consideration of the second class of Telementation, which we call "Generalized Telementation," or the use of the Force with a *general purpose* of affecting the desired result, without special attention to any particular person or persons. This form of manifestation of Telementation may be grouped into two sub-classes, *viz.*, (*a*) in which the general Desire or Will of the individual to attain certain results manifests itself in personal interviews, and induces Mental States in those with whom he comes in contact; and (*b*) in cases wherein the general Desire and Will manifest in Telementative Currents, or Waves, or Whirlpools, affecting all persons and things who are interested in any way in the enterprise, scheme, plan or undertaking of the individual, and tending to cause them to "fall into line" and obey the Will or comply with the Desires of the general plan of the individual.

HOW STRONG, POSITIVE MEN USE THE FORCE.

This last form of Telementative Influence is far more common than one would suppose. Strong, Positive men start into motion waves and currents that sweep over the country, gathering force with each added impetus, and using the principle of "mental contagion" to increase its influence. Great "leaders of men" are centres of these Mentative Whirlpools, and similar forms of Mentative Influence, and draw in, or suck in to themselves persons, things, and objects conducive to their plans and ambitions. They do not have it all their own way, of course, for there are many influences at work which tend to neutralize their efforts. Other men have conflicting schemes which interfere and often destroy the influence of these great Mentators, and then people are becoming educated regarding the nature of the forces they employ, and will not accept their suggestions or allow their vibrations to influence them. Still the force is still used to great effect by many politicians, and other persons who reach out for large numbers of people.

"Generals of Business" and What They Do.

Leading "generals of business" also make use of the force in this manner, and draw things "their way." In fact nearly everybody who does business with people scattered over a large territory, employs this force more or less, generally unconsciously. And many of these uses work no harm upon those affected, because many of these people are engaged in legitimate enterprises, and want always to give a "square deal," and a "good dollar's worth." I am not holding up this manifestation of Telementation as reprehensible—I am merely stating its general laws and forms of manifestation.

How to Repel the Waves.

One may repel these Mentative Waves in the same way, and by the same methods mentioned a few pages back in reference to the Repelling of Specialized Telementation. The rule is the same in both cases, for the principle involved is the same.

Justifiable Use of the Force.

Before leaving this branch of the subject, I would remind you that one may take advantage of this last mentioned form of Telementation to his own good, in a perfectly proper and justifiable way. One may wish to gain certain information and knowledge about certain subjects. If so, if he will hold a strong Desire that the desired knowledge will come to his notice and attention, and will at the same time Will that the Mentative Current flow forth in search of persons, things, and objects capable of imparting the knowledge or information, he will get results. He will find that after a while he will run across people who will be glad to give him the information he wants; or he will pick up a book that will either tell him what he wants, or else will refer to some other book or subject that will point out the path to him. These instances are quite common, and afford wonderful proofs of the laws herein stated. In this way no one is harmed, and mutual benefits are obtained. People are attracted to each other in this way, and each finds his own.

The Law of Attraction.

The above manifestation results from the operation of what has been called the "Law of Attraction," by the workings of which each person is continually drawing to himself the people, things, objects and even "cirtumstances" in harmony and accord with his prevailing Mental States. Like attracts like, and the Mental States determine that which one draws to himself. If you are not satisfied with what is coming to you, start to work and change your Mental Attitudes and Mental States, and you will see a change gradually setting in, and things that you want will begin to "come your way." This Law of Attraction has been much written about in works on Mental Science during the past ten years, so it is not necessary for me to go into details about it here. I have given you the general law, and rules, in this lesson, and you may apply it accordingly.

Like Attracts Like.

A most important fact about the effect of Mentative vibrations upon people lies in the principle that one is more affected by vibrations in harmony with their own accustomed feelings and Mental States, than by those of opposite natures. A man who is full of evil schemes, and selfish aims, is more apt to be caught up by similar vibrations than one who lives above that plane of thought. He is more easily tempted by evil suggestions and influences, than one to whom these things are abhorrenL And the same is true on every plane.

Illustrations Of This Law.

A man whose Mental Attitude is one of Confidence and Fearlessness, is not apt to be affected by vibrations of a negative, pessimistic, gloomy nature, and vice versa. Therefore, if you wish to receive the vibrations of the thoughts and feelings of others, you must place yourself in a Mental Attitude corresponding with those vibrations you wish to receive. And if you wish to avoid vibrations of a certain kind, the best way is to rise above them in your own mind, and to cultivate Mental States opposite to them. The Positive always beats off the Negative—and Optimistic Mental States are always Positive to Pessimistic Mental States. The sense of Individuality, and one's relation to the Universal Mind, is the strongest and most Positive Mental State one can attain. Therefore cultivate it, first, last and all the time.

THE "KEY" OF TELEMENTATION.

I now come to a phase of the subject that underlies all of the phenomena of Telementation, and really gives the "key" to much of its wonderful effects. I allude to what Occultists know as "Mental Visualization," or "Visualization," for short. This Visualization is to Telementation what the Pattern is to the maker of objects; what the Plans of the architect are to the builders; what the "mould" or "matrix" is to the casters of forms. It is the Skeleton around which the Materialization of Thought-Forms occurs. It is of the greatest importance to you to acquaint yourselves with its laws and effects.

"VISUALIZATION."

To "visualize" means to "see mentally"—that is to form a Mental Image of a thing—to "see it in one's mind," etc., Visualization, along the lines of one's daily occupation is a most important thing, but one that is very poorly appreciated, because little understood. The best workmen, writers, inventors, composers, etc., are those who are able "to see the thing in the mind," and then reproduce it in materialized form. Sir Francis Galton, one of the best authorities upon the subject, has said: "The free action of a vivid visualizing faculty is of much importance in connection with the higher processes of generalized thought. ... A visual image is the most perfect form of mental representation wherever the shape, position, and relations of objects to space are concerned. ... *The best workmen are those who visualise the whole of what they propose to do, before they take a tool in their hands.* ... Strategists, artists of all denominations, physicists who contrive new experiments, and in short, all who do not follow routine, have need of it. ... A faculty that is of importance in all technical and artistic occupations; that gives accuracy to our perceptions, and justice to our generalizations; is starved by lazy disuse, instead of being cultivated judiciously in such a way as will, on the whole, bring the best return. I believe that a serious study of the best means of developing and utilizing this faculty, without prejudice to the practice of abstract thought in symbols, is one of the many pressing desiderata in the yet unformed science of education."

VISUALIZATION AND TELEMENTATION.

And, all that Sir Francis Galton has said above, is equally true of the cultivation of the art of Visualization in connection with Telementation. The trouble with the majority of people is that they *do not know just what they do want.* They are not able to form clear Mental Images of that which they which to "create" or "materialize." The men who obtain the gteatest and most wonderful results through Mentative Influence, particularly in the form of Telementation, are those men who are able to "*visualize*" most clearly the things that they wish to "*materialize*"—who are able to form the Mental Image of the things they which to Manifest.

THE SECRET OF VISUALIZATION.

The secret of Visualization lies in the occult and psychological principle that "as is the mental matrix, so is the mental form; and as is the mental form, so is the physical materialization." In other words, the Visualized Mental Image is the Matrix or Mould into which the Mentative Energy is poured, and from which it takes form; and the form of the Mentative Energy, so treated, is what we have called the Mental Image; and around this Mental Image the deposit of Materialization forms—and thus does the Ideal become the Real.

In a Nut-Shell.

If you wish to get the best effects from Mentative Energy, you must create a Mental Image around which the material or physical materialization is formed—and the way to form the proper Mental Image is by Visualization, which thus builds up the matrix or mould into which the Mentative Energy pours, crystallizes and creates the Mental Image. And as is the Matrix so is the Image, and as is the Image so is the Materialization. Please read over this statement a number of times, until it is perfectly clear to you. For upon your understanding of it, depends your understanding of the laws of Materialization of Ideas of Mental Images, by means of Telementative processes.

What Is Necessary.

Before you can draw to you the material needed for building up the things or conditions you desire, you must form a clear Mental Image of *just what you want to Materialize*—and before you can make this Mental Image, you must *realize mentally* just exactly what you *do* desire. And the process of this is called Visualization. That is, you build up a Mental Matrix or Mould, little by little, until you have it before you clearly—then you pour into it the Mentative Energy of Desire and Will, until it stands out clearly formed as a Mental Image, just as you would see it if it were actually materialized. Then you must hold this Mental Image before you constantly, regarding it not as a *mere imagination*, but as a *something real* which you have created in your mind, and which will proceed to surround itself with the material necessary to give it material objectivity, or Materialization.

THE FIRST STEPS.

If you cannot see the whole thing at first, as a Mental Image—that is, if you are not able to build up a complete Matrix by Visualization, then do the next best thing—which is the *very best* thing for the majority of people—and build a Matrix of the *first step* toward the whole thing, that is, the first thing that is needed. Then concentrate upon this first thing until the Mental Image stands out sharp and clear, and you will find that things have been started in motion. Then, you may add little by little to your Matrix, and build up your Mental Image a little larger and in greater detail. And so on, and on.

AN IMPORTANT RULE.

And here is an important thing. You must mentally *see* the thing as actually existing, *right now*, and not as "going to exist" later on. You must realize that the Mental Image exists right now, else it will lack clearness and effectiveness.

THE NEXT STEPS.

Then, you must pour into that Mental Image a constant supply of strong, positive Mental Energy—Desire Force, and Will power, all of which will spread out in the proper directions and affect the material needed to Materialize your Mental Image. By so doing you impart to the Mentative Currents the necessary impetus and direction, and they will operate along these lines, and will proceed to Materialize your Mental Image for you. Things will come your way; people will appear who are necessary to your plans; information will come to you from strange sources, and in unexpected times and places; opportunities will open themselves up to you.

A CAUTION.

But remember this, that you must be prepared to act upon these openings, and opportunities. You must be alert and watchful, and *expectant*. You will have to do the work remember, yourself, although the Forces you have started into operation will supply you with the material. The door will be opened to you, but you must step in yourself; the tools and materials will be provided you, but you must use them; the information will be laid before you, but you must make it your own. Even Mental Magic will not avail the lazy man. You must learn to "do things" yourself.

THE WORKING PRINCIPLES.

This subject of Visualization would fill a book by itself, but I hope that I have been able to give you a clear idea of its *working principles*. Remember, always this rule—this Triple-Key of Attainment, as I have often called it: (1) You must DESIRE a thing most intensely; (2) then you must EARNESTLY EXPECT it; (3) then you must use your WILL in the direction of ACTION tending to bring it about. But first of all, as I have said, you must KNOW JUST WHAT YOU DO WANT, and then proceed to create the Mental Matrix or Mould by VISUALIZATION—that is, you must proceed to MENTALLY SEE it as already existing. In the above statement there is enough Occult Information to fill a series of books; boiled down, and concentrated.

CONCLUDING ADVICE.

And now, friends, I must bring this long lesson to a close. It must be read and studied in connection with the lessons preceding it, for they blend into each other, and the information "laps." I have given you certain Occult Teachings, in plain, practical form, which may seem so simple to you as to be passed over without the proper consideration and examination. Do not make this mistake, I pray you. Do not hanker after high-sounding terms and mystical verbiage. The Truth is capable of being expressed without these fancy trappings or drapery. I have tried to tell you the "How" of these things—but you must study carefully in order to grasp every point. I have boiled down, and condensed a great deal of information into this lesson—be sure that you do not let any of it get away from you. You cannot expect to acquaint yourself fully with this subject in one hasty reading. You must read and re-read many times, with careful study and thought. You must do some thinking on your own account, in order to apply these general principles to your own "symptoms" and needs—if you will read carefully, and then think a little. There is no Royal Road to Mental Magic, or anything else. I have tried to make the road a little easier for you—but you must do the traveling yourself. You cannot reach the heights by proxy. You must digest these things yourself—predigested ideas will do you no good.

THE SIMPLE UNDERLYING PRINCIPLE.

And, now in conclusion, look once more at the Magic Mental Picture in which you have seen all of these things in operation. You will see that underlying all of these wonderful manifestations of Telementation, there is just the simple principle that I have pointed out to you—Induction of Mental States by Desire Force and Will Power. Everything occurs by reason of this principle. You may think that the book that you needed, and which came to you so wonderfully, must have arrived in some other way. Not so, the book was placed here, and moved there, by PEOPLE, and these people have minds capable of being moved by vibratory waves, and so when once the thing was set into operation, all things worked together toward the given end. Even these lessons reached you under the Law of Attraction. There is no chance in these matters—there are Laws in operation everywhere, and always—and over all there is the Great Law of the Universal.

And, now in concluding this lesson, I would remind you to always realize that you are CENTRES OF LIVING MENTAL ENERGY in the Great Ocean of Mentative Energy. And that you are strong in the degree that you are POSITIVE. And that you are Positive in the degree that you are an INDIVIDUAL. And you are an Individual in the degree that you REALIZE THAT YOU ARE A "CENTRE OF

LIVING WILL." There is nothing to fear but Fear—you are capable of asserting your Individuality always, and everywhere—your only chains are those you forge for yourself—you are FREE right now, here, and always. Do not be deluded by the petty things of Personality, that pass away and perish over-night—but rest serene and firm in the consciousness that you are an INDIVIDUAL LIVING WILL CENTRE; and fear not to assert the Individual "I." There is no Devil but Fear—nothing but Fear can keep you from your own heritage and birthright. Assert the "I" and banish Fear.

Lesson VI

Mental Therapeutics.

The Ancient Forms—The Real Principle—Mind in the Cells and Organs—My Own Theory of Mental Healing—The Claims of the Cults—One Principle Under Many Names—The Suggestive Value of Forms and Beliefs—Various Temperaments Need Special Forms—The Effect of Confidence, Faith and Belief—The Potent Factor of Cure—Mental States and Physical Conditions—Mentative Induction in Healing—How It Operates—A Little Secret Disclosed—General Treatment—Local Treatment—First Steps in Treating—The Necessary Mental Conditions—Preliminary Suggestive Treatment—Visualization in Healing—Healing by Mentative Currents—Automatic Healing—Valuable Points of Practice—Simple but Powerful Methods—How to Conclude the Treatment—How to Give Absent Treatments—The Principles of Absent Treatment—Self-Healing by General Treatments—Local Treatment Explained; Theory, Principles, and Practice—The Basis of the Treatment—Good Suggestions Regarding Treatments—The Use of the Hands—A Plain, Simple Plan—The Degrees of Mind in the Various Organs—Treatment of Special Organs—What to Say, and How to Say It—Mind vs. Mind—Words and Their Inner Meaning—Local Treatment in Absent Healing—Local Treatment in Self—Healing—What This System of Healing Represents—Freedom from Cults and Organizations—You may adhere to your own favorite beliefs, and still make as many cures by the use of these methods, as are made by the best of those who believe and claim that the healing is done because of some fantastic theory, dogma, or belief.

Lesson VI.

Mental Therapeutics.

"THERAPEUTICS" MEANS "the healing art," therefore "Mental Therapeutics" means "the art or science of Mental Healing."

If I were writing this lesson from the standpoint of twenty years ago, I would think it advisable to fill page after page with a recital of the many claims of Mental Healing, but no such necessity exists at the present time. People have heard much regarding Mental Healing, and while they may differ in their theories and opinion regarding the nature of the cures performed, still they will nearly all acknowledge that that cures *have* been made and *are* being made by Mental Healing methods.

The Ancient Forms of Mental Healing.

The history of Mental Healing extends way back into the past, and the earliest pages of history treat upon it as if it were a long established and well accepted method. In fact the history of Mental Healing is the history of Mental Magic, so far as the older peoples and races are concerned. The ancient *Magi* used their mental powers in the direction of healing the sick, and restoring natural healthy conditions. People were brought to the Temples to be healed, and after the customary incantations, and ceremonies, designed to affect the imagination and respect of the primitive people, they were found to be benefited, and actually cured in time. But under and back of all these ceremonies and rites, the principle effecting the cure was the same principle that is being used to-day by all forms of Mental Healing, under whatever names it may be disguised and masked. There is but one Mental Healing Principle, and that has always been used; is being used now; and always will be used, so long as the race exists.

MENTATIVE ENERGY THE REAL PRINCIPLE.

And this principle is the application and employment of Mentative Energy. Mentative Energy is Positive to both Force and Matter, as we have seen in these lessons, and the Negative always yields to the Positive when the latter is properly and intelligently applied. The Mentative Energy really builds up the body from a single cell, and is inherent in every part and particle of the body. Every cell has its supply of Mentative Energy—the cell, and combination of cells, and the whole body in fact, is the result of conditions of manifestations of Mentative Energy. The Body is ALL MIND, at the last analysis. Mentative Energy manifests itself in countless ways in the Universe, and the physical bodies, and the cells of which they are composed are simply certain forms of manifestation of Mentative Energy. And, this being so, Mental Healing is not a case of "Mind over Matter," as is often taught, but is *a manifestation of Positive Mind over Negative Mind*. The Central Mind of Man is Positive to the Mind in the body of Man, and hence the curing effect.

MIND IN THE CELLS AND ORGANS.

Every cell has its share of mind, and Science shows us that each cell can and does live its life as a separate entity, always, however, subordinate to the whole system of cells, and the Mind controlling it. And the Mind in each cell, or system of cells, may be reached by the Positive Mind of a person, when properly applied. In order to fully grasp the significance of this statement, you must remember that every organ, part, bone, nerve, vessel, tissue and everything else in your body, is built up of cells which have formed certain combinations. There are individual cells in your blood and other parts of the body; and there are cell communities in your body, which perform certain functions, and which you call "my liver;" "my heart;" "my stomach;" "my kidneys," etc., etc. And there is Mind in every one of them. And the mind in every cell, and in every organ may be reached by Mentative Energy applied by the Mind of oneself or another person.

MY THEORY OF MENTAL HEALING.

And in this simple statement, I have embodied my idea of Mental Healing, which idea is based upon years of earnest study, experiment, and investigation, aided by personal acquaintance with and association with some of the most celebrated Mental Healers of this age. I have discarded fanciful theory, after fanciful theory, as unnecessary to account for the facts observed by the leading investigators of Mental Healing, and have at last "boiled down" the matter to this point and idea of *"Mind in the Cells and Cell Groups; which Mind is Negative to the Positive Central Mind of the Individual, especially when the latter is concentrated and intelligently applied."*

THE CLAIMS OF THE CULTS.

You may ask me the question "Well, but what about all the various meta-physical, religious, and semi-religious theories advanced to account for the cures performed by the various cults and sects of the 'New Thought' and similar movements?" Answering this I would say that the various cults and sects perform cures not *because* of their dogmas, but often *in spite* of them—the real cures being performed by Mentative Energy, pure and simple, called into operation, and employed, in various forms, and ways, under many coverings, disguises and draperies. It is all the same grand old principle, but "with fringe on"—the style of fringe depending on the particular theories and dogmas of the sects.

One Principle Under Many Names.

There has been much written, spoken, and taught concerning Mental Healing, under some name or other, but the majority of the writers have been attached to some particular cult, church, or organization, which claimed that the whole truth rested upon the acceptance of some particular theory, idea, doctrine or dogma advanced and held by it, in accordance with the particular views of some certain teacher or teachers. And, accordingly, the writings have been colored by the hue of such belief and dogma. One has but to look around him in order to see that the many conflicting schools of Mental or Spiritual Healing *are all making cures*, in spite of the claim of each that its particular school or sect, or church, has a monopoly on Truth, and a corner on "true metaphysical healing." The truth is that they *all make cures*—the percentage being about the same in each instance, taking the personal qualifications of the healers into consideration. In spite of the several claims that "we have the only Truth—all others are in error, and ignorant of the real Truth," etc., etc., *all* of these "erroneous people" are getting fine results. Their differing and often contradictory theories do not seem to cut any figure in the real work, and one who closely studies the subject is soon forced to the conclusion that *there must be some underlying principle of cure which they are all using.* And so there is! And I call this "underlying principle" the Effect of Positive Central Mind upon Negative Body Mind—you may give it any other name you choose, but you will get the results just the same.

Mental Therapeutics.

The Suggestive Value of Forms and Beliefs.

The various theories, statements, forms, observances, dogmas and what-not, have no other effect than giving a strong suggestion to people who are impressed by the same. Some people get better results when the Mental Healing is accompanied by some religious or semi-religious talk and explanation, whith appeals to the emotional parts of their nature and makes them more receptive to the healing process of the Mind. (Sacred shrines, images and relics cause cures in this way.) Others get better results when some technical mephysical theory is urged upon them, with a great show and use of long high-sounding words—they may not understand the words, but they think that there "must be something in it, for he used words that I couldn't begin to understand, and yet he knew all about them," etc. Others prefer the scientific explanation of the school of Suggestion, which avoids metaphysical or religious theories, and yet get the results. Others, still, adhere to the Mental Science idea of the Universal Mind, and the Personal Mind, and they, too, get results. Others like the Subjective Mind, and Objective Mind idea—and they get results, too. THEY ALL GET RESULTS—but some take more kindly to certain forms, and thus get better results.

Various Temperaments Need Special Forms.

I have frequently advised people to go to healers of certain cults and schools and churches, simply because I knew that the ideas of these particular schools, cults and churches would fit the particular temperament of the person in question, and thus the best results would accrue. I am most catholic in my ideas on this subject—I believe in a person employing any phase of Mental Healing, from Bread Pills to Christian Science—providing that the particular agency employed will invoke the Faith. Confidence and Belief of the patient to the utmost. Whichever form will best do this, that is the form I believe the best; for the patient.

Manifold Tastes Breed Manifold Forms.

I can see very well why a person of a warm religious temperament would be better benefited by Mental Healing in a religious form or phase than from mere Suggestion, or ordinary Mental Science—it opens up a part of the nature that is conducive to the cure. And I can see why others are impressed by technical, complicated Metaphysical talk, which causes them to wonder and be impressed, and thus causes an interest and an "expectant attention" which goes a long way toward making the cure. And I can see why others still, would rebel against either of the above mentioned forms, and would be better reached by a plain, scientific presentation of the subject. Every man to his taste—in Mental Healing as in everything else. In this respect I am like the Irishman who said he was glad that all people did not have the same taste, for if they did every mother's son of them would be wanting to steal his wife away from him.

The Effect of Faith, Confidence and Belief.

But, you may ask, why is it that Faith, Belief, Confidence, etc., play such an important part in the cures, if it be true that the real cure is effected through the mind in the Cells, and Cell-groups—what have Cells to do with Faith? This is a good question—and here is the answer. While it is true that the Mind in the Cells is the medium or cause of the cure, still it is a fact that these Cells are Negative to the influence of the Central Mind of the person. And if that Central Mind be filled with the Mental States of Disease, Fear, Undesirable Beliefs, etc., then the Negative Cells and Organs must be affected. And, if on the contrary the Mental States of the person be changed from Fear to Hope, Confidence, Love, Faith, Belief and Expectancy, then it will be readily seen that the effect upon the cells will be changed for the better. And, if in addition to these improved Mental States, a still more Positive State—a State of Conscious

Control and Power, then will the curative effect be greatly magnified and increased.

THE POTENT FACTOR OF CURE.

To tell the truth, I earnestly believe that the one great potent factor in Mental Healing, is the *removal of Fear* from the mind of the patient, by whatever means it may be accomplished, whether by Reason, Argument, Faith, Hope, or even by Superstition. Fear is the most Negative of the Mental States, and simply paralyzes the whole system. Fear and Worry actually *poison* the Cells of the body. This is a scientifically demonstrable fact. And if this pall of Fear can be lifted by any means, then a big step in the direction of a cure has been effected. *And Hope, Confidence, and Belief, will lift that pall.* That is why I believe in everything from Bread Pills to "C. S.," as I said a few minutes ago—whichever agency induces the greater degree of Hope, Belief, Confidence, and Expectancy, is the best for the particular case. But in all cases the Principle of Cure is the same—MIND.

MENTAL STATES AND PHYSICAL CONDITIONS.

It should not be necessary for me to recite the oft repeated facts of the phenomenon of disease being treated by mental states, and of cures arising from the same. Every man or woman who reads these lessons has heard this tale over and over again, many times. It is not longer a debatable question, this matter of the Effect of the Mind in Health and Disease. The books are full of it. It is as "old as the hills," and at no time in the history of the world has this form of Mental Magic been accorded greater attention and interest. And, therefore, I shall skip this part of the story, and get right down to business in the direction of telling you "just how" to apply the Mentative Energy in healing, both present and "absent."

"Mentative Induction" in Healing.

Well then, in the first place, the principles of Mental Healing are precisely the same principles that are applied in all forms of Mental Magic, as we have seen them in the previous lessons. It is all a matter of "MENTATIVE INDUCTION," first, last and always. And, as in the other phases of Mental Magic, this Induction may arise from either Mentative Currents, or by Mental Suggestion. Please fix this statement in your mind, so that I will not have to repeat it so often.

How Mentative Induction Operates in Healing.

Now, let us see what happens if Mentative Induction is set up in the mind of a person by means either of Mentative Currents, or Mental Suggestion, when what is called "General Treatment" is given. (What is called "Local Treatment" will be taken up later.) Well, we will suppose that the Mental State of the person has been changed by Induction (either from Currents or by Suggestion) to a strong Positive state—and that is what one must aim to produce in the patient. This Induced Positive Mental State in the Central Mind, is of course, strongly Positive to the mind in the body and its tells. The Mental Image of *a normal, perfect, healthy, well body*, being held in the Central Mind of the patient, it follows that the physical material of the body, and cells will begin to materialize in accordance with the pattern set before the mind of the cells, by the Central Mind of the person. It is the old story of Mental Visualization, and Physical Materialization over again. Of course, the effect is wonderfully heightened if the patient will direct his Desire and Will strongly to the recuperative or reparative action, in which effort he may be materially aided by the healer.

A Little Secret Disclosed.

The desired Mental State in the patient may be induced either by Auto-Suggestion (Self-Suggestion) on his own part; or by the Suggestion of the Healers (see where the ceremonies, and "frills and fringes" of the cults, come in, now, don't you?) or by the direct Mentative Currents of the Healer, applied as indicated in the previous lessons. In this form of healing, the Healer works *by arousing the mind of the patient, so that he really cures himself.* This "arousing" is of course affected by either Suggestion, or Mentative Currents—the effect being the result of "Induction" in either case, as you will readily understand.

The Phases of "General Treatment."

This form of Mental Healing, which I call "General Treatment" includes both the form of "present healing," that is when the Healer is in the personal presence of the patient, or else along the lines of what is called "absent treatments" or "distant treatments," when the Healer and the patient are not in each other's presence. We shall see both forms in operation, as we proceed with the lesson.

The Basis of "Local Treatment."

Leaving the subject of "General Treatment," for the moment, let us consider the broad principles underlying "Local Treatment." By "Local Treatment" I mean Mental Healing effected by the Mind of the Healer being directly and specially applied to the mind in the cells and organs themselves. You will remember what I have said about there being "Mind in the Cells and Organs"—well, "Local Treatment" is an application based upon that fact. The Mind of the Healer is brought to bear in a positive, direct, special manner upon these cells and organs, and the suggestions, and mentative currents are directed right to these organs and cells, without the intermediate stages of the Central Mind of the patient, as in the case of "General Treatment." Of course one may apply "Local Treatment" to himself, by directing his mind directly to the cells and organs, instead of indirectly by means of general Mental States. You may wonder why I speak of directing "Suggestions" to the cells—you may well ask, "can the cells *hear*?" No the cells cannot hear, but the utterance of the words of the Suggestion, by you, will enable you to direct your Mind more directly and forcefully upon the cells and organs. You will see, as we proceed, that I advocate "speaking right up" to the cells and organs of the body, and telling them just what you want them to do. You will be surprised when you try this and see how they respond.

CLOSE ATTENTION NECESSARY.

And, now that we understand the general principles of both of these phases of Mental Treatment, let us pass on to a consideration of the Practice of Mental Healing—the actual "how" of the subject. We will begin with "General Treatment," both present and absent,and will then take up the second phase of "Local Treatment." In both cases we will see the actual methods of treatment, in detail. But I must ask you to pay close attention to what I have to say about these treatments, for I am condensing a whole course of lessons in Mental Healing in this one lesson, and you will miss something unless you watch closely.

FIRST STEPS IN TREATING.

The first step in the Personal Form of General Treatment is to induce in your patient a Mental State of Calm, and Relaxation. This is quite important because this Mental State causes the patient to become receptive to the Impressions that you wish to make upon his or her mind. The best plan is to have the patient seat himself in a comfortable position (or if he is lying down, let him assume a comfortable attitude), and then talk to him a little in order to induce a comfortable, easy frame of mind, which will react upon the physical conditions. Have him relax every muscle, and withdraw the tension from every nerve, so that he will be relaxed, and "limber" all over, from head to feet. The best way to determine whether or not the desired condition has been effected is to raise one of his hands and then allow it to drop back to his sides or lap. If he is fully relaxed, his hand will drop just as if it were not attached to his body. The Mental State producing this physical condition may be best stated by the words "Let Go!" One must *mentally "let go,"* before he will be able to "let go" physically. The patient must feel perfectly at ease, and comfortable, in order that the best results be gained.

The Necessary Mental Condition of the Patient.

The Healer should endeavor to quiet the mind of the patient by an earnest, confident, sympathetic conversation, leading the subject toward bright, hopeful, happy topics, and especially avoiding anything likely to arouse antagonism or argument. He should throw earnestness and feeling into his tones, and speak as if his one object in life were to cure the patient, and of which cure he entertained not the slightest doubt. The Healer should forget himself, and concentrate his mentality completely upon the subject of *curing the patient*. He should be very careful to *act out* the part of the Confident, Successful Healer, because sick people are very suggestible, and take on impressions very easily, and so, if the Healer manifests an apparent lack of confidence in his outward demeanor, the patient will be most likely to accept the suggestion, and the work of healing will thus be rendered doubly difficult. If you have studied the lesson on Mental Suggestion, you will see the psychology of this fact.

Preliminary Suggestive Treatment.

It will be well to begin the treatment by a preliminary Suggestive Treatment, in a conversational tone. You should point out to the patient the conditions that you intend to bring about. You should endeavor to obtain the patient's co-operation by means of his holding a Mental Image of the desired condition. That is, if it be a case of stomach trouble, he should form a Mental Image of a strong, healthy normal stomach, doing its work properly, and digesting the food that is given it, and manifesting a good, hearty natural appetite. If the patient will do this he will be able to do much toward aiding you. You should then tell him that his stomach *is Strong*, *Strong*, *Strong*, (speaking the words *with intense feeling and force*) and that normal conditions are reasserting themselves under the power of the Mind. You should, in many ways and forms, keep before him constantly *a picture of the conditions you wish to bring about*, for by so doing you will change his Mental Image of Disease into a Mental Image of Health, and the best results is sure to follow. If you prefer the use of the hands in healing, by all means use them, as such practice gives a most powerful suggestion, as well as possessing other advantages.

The Value of "Visualization" in Healing.

You will find that you will be able to impart a wonderful degree of forceful, earnest intensity to your voice, if you will but practice "Visualization" in four treatments. That is, you must endeavor to actually *see mentally*, the conditions that you wish to bring about. And when you are able to do this, you will be able to hold the attention of the patient as his mind follows your words in your description of the successive steps of the cure that you intend bringing about. He will be able to see himself as gradually and surely improving, and growing well, not only in a general way, but also in the sense that he will be able to form a mental picture of the formerly diseased organ actually growing strong and normal. *Always keep before you the Mental Image of the conditions that you wish to bring about*—see them before you *as actually existing right now*—and your mind, and actions and voice will conform to that Mental Image, for by so doing the patient will receive the best possible Suggestion and Induced Mental States along the lines of Mentative Currents.

Healing by Mentative Currents.

And now to the actual work of Mental Healing by Mentative Currents. In this work I must again repeat my injunctions given a moment ago regarding the holding of the proper Mental Image in the mind of the Healer. In the degree that the proper Mental Image is held, will be the degree of success in the treatment. "Visualization" is the key-note of this form of Mental Healing, and the Healer should devote himself earnestly to acquiring the art of Visualizing. You must be able to see the patient as healed, and the organs, parts, and cells as functioning normally and properly. Cast aside all negative thought, and doubts, and throw yourself earnestly into the work before you. You will find that as the ability to Visualize is acquired, there will come to you a feeling of strength and power, and a sense of certainty about your work.

THE PROCESS ALMOST AUTOMATIC.

The process of transmitting the Mentative Currents is not especially difficult or strenuous. In fact, this part of the work seems almost "automatic." All that you will have to do is to concentrate your full attention upon the Mental Image that you have visualized, and earnestly Desire that the picture materializes, and do not bother at all about the Currents, for the latter will begin to flow freely without any voluntary effort on your part. Occasionally you may throw a little Will Power into the work, in order to stimulate the healing process, but ordinarily the unconscious use of the Desire Force will accomplish the result. It is not necessary to use the strenuous effort that so many Mental Healers employ in giving treatments—this is all waste energy, and tires one out without any corresponding advantage to the patient. The clear-cut Mental Image produced by the practice of Visualization performs the work for you, as I have said, almost "automatically." The more realistic your picture is made to appear to you, the greater the force sent forth, and the greater the degree of success will you have in your healing.

A VALUABLE POINT OF PRACTICE.

Some excellent healers have found that they gained additional force if they would add to their Mental Picture or Image, the picture of the Mentative Currents actually leaving their minds and travelling toward the patient, and then enveloping and surrounding the latter. One very good healer has told me that she always can see, mentally, the patient being "bathed in a perfect stream of her Mentative Energy." I feel that this lady was right, and that by adding this feature to the Mental Image very good results may be obtained. The student of these lessons will find this last image easy to produce if he will remember what we have said about Thought Forms.

Concluding the Treatment.

I do not advise too long treatments, for I believe that the best results are obtained in a treatment extending over say not more than fifteen minutes. You should then leave the patient with a few earnest words of encouragement and hope, bidding him aid you in your work by keeping the proper Mental Images of Health before him, and especially avoiding all Fear and Worry.

Simple but Powerful Methods.

The above process of giving a Mental Treatment may seem very simple to those who have not practiced it. But you will find that it contains the real essence of the healing process, without the "fringe" and "trimming." And more than that you will find it wonderfully efficacious—it will "do the work." You will never begin to even faintly realize the virtue of such a treatment, until you begin to practice it. You will then find yourself filled with such a sense of power, strength and healing force, that you will seem like another person. And your patient will likewise feel an immediate benefit. I might write page after page, giving you directions about the treatment, but, after I was through, it could all be boiled down into the plain, simple directions already given you. I have given you the essence of the practical treatment—you may add the "trimmings" yourself, if you feel that you need them. This same essence you will find to underlie all of the treatments of the various sects and cults, after you have trimmed off the "fancy additions," high-sounding words, and metaphysical terms. I have studied all these forms of treatment, and know just what I am talking about when I say this to you.

HOW TO GIVE "ABSENT TREATMENTS."

And now for the "Absent Treatments" along the lines of General Treatment. There is practically no difference in the methods. The principal additional process is that of the Healer endeavoring to form a Mental Image of the patient, as if he were right before him in person. If you have ever seen the patient you may easily reproduce his Mental Image. But if you have not seen him personally, you can form a Mental Image of "a man," or "a woman," without filling in the details of personal appearance, and the result will be similar. You will find the following method will help you in the treatment. Sit down in your chair, after drawing up another chair right before you, but about two or three yards distant. Then picture your patient as sitting in this other chair, and use your imagination to the fullest in this respect. Many practitioners of successful Mental Healing actually *feel* that the patient is sitting before them in this form of treatment. Then with your patient sitting before you (as a Mental Image) talk to him just as if he were present in person, using the same words, tones, and manner. Throw yourself earnestly into the idea of a personal treatment, and endeavor to forget that miles are between you. By so doing you will be able to start the Mentative Currents flowing freely in his direction, and he will be affected by them, and will obtain the best results. I have been told frequently by persons who have taken this form of healing from some of the world's best Mental Healers, that they could *almost see the Healer* before them—they could certainly *feel* his presence very distinctly.

The Particulars of "Absent Treatment."

This "talk" to the distant patient should consist of the same calming, quieting, soothing suggestions at first, followed by the positive, stimulating, forceful suggestions given afterward. Follow the precise instructions given for use in personal treatments, and you cannot go astray. There is no difference, in reality, between Personal Treatments and Absent Treatments—if you will remember this, and act upon it, you will have the key to the matter. And, then, after the suggestive talks, you should then give the same silent Mentative Treatment as indicated in my instructions regarding Personal Treatments. You should form the same kind of Mental Image, and proceed just the same, in every particular. Even bid him "good-bye" as you would in a personal treatment. If you have set a time for the Absent Treatment, your patient should place himself in a comfortable relaxed position. But this is not necessary—it is not necessary for the patient to even know the hour of treatment. All that he needs to do is to open his mind, receptively, to the treatment that you are to give him some time during the day—that is, he should express his mental "willingness," and thus take off the resistance of his Will which otherwise would have to be overcome.

The "Why" of Absent Treatments.

The Healer who wishes to give Absent Treatments should study carefully the lesson of this course, entitled "The Science of Telementation." In that lesson he will see the process of Telementative Influence along the lines of Mentative Induction, and will understand the details of the subject by reading what has been said regarding the Currents, Thought Forms, etc. Remember, please, that all the work of Mental Healing is done along the lines of Mentative Induction, just as is the process of all form of Mentative Influence. There is but one great law underlying all of these forms of manifestation, and if you understand the fundamental principle, you will be able to reproduce any or all of the manifestations of it. The instruction regarding Mental Healing is not confined to this lesson alone—it must be gained from a study of all of these lessons, for the reasons just stated. Strive always to acquire a clear knowledge of the Underlying Principles, and you need not worry about the details of operation or manifestation.

SELF-HEALING BY GENERAL TREATMENT.

And, now, just a word about Self-Heating, along these lines. *There is no difference between Self-Healing, and the Healing of Others.* I am going to give you the "ATKINSON METHOD OF MENTAL SELF-HEALING"—it is my favorite method. All that is necessary for you to do is to imagine yourself as a patient coming to yourself for treatment. Suppose your name is "John Smith," and you wish to treat yourself along the lines of the General Treatment. Well, all you have to do is to let the Central Mind part of you (or the "I") proceed to *treat the body* of "John Smith." *Talk to "John Smith" just as if he were an entirely separate individual.* Tell him what he should do, and what he should know, and what you expect to do for him. Give him the same Suggestions that you would give another patient. Talk up to him, and tell him just what you mean to do for him, and what he has got to do himself. Then give him the Silent Treatment just as you would another patient. Even give him the parting words, just as you would a patient. In short, treat him first, last, and all the time, as you would another patient. You will be surprised to note how efficacious this plan is. I believe that this is the first time that this plan has been stated in print—it is original with myself, so far as I know. There is a good, strong psychological, and occult reason for this plan of Self-Treatment, which is not necessary to go into here—the principal thing is that it "will do the work." Try it. The ordinary method of Self-Treatment, is to say "I am well" and so on, giving the suggestions in the first person. I consider that my own plan gives better results, but you may try both, and decide for yourself.

"LOCAL TREATMENT."

And, now for the "Local Treatment" methods of Mental Healing. Well, these are very simple also—so simple that I fear that some of you will undervalue them. But do not deceive yourselves, good friends, the "simplicity" represents years of hard work along experimental lines, and is really the "boiling down" of many methods far more complicated and technical. It is the "essence" of the thing, again. I wish that I could have obtained this information as easily as you are doing—but I couldn't, for I had to work it out for myself, in connection with other experimenters and investigators.

THE THEORY.

The Underlying Theory of this Local Treatment in Mental Healing is (1) that *there is Mind in every cell; cell-group; organ; and part, of the body;* and (2) that *the Mentative Energy in such Mind is NEGATIVE to that in the Central Mind of the Individual, and, consequently, yields to its Positivity when properly applied.* That is the whole story in a nut-shell. Now see if you can grasp its importance.

THE IDENTITY OF PRINCIPLES.

The above principle of the "Local Treatment" is really also employed in the General Treatment, because the Central Mind of the patient is stirred into induced activity and Positivity by Suggestion, or Mentative Currents of the Healer, or both. The Central Mind of the patient, so stirred up by induction, then acts upon the mind in the cells, organs, etc., unconsciously, and the cure results. Do you see just what I mean? Well, then, in the Local Treatment, instead of going about it in this way, the Healer brings his Mentative Energy to bear right directly upon the mind in cells, and organs themselves. So you see the process is really the same, at the last, that is it is the application of the Positive Central Mind upon the Negative Mind of the Cells, Organs and Parts.

Mental Therapeutics.

The Basis of the Treatment.

Now, then, how may one treat the cells and organs of another person, in this way? The process is very simple, when you once learn it. All that is necessary is for you to "treat" the organ, or part, just as you did the patient, in Personal, Absent, or Self, General Treatment, as stated a little while ago. You must learn to "talk to" the organ or part affected, and to give it Suggestions and Silent Treatment just as you did your personal patient. In short, the nearer you can come to *considering, and treating the cells or organs as if they actually were "personalities" or "entities,"* the better will be your success in this form of treatment. This is no mere trick, or bit of superstition—it is based upon good psychological principles, and has its reason in well defined occult laws. *There is Mind in the Organ and Cell, and you are reaching out to it.* Let us see just how to reach that Mind in order to properly Impress it.

The Practice of Local Treatment.

Well, the way to reach the Mind in the cells; cell-groups; ganglia; organs; nerves; parts, etc., of the body, is to *address yourself directly to it, just as you would to a person.* You must think of the Mind in the affected parts, as a "person" who is misbehaving. You must remonstrate with, argue with, coax, order or drive the "person" residing in the organ, just as you would different individuals. Sometimes coaxing is much better than driving, and sometimes the forceful method is necessary as we shall see. You may either talk aloud to the Mind in the organ, or else (and this is the better way in treating others) you may do your talking mentally. Tell them just what you expect of them—just what you intend they shall do—just what is right for them to do, etc. *And they will obey.*

A Good Suggestion.

I know a lady, who is an excellent healer along these lines, and who obtained the principles of this particular form of healing from myself. She tells me that she followed my plan, as above stated, with the exception that to her *the organs, nerves, and parts, always seem like disobedient children*, who must be managed one way or another. And so she proceeds just as she did when she was a successful schoolteacher. And, I am inclined to think that she is right, and has made an improvement on my original idea. For these "Cell-minds," or "Organ-minds" closely resemble the minds of undeveloped children, and are often unreasonably stubborn, although if they are reached the right way, by a firm though kindly tone in most cases, they will obey orders, and mend their ways.

THE USE OF THE HANDS.

It is well to use the hands at the beginning of this form of treatment, in the direction of tapping or patting the part of the body directly over the organ. This seems to have the effect of awakening the attention of the Organ-mind, so that it becomes more receptive. It is akin to tapping the shoulder of a man on the street, to whom you wish to speak. In such cases it is well to send the mental command: "Here, Listen to me!" The hands of the Healer may also be passed over the body as the mental commands are given, and they serve to give an additional and strengthened suggestion when properly used.

A PLAIN, SIMPLE PLAN.

A plain, simple way of giving this treatment is to awaken the attention of the Mind in the organ or part, as above stated, and then proceed to mentally lecture it, calling it by name, as for instance: "Here, Stomach!" or "Now, you Liver," etc. Don't smile at this advice—just try it yourself and you will stop smiling. *Then go on and tell the Organ-Mind just what you would tell it if it were an actual personality—a childish mind, for instance.* You will soon find how quick the organ-mind is to awaken to your words, and to act upon your suggestions or orders. Follow the laws of Suggestion in giving these treatments to the organ-minds—that is, remember the suggestive phases of Repetition, Authoritative Demand or Command, etc. Don't be afraid, but start in to give the Organ-mind "a piece of your mind," and it will obey you.

The Degrees of "Mind" in the Bodily Organs.

Dr. Paul Edwards, one of the world's most famous Mental Healers, whom I met quite often a number of years ago when he was living in Chicago, informed me that the result of his practice has taught him that there was a great difference in the "intelligence" of the Mind in the several organs. For instance, he believed that the Heart was *very* "intelligent," and quite amenable to mild, gentle, coaxing suggestions and advise or orders; while on the other hand, the Liver was a most mulish, stubborn, obstinate organ-mind, which had to be driven along by the sharpest and most positive suggestions. I have since investigated along this line, and I am now fully convinced of the correctness of Dr. Edward's theory in this respect. I have found the Heart to be very gentle, and obedient, as he said, and I have moreover found it needed but the slightest word to attract its attention. I have found the Liver to be brutish, stubborn, and obstinate, and needing the most forceful, insistent methods—something like driving a stubborn donkey along the road. I have also found the Liver to be lazy and sleepy, and needing much effort to rouse it into a receptive condition. The Stomach, I have found quite intelligent, particularly if it has not been brutalized by "stuffing," and it will readily respond to the treatment. A peculiar thing about the Stomach is that it seems to like "jollying," or "flattery"—tell it how good a stomach it is, and how well it can do its work; and how much you trust it to run things right for you; and lo! it proceeds to "make good," and justify your praise and commendations.

Treatment of Special Organs.

The Nerves respond readily to this form of treatment, along gentle coaxing lines. The Circulation of the Blood may be increased to certain parts, or restrained, in this way. In this way the Blood can be swept all over the body, creating a pleasant glow; or it may be drawn away from an aching head, or a feverish brow. The Bowels respond readily to a firm, kind treatment, in which they are to be told to move regularly—it being well to name a certain time at which you expect them to establish a regular habit, *in which case be sure to keep your appointment with them and give them a chance.* The organs peculiar to Women will respond quite readily to this form of treatment. Regular Menstruation has often been established by treating the proper parts in this way a month ahead, and keeping it up every day until the regular period—in this case, it is also well to "fix a date." Suggestions of "Firm, now—be Firm and Strong" have relieved many cases of Womb weaknesses. Profuse Menstruation has yielded to commands of "Slow, now; easy. easy; not so free a flow," etc.

What to Say, and How to Say It.

There are no fixed forms of treatment along these lines. You must acquire the "knack" by practice. The proper words will suggest themselves to you. The thing to do is *to know what you want done,* and then *command the organ-mind to do that thing; using the same words that you would use in talking to a real person In the place of the organ.* You will soon acquire the art, by a little practice. Those who have treated a large number of persons in this way have told me that the Mind in the organs and parts seem to instinctively recognize the Healer's power over them. Just as a horse or dog will recognize men who are accustomed to managing animals of their kind, so will these Organ minds instinctively recognize their Master in one who has studied this art of Mental Healing, along these lines.

Mental Therapeutics.

Mind Versus Mind.

Remember always that you are Mind talking to Mind, not to dead matter. There is Mind in every cell, nerve, organ and part of the body, and in the body as a whole; and this Mind will listen to your Central Mind and obey it, because your Central Mind is Positive to it—the organ is negative to YOU. Carry this idea always with you in giving these treatments, and endeavor to visualize the Mind in the organs, .etc., as clearly as may be, for by so doing you get them in better *rapport* with you, and can handle them to better advantage.

Words and Their Inner Meaning.

And, also remember, that it is not the mere sound of the words that happen to reach the Organ or Cells—they do not understand words as words, but they *do* understand *the meaning behind the words*—they recognize the Mental State of which the word is the outward symbol. But without words it is very hard for you to think, or clearly express the feeling—and so by all means use the words just as if the Organ-minds understood their actual meaning, for by so doing you can drive in *the meaning of the words*—and induce the Mental State conditions necessary to work the cure.

Local Treatment in Absent Healing.

While this Local Treatment is adapted especially to Personal Healing, still it may be also used to great advantage in Absent Healing, by combining it with the regular General Form of Absent Healing. That is, after giving the General Absent Treatment, proceed to place yourself *en rapport* with the Organ-mind in the patient, and then talk to it just as you would if the patient were actually present. Visualization will enable you to do this effectively. I have heard of some wonderful cures having been effected by the use of this form of Local Treatment in Absent Healing, in connection with the General Treatment.

Local Treatment in Self-Healing.

And, in case of Self-Healing this Local Treatment acts with wonderful force. One can, of course, "talk up" to his own cells and organs just as he can to those of another and with equal effect if he goes about it right. This opens up a wonderful field for Self-Healing. The methods and practice of Local Treatment in Self-Healing is precisely similar to those used in treating others. I am personally acquainted with a lady who has learned to make her body obey her perfectly. If the body looks tired or droopy or lack freshness and beauty, she just "talks up" to it and tells it how much she thinks of it and how much she appreciates all that it is doing for her, etc., and at the same time encourages it to manifest activity and interest, etc. The result is that the next morning after the treatment she will find that all of her suggestions have been accepted and acted upon by the body, and that the latter looks fresh, active and beautiful, manifesting all the appearance of youth and perfect health. I have heard of women managing to retain their youthful appearance in a similar manner. I have known men to "coax up" their bodies, when under the strain of unusual work, with the best of results. In fact, I believe that in this form of treatment of one's own Body there are possibilities as yet undreamt of by the race. Perhaps this hint may start some investigator to exploring the field to the limit—I have not found time to carry my investigations along this line quite as far as I would have liked. There is a great unexplored field here. There is a chance for some fine work here for the students of this book.

What This System of Healing Represents.

And now I seem to have reached the end of this lesson. Remember, please, that within its pages I have condensed information sufficient to have filled a good sized volume or two. Read it carefully and do not let the simplicity of my methods lead you to ignore the wonderful possibilities open to those who will practice them. I have not cared to dress up my "treatments" and methods in fancy garb for the purpose of bewildering the eye and creating an impression upon the foolish and childish minds of those who run after these things. I do not want a "following" of this sort—I want, rather, the earnest sympathetic cooperation of my students who appreciate the virtue in these apparently simple methods. As I have said before, these "simple" methods and forms of treatment represent the work and experience of myself and others extending over a number of years. They are the "boiling-down" of many systems and my personal lines of experiment. They embody the simplest, plainest, and yet the most effective methods known to the world of Mental Healing today. Take my word for this—I base this statement upon seven active years of earnest, patient, careful investigation, experiment and study along these lines under circumstances with which few are fortunate enough to be favored. I say these things not in the spirit of boasting or "booming my own wares," but merely that you may understand just what is behind and under these "simple" forms, methods and treatments.

FREEDOM FROM CULTS AND ORGANIZATIONS.

You will notice, I hope, that in order to practice these methods of Mental Healing you are not required to "join" anything—nor are asked to connect yourself with any new religion or semi-religion. *You may adhere to your favorite beliefs and still make as many cures as the best of those who believe and claim that the healing is done because of some fantastic theory, dogma or belief!* There is no more sense in building up a religion around Mental Healing than there is in building one up around Homeopathy, or Allopathy, or Osteopathy, or Hydropathy, or any other "pathy." There is but One Healing Power of the Mind and that is free and open to All. It is the gift of the Infinite to Its finite reflections. It is a Natural Force, working under certain laws—and FREE TO ALL. Take it and use it toward "the healing of the nations," beginning with yourself.

Lesson VII.

Mental Architecture.

The Meaning of the Term—The Brain and Brain-Cells—Phrenological Discoveries—Mental Muscle Development—Scientific Experiments—Remarkable Results—The Three Methods—Mental States and Physical Expression—Physical Actions Induce Mental States—The Secret of Making Yourself Over—Practical Use, not Mere Amusement—Opinion of Eminent Authorities—How to Cultivate or Restrain Mental Qualities—The Law of Auto-Suggestion—The Effect of Repetition—The Old and the New Methods—My Own New Method—How It Works in Practice—The Results of the Practice—Individual Requirements—The Faculties of the Mind—Building Up the Faculties—A Natural Law—The "Why" of It—Mental Architecture of Children—The Qualities of the Magnetic Man—The Magnetic Desire—The Hunger of Desire—Desire in Many Dresses—Desire Underlies All Action and Restraint of Action—Universality of Desire—How to Develop Desire-Force—Mental Images Awaken Desire—The Threefold Method in Desire—Why Desire Should Be Developed—The Magnetic Will—The Secret of the Resolute Will—Habit and Will-Power—Control the Physical Channels of Expression—Learn to Concentrate—Acquire the Will-Habit—The First Fight Is Hardest—Acquiring Second Nature—Judge, Weigh and Measure—Then Go Ahead—Fill Your Mind with Good Mental Pictures—Act Out the Habit—Practice Doing Disagreeable Things—Cultivate Fixity of Purpose—The Mental Faculties to Develop—Stability—The Will-to-Live—Courage—Barrier-Breaking—Getting and Keeping—The True Philosophy of Money Making—Some Plain Truths—Keeping Your Own Secrets—Prudence—Desire for Praise; and Fear of Public Opinion—Self-Confidence—Firmness—Earnest Expectation—Good Nature—Morals, Strength and Power—Mental States and Their Emanations—Concluding Remarks—My Message to the Individual—FINIS.

Lesson VII.

Mental Architecture.

"ARCHITECTURE" MEANS "the art or science of building or construction," and "Mental Architecture" means "the Art of Mind Building." By "Mind Building" I, of course, mean "Brain Building," for as I have told you in a previous lesson, I regard the Mind-substance as an Universal Energy, of and in which the Personal Mind is but a center of consciousness, strength, activity and power. The Brain is the "machinery" of the personal manifestation of Mind, or rather, the "converter" or "transformer" of the Mentative Energy. But as the word "Mind" is generally used as synonymous with "Brain," in the case of individuals, I shall speak of "Mind Building" in this lesson, although I always mean "Brain Building" when I so speak.

The Brain and Brain-Cells.

The differing manifestations of Mind in the various persons with whom we come in contact is at once recognized as depending upon the character, quality, degree and grade of their Brain-material. The brain is composed of a peculiar substance called "plasm," or elementary living-matter. The word "plasm" is derived from the Greek word meaning "a mould or matrix," and its use in connection with the Brain-substance is peculiarly appropriate, for it is in the cells of the brain that "Mental States" are "cast or moulded," as it were. The brain is composed of an enormous number of tiny cells which are the actual elements in the production and manifestation of Thought, or Mentation. These brain-cells are estimated at from 500,000,000 to 2,000,000,000, according to the mental activity of the person. There is always a great number of reserve brain-cells remaining unused in every brain, the estimate being made that even in the case of the wisest man, or most active thinker, there are always several millions of unused brain cells held as a reserve. And the most advanced science also informs us that the Brain "grows" additional cells to meet any demand upon it. And Brain-building is the development and growth of brain-cells in any special region of the brain; for, as you probably know, the brain contains many regions, each region being the seat of some particular function, quality, faculty or mental activity. By developing the brain-cells in any special region, the quality, activity or faculty which has that region for its seat is necessarily greatly increased and rendered more effective and powerful.

PHRENOLOGICAL DISCOVERIES.

The investigators along the lines of Phrenology have long since recognized the fact that brain-centers of regions could be developed by proper exercises, etc., and the text-books on that science give us many interesting facts regarding the same. These cases show us that not only is an individual able to develop and cultivate certain qualities of mind on the one hand, or restrain them on the other; but that also the very outward shape and size of the skull manifested a corresponding change, for the bony structure accommodates itself very gradually to the pressure of the increasing number of cells in some particular center of region of the brain.

Mental Architecture.

Mental Muscle-Development.

It is a fully demonstrated scientific fact that a man may "make himself over" mentally, if he will but devote the same degree of attention, patience and work to the subject that he would in the case of a desired development of some part of the physical body—some muscle, for instance. And the processes are almost identical in the case of muscle and brain-center—Use, Exercise and Practice along the lines pointed out by those who have investigated and experimented along the particular line.

Scientific Experiments.

Prof. Elmer Gates of Washington, D. C., one of the most remarkable men of this age, has given to the world an account of some remarkable experiments along the line of brain-growing, the experiments having been tried upon various animals. He tells us that his early experiments along this line were in the direction of training dogs to develop some one particular sense, that of seeing or hearing particularly. He would specially train a certain number of the animals according to his methods, and at the same time would keep a like number of the same animals of the same age, etc., without any extraordinary use of the particular faculty in question, and still a similar number without the opportunity of using that faculty at all. At the end of a certain time he would kill some of the animals belonging to each class, and upon examining the brains of each he made the discovery that the number of brain-cells (in the regions of their brains in which the sense or faculty was manifested) showed a startling difference, depending upon the degree of use and exercise of the particular faculty. His specially trained animals showed a much greater number of brain-cells than had ever been found in animals of the same breed and age.

REMARKABLE RESULTS.

Prof. Gates continued these experiments over a number of years and obtained some remarkable results. He specially trained the faculties of some of his dogs so that they were able to distinguish between seven shades of red and a like number of green shades. I have not the time here to speak at length of the wonderful results of Prof. Gates' experiments, but he has firmly established the scientific fact that brains may be "grown" at will, if the person will apply himself to the subject with sufficient zeal and ardor. I have conducted a number of interesting experiments (not with dogs, or through vivisection, however) which have proven conclusively to my mind that the entire natures, dispositions, characters and faculties of people may be entirely changed by intelligent psychological methods along the lines of Suggestion or Auto-Suggestion, accompanied with certain other methods to be mentioned in this lesson.

THE THREE METHODS.

The great school of "New Thought" people of the various sects, cults and associations have been doing some excellent work along these lines during the past ten years or more. Their systems of "affirmations" and "denials" really developed or restrained their brain-centers and desirable qualities were increased and developed and undesirable ones were restrained. But the mere use of "affirmations," "auto-suggestions" or even strong, positive suggestions given by another, forms only one-third of the work necessary in order to produce the best results. It is all very well to assert "I am Brave," "I am Industrious," "I am Active," etc., etc., but if the work stops there it remains only one-third done. It is true that these affirmations and auto-suggestions undoubtedly do stimulate and develop mental faculties and brain-centers and play an important part in Character Building. But in order that they be used to the best advantage there must be Visualization, and there should be a certain *physical acting out of the mental suggestion or affirmation*. There must be *Seeing* and *Doing* as well as *Saying*.

MENTAL STATES AND PHYSICAL EXPRESSION.

You will remember what I said in my lesson on Mental Suggestion regarding the fact that "Mental States take form in Physical Action," and its twin-truth that "Physical Action produces Mental States." It is a case of Action and Reaction in both instances. For instance, if you will start in to feel Angry, and keep it up a little while (even though the emotion is assumed for the experiment), you will find that your brows will form into a frown and that your hands will clench and your jaws will fasten into a savage "bite." You know this to be true, of course. But then, on the other hand, if you will assume the above-mentioned Physical Characteristics accompanying Anger and will keep them up earnestly for a short time, you will find yourself *actually feeling Angry*.

And, the same thing is true of the Feelings and Actions of Pleasure. Think intently of some pleasant thing and you will find your face breaking into an expression of pleasure—you will smile; your eyes will twinkle and you will manifest all the outward characteristics of pleasure. And, on the other hand, if you will "throw yourself into the part," and will smile and manifest all the outward signs of pleasure, you will find yourself beginning to feel "happy, jolly and pleasant" in a short time. I have seen a sign bearing the single word "SMILE!" in big letters cause people to change their mental states in a few moments. They would take the suggestion and being amused at the sign they would begin to Smile—then the Smile's physical actions would react upon their minds and they would begin to "feel good" and so on.

HOW PHYSICAL ACTIONS INDUCE MENTAL STATES.

I defy anyone to manifest the physical actions of any particular emotion or feeling, earnestly and actively, for a short time, without the corresponding mental state actually manifesting itself. Go into a business house manifesting the outward signs of Good Nature, Confidence, Self-reliance, etc., and you will not only impress others by Suggestion, but you will also *impress yourself*, and you will begin to actually *feel* the thing that you have been acting out. Go into the same place manifesting the outward appearance of Failure, Lack of Confidence, Fear, etc., and not only will your suggestions be taken up by the others, but you will sink deeper and deeper into the mental state you are acting out.

I have known people to acquire a masterful, confident, reliant character by a systematic and persistent "acting out" of the part—their "second-nature," so acquired, growing stronger than their original nature. The exercise of the faculty, in this way, developed the brain-cells in the proper area and the people were indeed "made over." I know men who, when feeling "blue" or "discouraged" will always force a smile to their faces and in a short time they will regain their accustomed or desired cheerful state.

An Interesting Illustration.

I have known at least one man to rouse feelings of Stern Determination by similar methods. This man was in a position in which there would frequently arise the necessity for the manifestation of the most Determined Sternness and an almost Angry display of Will. Well, the man in question was by nature a good-natured, easy-going, kindly person, and he found it almost impossible to manifest the desired qualities upon the occasions mentioned. But one day he was roused to a state of Angry, Determined Sternness by a most annoying exhibition of careless action in the office, which, although soon settled, left him with the physical reflex of the mental state just experienced. Before this physical condition had passed away there arose, unexpectedly, a case of genuine necessity for the exhibition of the Stern Determined Action, mentioned in the first place.

Meeting the man to whom this attitude must be manifested, our man found that, much to his surprise, he displayed a wonderful degree of the desired trait, and gave the other man a talking to that made his hair stand on end, and brought the desired result instanter. No one was more surprised at this occurrence than our man, and after it was all over he tried to "figure it out"—and he did. He came to the conclusion that when he was manifesting the physical conditions of the mental state, it required but a trifling effort to induce the state itself—in fact the state came almost "automatically." He had discovered, by accident, a well-established psychological law. And he made use of it ever after.

Thereafter, whenever he had to "work himself into a state," as he called it, he would walk about his office a few moments before he would see the other man, and during his walk he would "bite" hard and protrude his jaw; he would frown and clench his fists and make his eyes glare, etc., etc., and before long he would feel himself in the proper mood to see the other man and give him the necessary "laying out." The plan worked like a charm.

THE SEQUEL AND THE MORAL.

I almost hate to tell you the sequel, however. Our good natured "easy" man so developed these opposite qualities by this practice that in a few years he was known as a man to be dreaded by those who had occasion to receive treatment at his hands, and his whole nature seemed to have changed, and even his best friends would then hesitate to call him "easy" or "good natured." He had made himself over—that's all. And from this story you may build up a whole process of Character Building if you have sufficient Imagination and Ingenuity—for the principle is the same in all cases. Character is plastic—and may be moulded at will, by intelligent methods. But it takes more than "holding the thought" to do it—one must learn to ACT OUT THE PART DESIRED, until it becomes second-nature.

The Secret of "Making Yourself Over."

I wonder how many of you will realize what a wonderful field is here opened out for you if you will follow the idea taught by the past few pages? How many of you will realize that I have herein given you the "Secret of Making Yourselves Over?" I wish that I could fairly "pound into you" this truth. When I think of what many of you *are*; and then of what you *might be*, if you would realize the inner truth and importance of what I have just told you—well, then, I feel like printing the tale in big, black-faced type and capital letters—so that I could make you read it. But if you haven't "gumption" enough to "catch on" to the idea that I am presenting to you, I cannot help it—it's your loss, not mine.

Practical Use, Not Mere Amusement.

What in the world is the sense of you people paying me a dollar for this book if you do not intend to put into practice what I am teaching you? I have given you in these lessons information worth hundreds—yes thousands—of dollars to you, if you will but proceed to put them into practice. But the whole book isn't worth two cents to you if you merely "read" it idly and then after saying "it certainly is wonderful," forget all about it and what I have said. Well, now, that's all along that line. I have scolded you and have relieved myself of a certain amount of righteous indignation and now I shall proceed with my lesson. I haven't charged you for the scolding pages—I just throw them in extra, at my own expense. But, honest now, some of you people do need someone to get after you with a good stuffed-club once in a while. You're asleep! Wake up and make yourself over!

Mental Architecture.

Opinion of an Eminent Authority.

I think that the facts and principles above stated are self-evident and need little or no backing up by authorities. But I think I will give you a quotation or two to help fasten the idea in your minds. Prof. Halleck says: *"By restraining the expression of an emotion we can frequently throttle it; by inducing an expression we can often cause its allied emotion."* I wish that every one of you would commit the above words to memory—they are golden. By expression Prof. Halleck, of course, means the *physical* manifestation or expression—the physical action which springs from the emotion.

A Strong Statement.

Prof. Wm. James has this to say along the same line: "Refuse to express a passion and it dies. Count ten before venting your anger and its occasion seems ridiculous. Whistling to keep up courage is no mere figure of speech. On the other hand, sit all day in a moping posture, sigh, and reply to everything with a dismal voice, and your melancholy lingers. There is no more valuable precept in moral education than this, as all of us who have experienced know: If we wish to conquer undesirable emotional tendencies in ourselves we must assiduously, and in the first instance cold-bloodedly, go through the *outward movements* of those contrary dispositions which we wish to cultivate. Smooth the brow, brighten the eye, contract the dorsal rather than the ventral aspect of the frame, and speak in a major key, pass the genial compliment and your heart must indeed be frigid if it does not gradually thaw." Aren't those words fine? Read them over several times so as to be sure to grasp their full meaning!

How to Cultivate or Restrain Mental Qualities.

If you wish to *cultivate a quality* in which you are deficient, you must think about it, dream about it, concentrate upon it—live it out in your thoughts as a "day-dream" or "mental picture"—hold the Visualized Mental Image of it always with you—and last, and equally as important, if not more so, ACT OUT THE PHYSICAL MANIFESTATIONS OF IT—PLAY THE PART OUT. Act your part, earnestly, ardently, constantly, eagerly, steadily. On the other hand, if you wish to *repress a quality*, the best way to do it is to CULTIVATE THE OPPOSITE QUALITY, and the undesirable quality will be "crowded out." Do you see this last? Think over it! If you wish to get rid of darkness in a room, you don't have to shovel it out—just open the windows and "let a little sunshine in." Do you see what I mean, now? Prof. James has told you the same thing in the quotation given a few moments ago. It is a psychological law. Kill the Negative by cultivating the Positive. That's the Rule! But don't forget to ACT OUT THE PART!

The Law of Auto-Suggestion.

What is called Auto-Suggestion, or Self-Suggestion, is one of the most active agencies employed in Mind Building. Auto-Suggestion covers all the various forms of Affirmations, Denials, Statements, etc., employed by the several "New Thought" schools, and is the underlying principle of all forms of "Self-Impression." "Self-Impression" would be a better name than any of these terms, for it described the process exactly. One "impresses" his mind with certain ideas, suggestions, feelings and mental states. There is a dual aspect of mind which enables one to play two parts at the same time, *viz.* (1) the part of Teacher or Master, and (2) the part of Scholar or Pupil. One may charge his mind with the task of waking him up at a certain time in the morning—and he wakes up. Or he may charge his mind to remember a certain thing—and he remembers it. This form of Self Mastery may be carried to great lengths, and one may bid his mind collect data regarding certain subjects, from amidst its heterogenous collection of mental odds and ends of knowledge; and then bid it combine the information into a systematic form—and the mind will so act and the combined information will be at hand when needed. I find myself doing this, almost unconsciously, when I start to write a book—fact after fact, and illustrations, appearing at their proper time and place. The field of Self Impression has just had its outer edges explored—there is a great region of mentation here awaiting some of you.

THE EFFECT OF REPETITION.

And so, this Auto-Suggestion is a case of "says I to myself, says I." And the queer thing is that if you will impress your mind sufficiently, strongly, and with sufficient repetition, you will find it taking the impression and acting upon it. Repetition is a great thing in Auto-Suggestion. You remember the case of the man who told a certain lie so often that he got to actually believe it himself—well, repeated Auto-Suggestion works along the same psychological lines. Hearing a thing impressed upon it sufficiently often, it takes it as a fact, and proceeds to act it out accordingly. Constant Affirmation and Statement, made to one's self, will manifest in actual conditions.

THE VALUE OF AUTO-SUGGESTION.

Many a person has changed his whole physical and mental condition by a careful, persistent course of Auto-Suggestion. Of course, if one combines the Mental Image, or Visualization process with the Auto-Suggestion, he will obtain a doubly efficacious result. And if, in addition to these two he will practice ACTING OUT THE PART along physical lines, he will reap a ten-fold harvest of results. These three forms combined, employed and persisted in, will work miracles in anyone.

ILLUSTRATIVE INSTANCES.

For instance, if one suffers from Fear in meeting other persons—an abnormal timidity or bashfulness, commonly called "self-consciousness"—the course for him to pursue would be to brace himself up with constant affirmations or Auto-Suggestions of "Fearlessness;" then he should Visualize himself as absolutely Fearless; then he should endeavor to reproduce the physical appearance and outward demeanor (an Acting Out of the Part) of the Fearless man. And thus will he gradually develop into that which he desires. His ideal becomes real—his dream a fact—his feelings actions—his actions feelings. And this rule and example will hold good along the whole line of Personal Qualities or Characteristics. All come under the rule—the same principle works in all cases. Get the Principle and you have the secret of the whole thing.

THE OLD AND THE NEW METHODS.

But here I am going to suggest a little variation along the lines of Auto-Suggestion, which I have found to act admirably in this class of cases. The ordinary Auto-Suggestion, or Affirmation works along these lines, *viz.*, one affirms or suggests to himself something like this: "I am Fearless—I Fear Nothing—I am Courageous—I am filled with Confidence," etc., etc. Now this is fine—no one who knows anything about the subject will dispute the fact that a man "holding the thought" that "I Am Fearless," will be filled with Courage, and will manifest the qualities that he is claiming for himself. I have tried these things on myself and others and I can unhesitatingly testify as to their efficiency. It is the old tried and oft-taught plan of Affirmation or Auto-Suggestion that has worked wonders for so many people. And I positively advise you to follow this plan of "holding the thought," and *making the Affirmations or Auto-suggestions in the first person*, when you are "going into action." As a "bracer" it is unexcelled. But there is something else not so old—and here it is.

MY NEW METHOD.

You will remember that in my lesson on Mental Therapeutics in that part devoted to Self-Healing, I told you to imagine yourself as "John Smith," or whatever your name may be—that is, as a separate person, and then to "treat" him as such—just as you would a patient. Well, this plan also works admirably in cases of Character Building by Auto-Suggestion. While the "I am, etc.," plan is good as a bracer, and when going into action, still this last mentioned plan of mine operates far better when it comes down to steady "treatment" of one's self for mental failings, weaknesses and character-building. Just try both plans yourself and see if I am not right—but practice my plan a little until you acquire the "knack" before finally deciding the matter. Here is how it works in practice.

HOW IT WORKS IN PRACTICE.

Suppose you wish to cultivate Fearlessness in place of the Fear-thought that has bothered you so much. Well, in addition to the Mental Image or Visualization, and the never-to-be-forgotten Acting Out the Part, you wish to try Auto-Suggestion. The old way, you remember, was to claim to yourself, "I am Fearless, etc." Now my new way of "treating" yourself is to imagine that you are "treating" some other person for the same trouble. Sit down and give a regular treatment. Image Yourself as sitting before your Personality—The Central Mind giving a treatment to the "John Smith" part of you—the Individual "treating" the Personality. Do you see? Well, the Individual (that's YOU) says to the personality of "John Smith:" "Here, John Smith, you must brace up and do better. You are FEARLESS, FEARLESS, FEARLESS! I tell you you are FEARLESS! You are Courageous and Brave and Bold! You are Confident and Self Reliant! You Fear Nothing! You are filled with strong, *Positive* Mentative Energy, and you are going to manifest it—you are going to grow more and more Positive every day! You are *positive* this minute—do you hear me? Positive *this very minute*! You are Positive, Fearless, Confident and Self-Reliant *right now*, and you will grow more and more so every day. Remember now, you are POSITIVE, POSITIVE, POSITIVE—FEARLESS, FEARLESS, FEARLESS," etc., etc., etc.

The Result of This Practice.

You will find that by this plan you will be able to fairly pour in the Positive suggestions to "the John Smith part of You," and the latter will take them with the same effect as if there were two persons instead of one. And there *are* two persons, according to the Occult Teachings—the Individual and the Personality. This plan will afford a welcome variation to the monotonous "I Am this and I am That" methods which have caused so many once-ardent followers of the "New Thought" to throw up the whole matter in disgust. This wholesale "I am this and that" business has tired many a good soul who thereby let go just when in sight of Attainment. To such and to all others I would say "Try this New Plan!" Learn to actually "treat yourself" by this method and you will be surprised at the rapid progress you will make as compared with the old plan. But don't forget to impress upon the "John Smith" part of you that he must hold the Mental Image or Visualization; and that he *must* start right in to ACT OUT THE PART! Don't let him get away from this—insist upon it—cross-examine him about it before each treatment and hammer it into him hard. For as our colored brother would say: "He sure needs 'em all" to carry him through.

Try It On Yourself and Find Out.

Now, please experiment with this method on yourself and find out its wonderful possibilities by your own experience. Don't rest with my say-so but prove it for yourself. When once you have found out just what this method will do for you you will wonder that you had never thought of it before. You will cultivate a sense of Individuality which will recognize the Personality as a plastic something that can be moulded and shaped at your Will by this "treatment." And, best of all, you will learn to know that the Individual is YOU, and YOU are the Individual, and that the Personality is merely something that "belongs to you." When you have reached this stage you will have called to your hand the forces of the Great Mentative

Energy and will indeed have a right to call yourself "Positive" and an "Active Center of Power" in the Great Ocean of Power. And all this will have been brought about by this new plan of "Says I to myself, says I." Is it not "worth while?" Then start in to "make yourself over as YOU will!"

INDIVIDUAL REQUIREMENTS.

But now comes the question "In what respect shall I make myself over?" And this is a question that I cannot answer for you in these lessons, because each one of my readers would have to be answered differently, and I would have to understand the requirements of each particular case before I could so answer. But, after all, each and every man or woman who studies these lessons has a very good idea of his or her particular strong or weak points of character. Each one knows just about what qualities need to be strengthened and built up, and just which ones need to be restrained. Every person knows his shortcomings in the lines of personal qualities or character, for he or she has been forced to this knowledge by coming in contact with the world. If you are considering the question of Character Architecture in your own case, I would advise a strict Self-Examination with a pencil and paper, in which you must set down the degree of development of each particular quality, with fear or favor toward yourself. When you have done this you will know just how to proceed. You will have given yourself a Mental Diagnosis. I herewith give you a general list of qualities, etc., as an aid in this work of Self Examination as a basis of Mental Architecture. In using it ask yourself the question : "WHAT DEGREE OF THIS QUALITY DO I POSSESS?" And answer the question "on honor."

THE FACULTIES OF THE MIND.

Below I give you a list of the "faculties" usually given in works on Phrenology, which will aid you very materially in preparing your report on yourself. Each faculty relates to some quality of character possessed by you, and regarding which you are asking yourself the question mentioned above:

Sexuality.	Ideality.
Friendship.	Mirthfulness.
Love of Life.	Sense of Size.
Physical Appetites.	Sense of Order.
Cautiousness.	Memory.
Firmness.	Language.
Faith.	Judging Human Nature.
Ingenuity.	Parental Love.
Imitation.	Stick-to-it-iveness.
Sense of Shape.	Determination.
Sense of Color.	Secretiveness.
Sense of Locality.	Self Esteem.
Musical Taste.	Hope.
Comparison.	Sympathy.
Domestic Qualities.	Sublimity.
Love of Places.	Observation.
Fighting Qualities.	Sense of Weight.
Acquisitiveness.	Sense of Number.
Love of Praise.	Sense of Time.
Integrity.	Originality.
Veneration.	"Blarney," or Agreeableness.

Building the Faculties.

Every one of the above mentioned faculties or qualities may be increased or decreased by the practice of the methods given in this lesson. Auto-Suggestion, Visualization and Acting-Out-the-Part—that Triple Method of Character Architecture will enable anyone to "make himself over" in any one or more of the above qualities. You will, of course, always remember that the methods named act in the direction of stimulating the growth of the brain-cells in the particular centers, areas and regions in which the particular faculty or quality is manifested. The immediate cause of the growth of the brain-cells is the DESIRE of the individual manifesting itself along physical lines; coupled with that law of Nature which causes increased physical or mental growth in accordance with NECESSITY or Need. The earnest Desire, heightened by Visualization and Auto-Suggestion, stimulates the brain centers manifesting the desired qualities, and by so doing causes a more rapid production of new cells and the greater development of the existing ones. Then the Acting-Out-the Part, with its physical manifestations, creates a direct demand upon the brain for means of manifestation, and the brain responds by growing additional cells to meet the demand.

A NATURAL LAW.

There is in Nature a law that tends to furnish the organism that which is needed for its development and necessities. The horse has evolved from a three-toed animal into a one-toed one, in response to the demands of its environments, and the necessities of its life. Birds of prey have claws and beaks adapted to their needs and wants; beasts of prey have great teeth, claws and shape of body adapted to their wants and necessities—and so it is all through Nature. But remember this, that animals constantly change as their environments alter, for Nature always is ready to supply that which is demanded by the necessities of the organism.

THE "WHY" OF IT.

Evolution gives us many convincing illustrations of this fact, which I regret not being able to mention here. If a part of the body is brought into unaccustomed use, it becomes tired at first and then Nature sends to its relief increased nutrition and development so that in time it can meet the new requirements with ease. And so it is in this matter of the brain-cells. Make a demand upon Nature for increased Power along certain lines and she responds. And the way to make the demand for new brain-cells in order to manifest certain qualities to a higher degree is to follow the methods given you herein - Auto-Suggestion; Visualization and Acting-Out-the Part. I trust that you now understand not only the "how" of this subject, but also the "why" of it.

It is impossible in the space of a lesson to give detailed instruction regarding the development of each separate faculty of the mind. That would require a good sized book by itself. But I have given you the general principles and directions and you should be able to work out the rest of the problem yourself. I will, however, give you special directions for the development of the particular qualities most necessary to the Positive Magnetic Man mentioned in my lesson on Personal Influence. That special instruction falls naturally within the field and scope of this lesson. I will condense a mass of this information within the remaining pages of this course.

MENTAL ARCHITECTURE OF CHILDREN.

Before proceeding to this last mentioned phase of the work, however, I wish to say that not only may one "make himself over" by the methods given, but he may "make over" other people by the same methods applied in the form of Suggestive Treatment. This is particularly true in the case of children, whose characters are extremely plastic, and who yield readily to constructive shaping and guidance. It is not necessary for me to go into this matter in detail, for in my lesson on "Mental Suggestion" and in my instruction in "Mental Therapeutics," as well as in the present lesson, I have given the principles of such treatment and the methods of applying the same. I trust that every student of this course has paid sufficient attention to what has been taught to be able to understand and apply this form of Suggestive Treatment to others.

What I have said about treating the "John Smith" part of you is true when you are actually treating others. The same principles apply. In addition to these you may advantageously use treatments by Mentative Currents, which will tend to induce in the mind of the other person the desired Mental States, which in time will result in the production of the new brain-cells needed to "establish" the mental character-cure. In treating others for a change of character, proceed exactly as you would in treating them for a physical ailment—the principle is the same, for the trouble arises from a similar underlying cause. In both cases you are treating Mind, remember.

THE QUALITIES OF THE MAGNETIC MAN.

And now to the building up of the Positive Magnetic Man. We have seen, in the fourth lesson, what he was like, and now we must try to "make ourselves over" to resemble him. The methods given in the present lesson apply to this work, of course. Let us now form a Mental Picture of the Positive Magnetic Man and see what qualities he possesses, and then learn how to develop and cultivate those qualities.

THE MAGNETIC DESIRE.

Well, then, first our Magnetic Man is possessed of a strong Desire. He knows how to "want" a thing the right way. No mere "wishing" or "sighing" for a thing—when he wants a thing he WANTS it. We all think that we *want* things, but the majority only want them in a halfhearted way. The flame of Desire burns feebly and gives little light or heat. One of the first things you will notice in coming in personal contact with the men "who do things" in the world is that they are filled with that intense, eager, longing, craving, hungry, ravenous Desires that stirs them on the mighty effort and achievement—which makes them DEMAND things instead of begging for them.

Even among the animals that we speak of as "strong" and "masterful," you will find that this Desire quality is strong in them, so much so that it impresses itself in their every movement and action. And on the other hand, you will find a lack of that same quality in the species of animals that are preyed upon, hunted and devoured by the others. This class of weak-desired animals impress us as "weak" and "spiritless."

THE HUNGER OF DESIRE.

And so it is with men. No one ever did anything or got anything unless he was filled with a strong, hungry desire for that thing. If a man feels a hunger for attainment, just as he feels a hunger for his meals, he will make mighty efforts to satisfy that hunger. Just think of what you would do to satisfy a craving hunger! Well, these men feel the same way about other things for which they are hungry. Desire *is* a form of Hunger. And the hungrier a man is for a thing the more Desire-Force will he manifest and the greater efforts will he make to get that thing.

DESIRE IN MANY DRESSES.

People have gotten into the habit of speaking and thinking of "desire" as an unworthy, low, animal, selfish quality—but they are seeing only a half truth while thinking that they are seeing the whole thing. They dodge the question by speaking of "high desires," "aspiration," "ambition,' "zeal," "ardor," "love," and a number of similar terms—but these things are merely our old friend "Desire" with a new name. Let me give you a few words used in speaking of some form of Desire. Here they are: Desire, wish, want, need, exigency, mind, inclination, leaning, bent, animus, partiality, penchant, predilection, propensity, willingness, liking, love, fondness, relish, longing, hankering, solicitude, anxiety, yearning, coveting, aspiration, ambition, eagerness, zeal, ardor, appetite, appetency, hunger, thirst, keenness, longing, craving, etc., etc. Quite a formidable list, isn't it?

DESIRE UNDERLIES ALL ACTION AND RESTRAINT OF ACTION.

The truth is that all of the "feelings" that incite one to action of any kind or sort, are forms of Desire. Without Desire one would cease absolutely from action. Proceeding every action there must be Desire, either conscious or unconscious. Even those people who make a virtue of Renunciation of Desire, and who claim to have "conquered Desire absolutely," are acting in response to a more subtle form of Desire. How is this, you ask? Well, simply because they are carrying out *a Desire not to desire certain other things*. Desire is at the bottom of the Renunciation, just as it is at the bottom of the very Desires they wish to renounce. This must be so always, for Desire is a fundamental Natural Law, and is always manifest. Not only in the *doing* of things is Desire manifest, but also in the *refraining from doing* the same things. One man desires to smoke—another desires not to do so. Desire in both cases! "Lack of Desire" to do a certain thing simply means a desire to pursue an opposite course of conduct and action. And so it goes—Desire is manifest in every action and refraining from action—so long as one has the capacity for action.

UNIVERSALITY OF DESIRE.

Nothing has even been done, created, or manifested without Desire. The very atoms manifest Desire in their combinations. And so, all the Universe has been built up through the operation of the law of Desire, and the law of Will—both of which are phases of the one law. Desire underlies all Life—it rests in the very heart of Life itself. And the greater the manifestation of Vitality, the greater the force of Desire. But remember always, that there are *wise* desires and *unwise* desires. And the Positive Magnetic Man learns to distinguish between the wise and the unwise desires—between the "good" and the "bad" ones—and governs himself accordingly. He examines his Desires and picking out the "good and wise" ones he discards the "bad and unwise" ones—then he proceeds to develop and build up the ones he has selected.

How to Develop Desire-Force.

And how does our man develop his Desire when Desire in itself is not a separate Mental Faculty, but, instead, manifests through and in each faculty? Well, he proceeds to *hold up to it the Mental Image of the things to be desired*, and the Desire Force within him flows forth, and manifests more and more energy according to the stimulus. Desire Force is always inherent in the person just as is Will Power, but both need *an incentive to action*—a stimulus to manifestation. It is a well-known law of Psychology that Desire flows out and manifests itself in response to an Object. This Object of Desire is always something that affords pleasure, satisfaction or content to the individual, or else that will rid him of pain, discontent, discomfort, of dissatisfaction, either immediate or remote in both instances, and sometimes indirectly, that is, the pleasure or pain may be occasioned by the pleasure or pain, immediate or remote, of some other person in which the original person is interested.

Mental Images Awaken Desire.

The clearer the Mental Image of the Object of Desire, the greater will be the degree of Desire manifested, all other things being equal. A child may be filled with discontent—it wants something, but does not know what it wants. Then the child thinks of "toys"—and it begins to want still harder. Then it *sees* a toy—and then its want becomes very intense. One may feel hungry in a degree, but when he *sees* some particular object of taste, the hunger becomes far more intense. And so it follows that if one will keep on presenting to his Desire the Suggestion and Mental Image of the Object, then will the Desire begin to burn more fiercely and strongly and may be cultivated to almost any degree.

We all know how one may awaken Desire in another in this way, by means of Suggestion, and by presenting the Mental Image of the Object, in conversation, etc.—how many of us know to our cost how the "sight" of an unthought of thing makes us begin to "hanker" after it and long for it? The book agent plays upon this trait of character in us—and so does the department store man on bargain days and by his window displays. You will remember what I told you in the lesson on Suggestion, about the steps in "Salesmanship," the important point being to "arouse desire" in the customer—and what I said about the same thing in the case of the Advertiser. This idea underlies all forms of Suggestive Influence and is manifest in the lives of every one of us, every day of our lives. And if this be so, can you not see that by Auto-Suggestion you may arouse the same degree of Desire in yourselves that others arouse in you and you in others?

THE THREEFOLD-METHOD IN DESIRE.

So, then you see that our Threefold Method—Auto-Suggestion, Visualization and Acting-Out-the-Part, will develop Desire in you. In Auto-Suggestion, along these lines, you must "treat" yourself as I have told you for Desire. Tell the "John Smith" part of you how much he Desires this or that—how much he aspires to this or that—how strong is his ambition for this and that, etc. Then Visualize the Object, that is the thing desired, until you can see it plainly and clearly. See yourself in possession of, or as having attained it. Keep this Mental Image always with you, for it will act powerfully in arousing your Desire Force. Then Act-Out the idea of you gaining headway and moving on to the possession or attainment. Cultivate the outward actions and demeanor of Yourself as you can image yourself to be when you have attained. If you are after Success, then Act-Out the part of the Successful Man. You need not be told *why*, after what I have said.

WHY DESIRE SHOULD BE DEVELOPED.

In conclusion, I will again remind you that the objects of this development of Desire are, (1) that your Will may be called into play, and (2) that your Desire Force may be set into activity and thus begin in its "drawing," "attracting" work. Read what I have said about Desire Force in the second lesson. Now, do not dismiss this part of the subject lightly. It is most important to you. Desire and Will are the two phases of the Underlying Force, and you must develop both of them in order to get the best results. Keep the flame of Right Desire ever burning brightly. Feed its lamp with the ideas of the Objects of Desire by Auto-Suggestion, Visualization and Acting-Out. Remember my parting words about Desire: The first thing in the direction of Doing Things, or Getting Things, is TO WANT THE THINGS HARD ENOUGH! A strong, ardent, keen Desire will clear away the undergrowth of the Path of Success. It will attract you to the people and things needed for its satisfaction, and will attract to you the people, things, circumstances, environments, etc., needed for its satisfaction. DESIRE IS THE SOUL OF THE LAW OF ATTRACTION.

THE MAGNETIC WILL.

And now let us consider the second attribute of our Positive Magnetic Man. It is WILL POWER. Our man is an example of LIVING WILL. He is filled with the force of Action. He is Determined. He keeps his Will on an object just as a machinist keeps his chisel on the hard metal, letting it bite in deeper and deeper until the desired impression and end is obtained. I have told you how the Will is always set into operation by the urge of Desire. When you develop and cultivate Desire you are doing much to cultivate Will Power. So I need not repeat this part of the process—I have just told it to you under the head of Desire. But there is another feature about the use of Will which I must call to your attention. It is the feature of its Determined Application and Manifestation. It is all very well to have a Strong Will, but it will avail you nothing unless you learn how to apply it.

THE SECRET OF THE RESOLUTE WILL.

The secret of the Resolute Will lies in Determination and Persistency. And the first thing to be acquired is Attention for Attention. Writers on psychology will tell you that a "tenacious attention is one of the strongest factors of a cultivated will." That is it—you must acquire Tenacity of Attention. You must acquire the art of patiently dwelling upon a thing until you accomplish your purpose. You must learn to do things thoroughly and completely. You must learn to concentrate your will upon a thing and not allow it to be distracted or to wander off until you do what you set out to do. You must cultivate stability, decision, perseverance, tenacity and stick-to-it-iveness. And you can do all of these things by the Triple Method given in these lessons. Each quality is capable of cultivation and development in the same way. You can do these things *"if you want to hard enough."* First stir up your Desire to accomplish the task—the Will that you shall do it—then DO it. Thousands of others have done these things—and so may you if you are an Individual and not a mere Personal Shadow. I shall now give you some advice regarding Will Development, to which I ask you to pay close attention.

HABIT AND WILL-POWER.

The first obstacle to be overcome in the work of Cultivating Will Power is to overcome the old habits of Weak Will, and to replace them by new habits of Strong Will. This question of Habit is a most important one, for we are all more or less slaves to habit. Habit is second-nature which is often much stronger than our ordinary natural impulses. In order to develop the Dominant Will you must cultivate some new habits. And of these things I shall now speak. The following rules for the development of new habits will prove of great benefit to you, if you will study them carefully and then put them into practice.

Control the Physical Channels of Expression.

Rule 1. Get control of your physical channels of expression and master the physical expression connected with the mental state you are trying to develop. For instance, if you are trying to develop your Will along the lines of Self-Reliance, Confidence, Fearlessness, etc., the first thing for you to do is to get a perfect control of the muscles by which the physical manifestations or expressions of those feelings are shown. Get control of the muscles of your shoulders that you may throw them back manfully. Look out for the stooping attitude of Lack of Confidence. Then get control of the muscles by which you hold your head up, with eyes front, gazing the world fearlessly in the face. Get control of the muscles of the legs by which you will be enabled to walk firmly as the Positive Man should. Get control of the vocal organs, by which you may speak in the resonant, vibrant tones which compel attention and inspire respect. Get yourself well in hand physically in order to manifest these outward forms of Will, and you will clear a path for the Mind to manifest itself—and will make the work of the Will much easier. But it takes Will to do these things and you must be prepared to use it. Keep your attention on these outward forms of expression until you acquire the habit and make it "second-nature."

Learn to Concentrate.

Rule 2. Learn to Concentrate. By so doing you will be able to focus your Will upon any object desired, and thus get the greatest effect. In using the Will endeavor to make it "one-pointed" as the Orientals say. That is, have for the object of the Will One Main Object and then focus the Will firmly upon that object. Cast from your mind all ideas and thoughts not in harmony with the One Idea upon which you are concentrating your Will. In the beginning it will be well to avoid all persons, environments, etc., calculated to distract you from the Main Idea. But after a bit you will be able to interpose a resistance to these distracting things and banish them from you by a mental command. While acquiring Will in this way you will find that it often takes even more Will to turn away from these outside objects than to follow your main object. You must learn to master these temptations even if in so doing you must needs act like Ulysses who made his companions stop up their ears with wax lest they be fascinated by the song of the Sirens.

ACQUIRE THE WILL HABIT.

Rule 3. In acquiring a Will Habit use every occasion in order to *repeat the effort of the Will* along the lines of the habit. Give your Will much exercise. Every time you do a certain thing the easier does it become to repeat it, for the habit becomes more firmly established. Habit is a form of "impression," and the oftener you sink the die of the Will into the wax of the Mind, the deeper is the impression. Exercise, exercise, exercise—practice, practice, practice.

THE FIRST FIGHT IS THE HARDEST.

Rule 4. The greatest struggle is at the beginning of the practice or formation of a new Will Habit. Here one has to fight with all his might—but the first battle well won, the after-fights moderate and finally become mere skirmishes. There it behooves one to gird on his armor firmly and grasp his sword with strength at this first fight. Try to stop smoking or drinking, for instance, and you will find that three-quarters of the entire struggle is condensed in the fight of the first week if not the first day. Remember the case of Rip van Winkle with his "well, this glass don't count"—he *never could* get started. And, beware of a single slip at the start, for such slips weaken one more than he can regain in a whole day of success. After having made up your Will to acquire a habit, you must not allow a single slip for this reason. A well-known writer on the subject has compared these slips to a ball of cord which one is endeavoring to wind—

each drop of the ball unwinds more than many windings can replace.

ACQUIRING "SECOND-NATURE."

Rule 5. Endeavor to fix the habit as a strong Mental Impression by any and every means that suggest themselves to you. For when this habit becomes firmly impressed upon your mind you will find it most "natural" and easy to act along its lines, and most difficult to break away from it or to act contrary to it. You are building "second-nature," remember.

JUDGE, WEIGH AND MEASURE—THEN GO AHEAD.

Rule 6. "Look before you Leap," and "Be sure you're Right, then Go Ahead." Always take a good look at a thing before plunging in. Give it the benefit of your judgment and do not be carried away by the judgment of others. Use your Reason and Judgment—that's why you have them. But, after once having decided that a thing is "right" for you to do, then you must learn to *"go ahead" to the finish*. Learn to *"Place your hand upon the plow and look not backward."* Learn to control your Will Power and do not let it leap into action until you are sure it is right to do so. And all of this means rigid self-control and mastery of one's moods as well as one's passions and emotions. Guard yourself against yourself. And also guard your Desire from the influences of others, for through your Desires your Will is called into action.

Children, savages and undeveloped Individuals manifest little or no Mastery over their Desires but allow themselves to be affected by every little wave from within or without and then let their Will fly into action in response thereto. The Individual learns to "inhibit" (that is to "check, restrain, hold back, forbid, prohibit," etc.) Emotional States and Feelings. By so doing he will hold his Will Power under control for use when it is advisable. Pull the trigger of your Will Power *yourself* after you have taken deliberate aim and at some object worth while.

Do not allow others to pull it for you nor do you, yourself, pull it in response to a whim, a dare, an unrestrained feeling. A useful rule along these lines is given by Prof. Hoffding, who says: "Even if we cannot prevent a feeling from arising, we may possibly prevent it from spreading, *by inhibiting the organic movement which accompanies it*, the indulgence in which augments it." In other words, retrain the physical action and the feeling dies. Do you see how this idea of physical expression and "acting-out" runs shoulder to shoulder with the idea of Mental States all through the subject of psychology?

FILL YOUR MIND WITH GOOD MENTAL PICTURES.

Rule 7. Keep the mind filled with Mental Pictures of the thing which you wish to become a habit, for by so doing you are constantly adding oil to the flame of Desire—and Desire is the cause of the manifestation of Will. The Feminine Desire *asks*, and the Masculine Will seeks to gratify the request of his mate in any direction indicated by her. Therefore, the more she *sees* what she wants the more she *asks*—and the more she *asks* the more eager does he become to please her. The Apple was *shown* Eve, then she *told Adam it was good* and asked him to take a bite, and then Adam ate and the mischief was done. But this rule works for good as well as for bad—"it's a poor rule that won't work both ways." But the principle is the same in both good and evil cases.

ACT OUT THE HABIT.

Rule 8. Act out the Habit as often as possible, and as well as possible. Learn to go through the motions until the part becomes perfect and easily performed. I needn't tell you students the reason for this again—it should be an old story with you by this time.

Practice Doing Disagreeable Things.

Rule 9. Practice doing disagreeable things. This will strengthen the Will wonderfully, for reasons that should be apparent to every student. What would be the condition of your muscles if you never had to use them? And what will be the condition of your Will if you never have to exercise it by doing something unpleasant or disagreeable. Anyone, even the weakest, can do a thing along the lines of no resistance—pleasant, agreeable things, without opposition or resistance. But it takes a true Man or Woman—a true Individual—to do things against resistance from without or from within. And when one has learned to master *himself*, that is, his own moods and feelings—then he is able to Master the Outside World. And not until then, either! Therefore often set yourself an unpleasant or disagreeable task to perform, for by so doing you acquire Mental Muscle, which is but another name for Will.

Prof. James, the eminent psychologist, advises his readers to systematically exercise themselves in the direction of doing some particular things *for no other reason than that lhey would rather not do it.* Even if the task be nothing more than rising and giving up a seat in a streetcar *when you want to retain it very much indeed.* Prof. James compares this exercise to the paying the premiums on insurance on one's property—one is laying up reserve resources for a day of need. He tells us that a man who trains himself in this way can be counted upon in any emergency—*he may count on himself* to manifest Will Power. As Prof. Halleck says, in speaking of such a man: "While another would be still crying over spilt milk, the possessor of such a will has already begun to milk another cow." The men who have attained great success have, in nearly every case, so trained their wills that they could undertake a difficult or disagreeable plan with a minimum of effort. *They had acquired the habit.* When one learns to say "Yes! or No!" to himself, he can say "YES!" or "NO!" to others with the greatest force.

Cultivate Fixity of Purpose.

Rule 10. Cultivate Fixity of Purpose. The man of strong Will must learn to see an Object ahead of him and then to "want it hard enough," and then to fix his Will upon it and hold it there, while he moves to it in as straight a line as possible. But no matter how he may have to swerve from his straight line of approach, by unforseen obstacles, nor how many times he may stumble, *he still always remembers what he is after*—AND HE KEEPS AFTER IT. The shifting, changeable, weathercock sort of men manifest but little Will, and accomplish little or nothing. The successful men are those who *know what they want and never forget it*. It may take them some time to find out just what they *do* want, but when once they find it out they hold firmly to it to the end with an invincible determination and unswerving purpose—and these qualities always win in the long run, if for no other reason than because so few possess them and the majority of men get tired of the struggle and drop out of the race. It's the fellow with the "staying qualities" that pulls through in the end no matter how much of a start the others may have had on him in the beginning. Concentrate and cultivate "Stick-to-it-iveness."

Develop These Mental Faculties.

I shall now briefly run over the Mental Faculties most necessary of development in the case of the man who wishes to gain the Magnetic Will. And I shall add a few words of advice regarding the development of each of the said qualities.

The Faculty of Stability.

I. Continuity. This faculty has been so named by the phrenologists, and defined as the faculty that enables a man to "stick-to-it" until it is done—that gives him patience to complete his task—that gives him stability. Its lack makes a man restless; changeable; shifting; disconnected; scattered; unstable; and unreliable. To cultivate this faculty follow the Three-fold Method, in the direction of concentrating, dwelling upon, and sticking to a matter once undertaken; doing thorough work; and fighting against distracting ideas and things, or temptations to "make a change."

THE FACULTY OF THE "WILL-TO-LIVE."

II. VITALITY. This faculty is defined by phrenologists as one that makes a person tenacious of life; and which causes him to fight off death, sickness, or weakness. This is a necessary faculty for the Magnetic Man to develop, for by so doing he not only becomes stronger, but also imparts a certain quality of Strength and Resistance to his personality that will be felt by others. As an example, contrast the "fight for life" in an animal of the cat family, and then the lack of it in a sheep or rabbit—then think which of them is more respected and regarded in the world of animals. By all means cultivate that Resolute Fight for Life, that is manifested by all strong creatures. Try the Threefold Method along the lines of holding on to life, and manifesting the "Will to Live."

THE FACULTY OF COURAGE.

III. COMBATIVENESS. This phrenological faculty manifests in the direction of Resistance; opposition; courage; boldness; defensiveness; defiance; spirit; self-protection; determination; "let me alone"; "get-out-of-my-way"; etc. It goes with all strong characters. It is true that its perversion renders one a nuisance and a quarrelsome and brawling person, and such state is to be avoided. But its absence makes of one "a human door-mat," and the world proceeds to wipe its feet on him. The strong Magnetic Man must have this faculty well-developed, and also well-controlled. It must be the case of the "soft voice and the big stick," of which we have heard so much of late. The world loves the brave man, and hates a coward. And this means Mental Bravery, and Mental Cowardice, principally, in these days of Mental Struggle. By all means learn to stand up like a man, and, looking the world firmly and calmly in the face, say in the words of the old verse: "Come one; come all! this rock shall fly from its firm base, as soon as I." Don't be a brawler, but don't be a Weakling. Avoid the Rabbit and Sheep mental attitude. Develop this faculty by the Threefold Method, along the lines of debate; argument; mental conflict; mental resistance; asserting your Individuality; insisting upon your rights; self-confidence; self-assertion; and "I Can and I Will."

THE BARRIER-BREAKING FACULTY.

IV. DESTRUCTIVENESS. This name is not well-chosen, in my opinion, by the phrenologist's, but I shall not attempt to change it here. It is used by them to indicate the faculty that manifests in: Determination to overcome obstacles; beating down resistance; brushing away barriers; making headway; pushing to the front; clearing away underbrush; pushing through the crowd; holding your own; etc. Its perversion renders one a hated man, and one who is not sufficiently regardful of the rights of others, and whom it becomes the duty of society to restrain. But, still it is a quality that is needed by the Magnetic Man, lest he allow himself to be walked over with impunity; outraged; and treated with contempt by the world; or which will cause him to be pushed aside and imposed upon. Its absence also causes one to be overcome with impotence when obstacles confront him, or resistance shows itself. Its absence causes one to be a whining "I Can't" person; and also causes one to be too much subject to precedents, pretended authority, etc., and kills off his originality. To develop this faculty, use the Threefold Method along the lines of breaking new mental ground; striking out into new paths; breaking down barriers; overcoming restraint; holding your own ; pushing to the front, even if you do have to elbow the crowd, etc.

THE "GETTING AND KEEPING" FACULTY.

V. ACQUISITIVENESS. This term is used by phrenologists to indicate that faculty which manifests in: Getting; acquiring;

possessing; drawing to oneself; obtaining and securing desired things; etc. It may be perverted into miserliness; penuriousness; meanness;. hoggishness, etc., but nevertheless its proper use and development is necessary to the Positive Man. Unless one has a Desire to Have and Hold, he will not be apt to make any progress in the world. One must want to get things, before he will act energetically. And so far as money is concerned, while I freely admit the evils of an extreme greed and desire in this respect, yet I am just as fully convinced that a man must possess a certain amount of this "money-wanting" quality in order to make him an active centre of force.

For, when one wants money, he really wants the things that money buys. Money stands for nearly all that is necessary for a man's well-being and sustenance. Money in itself is nothing—and a man is a fool who loves or seeks it *for itself*. But it is also a "symbol" of almost everything else, and without it he can get practically nothing else. So, just as I think it justifiable and proper for a plant to desire and seek, and draw to itself the sustenance of the soil, air, water, and sunlight, so do I think it proper, desirable and praiseworthy for a man to desire, and insist upon drawing to himself the proper sustenance of life—and Money means just that, to the sane man, and nothing more.

The people who decry this "desire for Money," are principally those who either (1) have failed to accumulate money themselves, by reason of lacking the necessary qualities (the really *unfortunate* ones do not join in the condemnation of the *desire*); or (2) those who have inherited Money of which they did not know the labor, excitement, or satisfaction of making for themselves, and who, therefore, grow rightly disgusted at the money which they did not have to use their heads or hands to acquire. These people are like those who take no exercise, and get indigestion at the sight of a good dinner; while those who have worked well come to the dinner with a good appetite, and cannot understand the "sick-feeling" of the others. It is a law of Nature that makes both of these classes of people "sick" at the sight of that for which they have not worked; or (3) that class of "parasites" who live by the hard work of others, doing nothing themselves, and deeming themselves far above those "muckers," or "money-grubbers," who work, and toil and labor to support these "parasites."

Among this last mentioned class—the "parasites"—I cheerfully include that class of pampered wealthy women, who take no part in the world's work, even refusing to make their own beds, or sweep their own rooms. These good souls often think that they are "living the higher life" in this way, and they consider Money as "something sordid, and unworthy of us who dwell on the higher spiritual or artistic planes of thought." They look down upon their husbands or fathers, who are right in the thick of the "money-making madness" which is made necessary by the demands of these very "high souls" for seal-skin sacks, diamonds, automobiles, etc.

This last mentioned class—the Female Parasites of Society—are the ones really responsible for much of the inordinate and excessive development of the faculty of Acquisitiveness noticeable in the world to-day. They lead their "beautiful lives," far above the roar and bustle of the mart—but every dollar that procures them this privilege comes from the same "desire for Money" which they hypocritically decry. For very few normal men will work themselves to death to pile up accumulations for themselves alone—it is always for "those dependent upon me."

And, in this class of "parasites" I, of course, include those sap-headed youths, who with their cigarettes sticking between their foolish teeth, speak pityingly of their fathers who are "down among the muckers" grubbing for Money. I am not trying to preach a sermon, but this hypocrisy makes me sick. They're all after money—every blessed mother's son and daughter of them—in one way or another. And what's the use of denying it. Some day we may have better economic conditions—I pray to God that we may—but until that time all of us must chase the nimble Dollar to the best of our ability. For unless a man does this thing, "then shall he not eat; nor be clothed; nor have shelter; nor books; nor music; nor anything else that makes life worth living for one who thinks and feels." Therefore I feel justified in saying to you: *develop a normal degree of Acquisitiveness*, if you wish to amount to anything in the world's work. Develop it by the Threefold Method, along the lines of Realization of What It Means, and What it Will Do for You, in this stage of the World's Economic Evolution. But—Don't Be a Hog! And "while you're getting, get all you can," *but give the other fellow a chance.* "Live and Let Live!"

THE FACULTY OF KEEPING YOUR OWN SECRETS.

VI. SECRETIVENESS. This is the name given by the phrenologists to that faculty that manifests as: Policy; tact; concealment; self-repression; self-restraint; etc. Its perversion leads to deceit; double-dealing; duplicity; lying; false-living; etc. But a certain amount of it is necessary for the Magnetic Man, lest he fall into the error of wearing-his-heart-on-his-sleeve; transparent-simplicity; loose-mouthedness; "blabbing"; lacking ordinary prudence; indiscretion; etc. Develop this faculty by the Threefold Method along the lines of tact; diplomacy; reticence; cautiousness; politeness; etc., the main object being to acquire a faculty of keeping your own secrets; keeping your affairs to yourself; avoiding that "leakiness" that has ruined so many men—and women. Regarding this "—and women," I would say that my business experience has taught me that in spite of the alleged "secret-telling" of women, it is true that the women stenographers in an office are far less liable to disclose their employers' secrets, than are the men employees. And then again, while a woman may have a tendency to "pass on a secret," still she knows how to keep certain secrets that concern herself, or the man she loves—or the child she loves—in a manner, and in ways that cause a man's hair to raise in bewilderment. And, why should I say anything about this matter anyway—am I not telling you the "Secrets of Mental Magic" in these lessons?

Mental Architecture.

The Faculty of Prudence.

VII. Cautiousness. This faculty manifests in Carefulness; prudence; watchfulness; foresight; judgment; etc. Perverted it leads to timidity, irresolution; etc. But a certain amount of it is necessary. One should learn to use Judgment and Reason—to "be sure he is right, before going ahead." If deficient in this quality, develop it by the Threefold Method along the lines of care, prudence, watchfulness, thought, use of judgment, etc., and by "looking before you leap." If you have too much of it, restrain by similar methods, along the lines of boldness, daring; "don't worry"; take-a-risk-on-it, etc., and a general spirit of not crossing a bridge until you come to it.

The Faculty of "What Will People Think"?

VIII. Approbativeness. This faculty manifests in a desire for approval; praise; flattery; fame; show and ceremony connected with one's personality; etc. It is seen frequently in a perverted sense. Very few of us need to develop this quality—we have enough, or more than enough of it already. If you wish to restrain this faculty, you may use the Threefold Method along the lines of indifference to public approval or opinion; "what-does-it-matter-anyway"; "they say; what do they say? let them say"; "do not worry about it—your friends will not care, and you enemies will persist anyway, so what's the use"; "what care I for the opinions of the crowd, anyway—they are 95 per cent fools at the best"; etc., etc., etc. Learn to live your own life, and stand upon your own feet. Other people would like to even "breathe" for you if you would let them—but say "scat" to them, and shake them off when they bother you. You've got to live your own life, and why bother with the people who are always telling you "you mustn't do it this way—do it as I say," when their own lives are glaring examples of the folly of "*their* way."

Pick out a right object—follow a right course—and let the crowd mind its own business, if it will—and *if it won't, forget it.* You will find it ready enough to shower favors upon you when you finally succeed. And do not be deceived by its praise or flattery—the same people who are singing your praises to-day, will damn you to-morrow if occasion offers. They are throwing roses at you now—to-morrow they may throw rocks with equal grace and delight. Don't be a slave to the crowd or its opinions—make yourself Master of it, if you would rule it. It is managed through its selfish fears and interest, rather than through its love. It has a mean trick of turning on the thing it loves, and tearing it to pieces, just as a female-spider devours her mate. But when it Fears—*well then it let's you alone.* Not high spiritual teaching, perhaps—but a bit of Worldly Wisdom. Shake off the crowd from your heels—you mind your own business, and tell it to do the same. And look it in the eye while you are telling it, too. It will understand you, if you don't truckle to it. But never cringe to it—else it will rend you to pieces.

The Faculty of Self-Confidence.

IX. Self-Esteem. This is the faculty of Self-Respect; Self-Reliance; Self-Love, etc. Perverted it means tyranny; superciliousness; imperiousness; hauteur, and other forms of egotism carried to extremes. This quality is necessary to be developed, normally, in the Magnetic Man. He must learn to respect himself; value himself; rely upon himself; love himself; hold his head high; look the world in the face; Believe In Himself; and Take His Own Place in the World, without false modesty, or shrinking. Develop it by the Threefold Method, along the lines of realizing just what you are—a Centre of Energy, Power, and Strength in the Universal Ocean of Energy. Think of yourself in the word of Black Hawk, the Indian chieftain, who said to Jackson: "I Am a Man!" Be a "Man among men," and insist upon the fact. Learn to say "I Am." Feel that back of, and under you, is the great Ocean of Universal Mind Energy and realize that you are Of and In this wonderful thing.

Believe in Yourself; love Yourself; look out for Yourself. I tell you students, I believe in you, everyone of you, for I know what you are and what you have *in* you—and I want you to Believe In Yourselves. I want you to say "I" without being afraid. Don't be afraid to "Assert the I." Don't be afraid to say "I." Say "I; I; I; I; I; I; I," until you begin to realize what a wonderful thing that "I" of you is, after all. Recognize the "Ego" as a Centre of Power, and stop all this foolishness about being a "worm of the dust." Don't be "meek and humble" like Uriah Heep. On the contrary, stand up, with head thrown back, looking the world straight in the eyes, without Fear, and say firmly and positively: "I Believe in God—and I Believe in Myself." You have heard it said that "God helps those who help themselves"—and He *does*, unquestionably. But this is also true—God *Believes* in Those Who Believe in Themselves. And so does the World, because God has made it so! So start in now, and say, early and often, "I Believe in Myself!"

THE FACULTY OF FIRMNESS.

X. FIRMNESS. This term does not have to be defined—you all know what it means. It is the faculty of stability; fixity; decision; perseverance; tenacity; manifestation of the Determined Will. Too much of it may make you mulish, and stubborn—but very few of you have too much of it, along the right lines. You need to develop it by the Threefold Method along the lines of "putting your hand to the plow, and looking not backward"; sticking to your original plans, despite the talk of others; resisting tendencies to "side-track" you. This is the faculty that keeps the Will to the task, like the Chisel to the Metal, until the work is done. Be firm as a rock against which beats the storms, but which yields not an inch, nor is it hurt a particle. Have a mind of your own, and hold to what you believe is right. *See your object, and match straight to it, firm in your determination and purpose.* By all means develop the faculty of Firmness.

THE FACULTY OF "EARNEST EXPECTATION."

XI. HOPE. This is the faculty of Expectation, and Anticipation. It gives us one of the three features of Success—"Earnest

Expectation." You must Believe in your Success and must "Earnestly Expect" it. Cultivate Hope and "Earnest Expectation" by all means. Be not a mere dreamer or visionary, through excessive hope—but Cultivate Desire; then develop Earnest Expectation; then Will to Act. Each of these features is necessary to the Great Three. Develop it by the Threefold Method, along the lines of "looking on the bright side," visualization; "looking aloft"; not worrying; and Belief in the Efficacy of Earnest Demand accompanied by Earnest Work. Visualization is the greatest incentive to Hope and Earnest Expectation. When you can see the thing done "in your mind's eye," you have started to build in earnest—the rest is a mere matter of detail and work.

THE FACULTY OF GOOD NATURE.

XII. MIRTHFULNESS. This is the faculty of Humor. By all means cultivate the sense of Humor. It will save you from more follies and ridiculous positions than anything else. And cultivate the Cheerful Spirit for it will make life easier for you, and will lubricate the machinery of Work and Endeavor. It will also make friends for you, and will tend to remove the obstacles which the world throws in the way of people who are sour, disagreeable and "grouchy." Smile and the World smiles with you; Frown and you get a Frown. Develop this faculty, by all means, by the Threefold Method, along the lines of Humor, Joy, Cheerfulness.

MORALS, STRENGTH AND POWER.

And, so, now I have called your attention to the faculties most prominent in the Magnetic Man. I have not spoken of his Religious or Moral faculties, because these lessons are dealing with another part of his make-up. But do not imagine that the qualities named here have no connection with the religious or moral life. There is nothing that I have recommended here that will not apply as well to the Minister as the Business man—to the Priest as well as the Salesman. The same mental qualities that make a bad man "great" and "strong" will make a good man "great" and "strong." Morals are one thing and degrees of Strength another. Good men may be strong or weak; bad men may also be strong or weak. And in the degree of "Strength" will be the degree of Influence, for good or evil, that a man will manifest. With this in mind, I think that it would be a great thing for the world, if some one were to distribute this book among the "good" men of the world, who have imagined that there was nothing but selfish knowledge in "Mental Magic."

MENTAL STATES AND THEIR EMANATIONS.

And, now, in closing this last lesson, let me remind you that these Mental States, cultivated and developed as I have shown you, will manifest themselves in your outward manner and demeanor, as Mental Suggestions to those with whom you come in contact. The symbol will spring from the inner Reality. And they will also manifest in the shape of Currents of Desire Force and Will Power, which will sweep far and wide, as well as near and close, influencing and affecting those within their field of Induction. From these Mental States will flow a strong stream of Magnetism which will tend to "draw" to you that which you demand and desire; and which will also tend to "force and compel" the things that you so Will. You are a great Centre of Force, which radiates from you continually. Realize this, and endeavor to charge that Force with the best qualities and properties, that while you are Asserting your Own Individual Rights, you will still be doing something toward the great work of Strengthening the Race, to the end that it may produce more real Individuals ready and capable of playing their part in the great Drama of Life, on the Stage of the Universe.

CONCLUDING REMARKS.

I consider these lessons to be my most important work. They are along new lines, and are radical in the treatment given the subject. They are as "meat for strong men, and not milk for babes." There is no "bromide" or "pink-tea effects" in them. They are vital, radical, and positive. Their Message is "Strength." All Truth that is worth while, renders its possessor Stronger—if any teachings cannot stand this test, discard them. Nature's Law is toward producing strong Individuals—fall in with it, and Nature will come to your aid, for then you will be one of its Chosen Ones. Fall in with the Law of Evolution—do not run contrary to it. In the one case, you are nourished, supported, strengthened and encouraged—in the other, you are relentlessly crowded out by the operations of the Law.

For Whom These Lessons Are Written.

If you get one-half the benefit from the study of these lessons that I obtained from the writing of them, you will be well repaid for your task. They are as a "live wire," charged with the elemental force, energy and truth about certain occult natural laws. They contain a message for you, which I trust you will heed—for you need it. If you are an Individual, this teaching is just what you want. And the same is true if you are *not* one, but *want* to be one. But, if you are a Weakling, and prefer to remain so, instead of rising and claiming your birthright of Strength—your heritage of Power; then by all means remain as you are, and go on your own way. Leave these teachings for the others of your brethren, who will not sell their Birthright of Power for the Mess of Pottage of Negative Content, and Sheep-like Passivity, but who are boldly claiming their own, and demanding their rightful portion—these Strong Brothers of yours, the Individuals who are the coming Inheritors of the Earth.

My Message to the Individual.

I have tried to infuse my words with the strong, vital energy, which I feel surging through me as I write out this Message of Strength to you. I trust that these words will act as a current of verbal "electrons," each carrying its full charge of Dynamic Power. And I trust that each word will act to so fill you with the

Mentative Energy that gave them birth, and will thus awaken in you a similar Mental State, Desire and Will, to be Strong, Forceful, and Dynamic—determined to assert your Individuality in Being and Doing that which the Universal Creative Desire and Will is hoping that you will Be and Do. I send to you this Message charged with the very dynamic vibrations of my Brain, as it transforms and converts the Mentative Energy into thoughts and words. I send it to you—yes, You, who are now reading the words—with all the Energy, Force and Power at my command, to the end that it pierce your armor of indifference, fear, and doubt, and "I Can't." And that reaching into your Heart of Desire, it may fill you with the very Spirit of Individuality, Conscious Egohood, Perception of Reality, and Realization of the "I." So that from hence on your battle cry will be changed, and you will plunge into the thick of the Fight, filled with the Berserker Rage, like the Icelandic Hero of old, and shouting your Positive Cry of Freedom, "I Can and I Will," you will mow your way clear through the ranks of the horde of Ignorance, and Negativity, and reach the heights beyond. This is my Message to You—the Individual!

FINIS.

THE "SIDE LIGHT MANUALS"

I PURPOSE ISSUING a series of manuals, supplementary to "The Secret of Mental Magic," which will contain specific directions for developing and cultivating the principles of certain particular phases of Mental Magic, described in my "Seven Lessons." These manuals will be in the nature of Special Instruction along the particular lines indicated by their titles. They will have very little to say regarding basic laws or principles, for those points are fully brought out in the main work on "Mental Magic," of which these manuals will be as "Side-Lights." But they will be filled from cover to cover with plain, practical information concerning the actual operation or workings of these principles, together with special instruction, and exercises, whereby one may use the same in his every day life, on the one hand; or recognize and prevent the improper employment of the same against him on the part of others, on the other hand.

These little manuals will not be as large as the main work, but will be filled with the very cream of the subject, along the "just how" lines. They will be sold (as are all of my books) subject to 24 hours' examination, with privilege to return and refund of money, if you are not perfectly satisfied. The first one of these "Side Light" Manuals will be entitled was issued on June 1, 1907. The remainder of the series will be issued from time to time—if you desire I will notify you as each comes from the press. I am sure that every one who is interested in the main work: "The Secret of Mental Magic," will be more than pleased with Manual No. 1, above mentioned.

Masonic Temple, Chicago, Ill. William Walker Atkinson.

Bibliography

Atkinson, William Walker. *The Secret of Mental Magic*. Chicago, IL: William Walker Atkinson, 1907.

Atkinson, William Walker. *Mental Fascination: Reveals the fantastic powers of the mind. Contents: What is Mental Fascination; Among Animals; Impressionability; Experimental Fascination; The Dangers of Psychism; Oriental Fascination; Future Impression; Establishing a Mentative Centre; Personal Atmosphere; Direct Personal Fascination; Eye Impression; Fascination of the Eye, plus more.* Chicago, IL: The Fiduciary Press, 1907.